D1559698

BIZ JETS

Economics of Science, Technology and Innovation

VOLUME 1

The titles published in this series are listed at the end of this volume.

BIZ JETS

Technology and Market Structure in the Corporate Jet Aircraft Industry

by
ALMARIN PHILLIPS
Professor Emeritus,
University of Pennsylvania,
and
Chairman of the Board,
Econsult Corporation

A. PAUL PHILLIPS

and

THOMAS R. PHILLIPS

KLUWER ACADEMIC PUBLISHERS
DORDRECHT / BOSTON / LONDON

338.476291
P55b

Library of Congress Cataloging-in-Publication Data

Phillips, Almarin.
   Biz jets : technology and market structure in the corporate jet
aircraft industry / by Almarin Phillips, A. Paul Phillips, Thomas R.
Phillips.
      p.   cm. -- (Economics of science, technology, and innovation ;
v. 1)
   Includes bibliographical references and index.
   ISBN 0-7923-2660-1
   1. Aircraft industry--United States. 2. Jet planes. 3. Market
surveys--United States.   I. Phillips, A. Paul. II. Phillips,
Thomas R.   III. Title. IV. Series.
HD9711.U6P48 1994
338.4'762913334'0973--dc20   93-42692

ISBN 0-7923-2660-1

Published by Kluwer Academic Publishers,
P.O. Box 17, 3300 AA Dordrecht, The Netherlands.

Kluwer Academic Publishers incorporates
the publishing programmes of
D. Reidel, Martinus Nijhoff, Dr W. Junk and MTP Press.

Sold and distributed in the U.S.A. and Canada
by Kluwer Academic Publishers,
101 Philip Drive, Norwell, MA 02061, U.S.A.

In all other countries, sold and distributed
by Kluwer Academic Publishers Group,
P.O. Box 322, 3300 AH Dordrecht, The Netherlands.

Printed on acid-free paper

Table of Contents

List of Tables

Preface

This book grew from long-term interests in the economics of technological change and the aircraft industry. The senior author has argued for many years that opportunities created by advances in science and technology play a large role in the determination of market structures. The argument was made explicit in "Patents, Potential Competition and Technical Progress," *American Economic Review*, May 1966, and more fully explicated in *Technology and Market Structure; A Study of the Aircraft Industry*, 1971. At that time, the so-called structure-conduct-performance paradigm reigned in industrial economics. The idea that market structure was even partially endogenous to the market process was quite foreign to the main body of microeconomics, including the economics of technological change. Even the works of Joseph Schumpeter had been popularized to say that the important relationships to be studied were those that explained differences in the rates of technological change in terms of differences in market structures. It is probably correct to say that the latter approach still dominates economic research in the area, despite a growing number of influential theoretical and empirical studies that emphasize the endogenization of market structure.

The senior author was commissioned to conduct a study of the market for business jet aircraft in the mid-1980s. This work sparked a renewed interest in describing changes in market structure in terms of the degrees of success various sellers achieve in seizing on the opportunities created by advances in technologies. As was the case in the 1971 study of commercial aircraft, detailed research could unearth the stories of the failures as well as the successes in these endeavors. Interest was heightened as well by the large volume of related research that had appeared in the intervening years. The two junior authors — sons of the senior author — volunteered their services enthusiastically.

Almarin Phillips was responsible for the first draft. His work was based primarily on research conducted by Thomas R. Phillips. A. Paul Phillips edited the work with such care that he literally became co-author of subsequent drafts.   Thomas Phillips continually reviewed the manuscript to check on accuracy and to contribute to content.

We are indebted to many people.   The story of PPG's converted C-47, *The Glasshopper,* is woven into the text.   Almarin Phillips had the pleasure of traveling on that old plane a few times in 1957.   The history of *The Glasshopper* and its successor aircraft at PPG was supplied by W.T. Branthoover and Guy A. Zoghby.   We appreciate their courtesy.   A condensed version of the first three chapters was presented at a conference sponsored by the Department of Industrial Management and Economics, Chalmers University of Technology, in Marstrand, Sweden, in 1991.   This paper appears as "The Formation of the U.S. Market for Business Jets" in *Economics of Technology*, Ove Granstrand (ed.) (forthcoming).   Giovanni Dosi, Ove Granstrand and other participants at that conference provided a number of helpful comments.

Arthur Schmauder reviewed an early version of the manuscript and made a number of very useful suggestions.   Richard Wingfield, a friend who has considerable experience as a pilot of business aircraft, answered numerous questions and encouraged us with his interest in what we were doing. Holly Schifflett and Sandra Hicks, librarians at the Science and Engineering Libraries of the University of Virginia, were extremely patient and helpful. So, too, were Renée E. McHenry, Jo A. Cates and Mary A. McCredie at the Library of the Transportation Center, Northwestern University.

Kathleen Duffy supervised the production of the book.   The several drafts were typed by Tanya Brown.   Marlene Granitz checked the work for accuracy and consistency.   The manuscript was put into photo-ready form by Function One Computing of Haddonfield, NJ.

We are pleased that Kluwer Academic Publishers and their consulting Editors, Bo Carlsson and Christiano Antonelli, have accepted this book as the first of the new series of books on the Economics of Science, Technology and Innovation.   Marie M. Stratta, Senior Editor at Kluwer, has been especially supportive.   We are grateful also to Aaron Gellman, Director of the Transportation Center, Northwestern University, for sponsoring this book as one in the Center's series on transportation industries.

It has been a lot of work — and a lot of fun, too.

Almarin Phillips
Wynnewood, Pennsylvania

A. Paul Phillips
Wellesley, Massachusetts

Thomas R. Phillips
Scottsville, Virginia

Chapter One

Technology and Market Structure

The Setting

In 1950, the Pittsburgh Plate Glass Company (now PPG Industries) purchased a used C-47, the military version of the DC-3. The plane was converted to business use, with accommodations for 12 passengers and a crew of two. A caricature of a grasshopper was painted on the nose of the plane with the name, "*The Glasshopper*," inscribed below it. A former military pilot was hired, and PPG had an "executive aircraft" available for its use.[1]

The Glasshopper was treated with the affection rightfully accorded DC-3s, but its shortcomings did not go unobserved. The plane was noisy, slow, unpressurized, expensive to operate and maintain, and uncomfortable to occupy on the ground. Still, the number of DC-3s in corporate fleets was growing. The selling price of converted models ranged to as high as $275,000 by 1955.[2] While businesses wanted "a $200,000 pressurized-cabin multi-engine craft that [would] carry about 12 people [over a] 1,000-mi. range [at] about 300-mph. cruising speed," they knew that it would "be several years before [they would] be able to get anything but a compromise of some of [these] requirements."[3] The technology to produce such a plane was not yet available.

PPG operated *The Glasshopper* until 1960 when a Grumman Gulfstream G-159 twin-engined turboprop was purchased to replace it. In the interim, PPG had acquired a second DC-3. That plane was given to the University of Ohio in the mid-1960s and replaced with a Hawker Siddeley HS-125 business jet. The HS-125 proved to be too small and a Gulfstream G-II business jet was purchased in its place in the late 1960s.

The G-II had capabilities hardly imagined for a business airplane when *The Glasshopper* was acquired. The G-II could be configured for up to 30 passengers, had a cruise speed in excess of 500 mph and a range of 3,200

1

statute miles. It was priced in 1967 at about $2,300,000 green (i.e., without interior and exterior finishing and complete avionics).[4] The technologies involved in producing business aircraft had altered fundamentally in less than two decades. Engines, airframes, avionics, construction materials, manufacturing techniques — all had changed. Moreover, these new technologies were for the most part introduced by companies that had not made business or commercial aircraft prior to their entry into the market for business jets.

The Scope of the Study

The market for business aircraft has been and continues to be profoundly affected by rapid and far-reaching changes in technology. The history of business jets — "biz jets" — affords an excellent opportunity to investigate a number of important questions bearing on relationships between technological change and the structure and functioning of markets. While case studies are of limited value in developing and testing broad hypotheses about such relationships, they do permit explorations into the complexities of real-world markets in ways that are difficult to capture in theoretical and econometric studies.

Our approach is Schumpeterian in several respects. First, we emphasize "competition from the new commodity, the new technology, the new source of supply, the new type of organization."[5] In this context, we are dealing not with the analysis of market equilibria, with price as the equilibrating variable, but rather with the analysis of market disequilibria, with actual and potential innovations acting to disrupt existing market relationships.

This is not to say that price is unimportant. In the case of business jet aircraft, however, the products are complexly multidimensional. Customers have preferences that run in terms of variables defining such things as range, speed, payload, runway requirements, operating efficiency, maintenance costs, and avionics capabilities. Thus, what is relevant is not price per (simple) unit, but instead a vector of price-performance attributes that need not be ranked consistently across airplanes or across customers. Moreover, since acquisitions of business aircraft represent capital investments, the decision to buy is likely to be made through something like a discounted cash flow analysis instead of through simple price comparisons.

The analysis is Schumpeterian in another important respect. We view market structure as being essentially endogenous to the competitive process. Indeed, explaining the factors that give rise to entry — to the successful introduction of new products and increasing market shares (or, conversely, to failure in the marketplace and eventual exit) — is a primary focus of the inquiry. In investigating the determinants of market structure, we also recognize that the behavior (or conduct) of firms in the market is, at least to a degree, endogenous. Thus we look for possibilities of different firms in different circumstances pursuing different R&D strategies — perhaps successfully and perhaps not successfully.

Within this Schumpeterian framework, there are other matters to be investigated. One of these is the so-called "over-bidding" question. Is it possible that, given a changing and largely non-proprietary technology base, firms continue to enter the market even though negative returns are being realized by the incumbents? Can this occur over a considerable period of time and through a sequence of innovations? Or, again looking at Schumpeter, is overbidding more of a once-and-for-all phenomenon associated with a "swarming" of firms immediately after a successful major innovation? If negative profits persist, what are the incentives and (expected) rewards that lead to continuing participation in the market? [6]

We look, too, at the question of "first-mover" advantages. Can a follower, possibly disadvantaged at one stage, become an advantaged leader at another stage?[7] May there be advantages to not being first? And what of the related question of whether firms with small (or zero) shares of the market are more willing to introduce major innovations? [8]

Studies of commercial aircraft have found that governments have played key roles.[9] That turns out to be true with business jets as well. Various aspects of government policies — particularly government-sponsored R&D — were critical in creating the basic technologies on which the aircraft depend. But governments did more than create technologies to provide the "push" for private developments. In the case of business jets, governments were involved in defining the initial requirements and for a large part of the early demand for the planes themselves. That is, there is an element of demand "pull" as well as technology "push" in the government involvement.[10]

A recent strand of literature suggests the existence of "technological trajectories."[11] Technological trajectories describe the patterns and multidimensional directions of change within major technological paradigms. The question of whether those patterns and directions are naturally ordained by the technologies themselves or are the result of responses to economic factors is related to the technology "push," demand "pull" controversy. We examine the apparent trajectories and, among other things, find a persistent tendency for operating costs to fall even while the performance characteristics of the aircraft show pronounced improvement.

We look also at entry barriers and other factors that may limit the ability of new firms to contest the success of initial innovators. A number of such factors may be at work in markets characterized by rapid technological change. It is clear that there are substantial "learning costs" and other sunk costs involved in developing, producing and selling a new aircraft. Viewed prospectively, when entry is being considered, unit costs fall as the cumulative output of a particular plane increases. The extent to which sunk costs, including learning costs, can be transferred from one model to another and from one manufacturer to another may also be important.

We also look at the stability — or, in this case, the instability — of market shares during the first three decades of sales of business jets. It turns out that entrants quickly displaced the first-movers, largely it seems because the latter failed to improve on their initial offerings. Some of the later entrants experienced the same difficulties, while others maintained or improved their market shares through successive innovations.[12]

Finally, we explore briefly the public policy implications of the study. Two facets of policy are examined. First, while governments played an important role in creating a friendly environment during the time the industry was getting started in the late 1950s and early 1960s, it is now argued by some that, at least in the U.S., policies have shifted and that a distinctly hostile environment now exists. New tax laws and increased exposure to product liability claims are blamed for the present depressed condition of the industry.

Second, some observers believe that the U.S. business jet industry, in particular, and the U.S. aviation industry, more generally, should be beneficiaries of a new industrial policy. Proponents suggest that targeted government R&D programs as well as relief from taxes and excessive product liability claims are essential to preserve the ability of U.S. firms to compete in the global economy.

Where We Go From Here

The next chapter picks up the story of business aircraft during the 1950s, prior to the appearance of turboprop and turbojet planes. PPG's converted DC-3s are one part of the picture. There were many other planes in business fleets and, not surprisingly, more than a few attempts to develop new planes within the confines of the technologies of propeller-driven, reciprocating engine aircraft. There were as well attempts from the mid-1950s onward to escape the confines of the older technologies through the development of business jets. These development efforts are traced in some detail, with attention to the differences between the technical and the economic aspects of those aircraft that eventually achieved a degree of market success and those that did not. This part of the analysis ends in about 1960, when two U.S. manufacturers of business jets were poised to enter the market.

Chapter Three looks at the next decade of technological and market rivalry. The first two manufacturers come into the market, one with a relatively small aircraft, the other with a much larger plane. One was very successful in obtaining military sales, the other was not. Despite the lead of the first two — and, indeed, despite the extremely limited success the first two had — new manufacturers entered with new types of aircraft and new marketing strategies. Some of these entrants achieved considerable market shares while others did not. By the end of the 1960s, the structure of the market was in a state of apparent flux.

The relatively late but successful entry by Cessna at the small, low-performance end of the business is covered in Chapter Four. Here we find successful entry by a manufacturer which, by reason of extensive experience in the production of a military jet trainer, could seemingly have come into the market years earlier. We find as well the failure of several other entry attempts during the same period. The most notable of these is the effort by Aerospatiale to introduce its Corvette, a project that went awry in many ways. While Cessna ended up with a large share of the total output of the lighter jets, its success did not deter others from trying.

Chapter Five presents the picture of developments at the heavy, high-performance end of the market in the period after 1970. Here the primary focus is on the Gulfstream, with considerable attention as well to the Canadair 600/601 and the Falcon 50 and 900 entries. The Canadair story is of special interest since it represents the concluding part of William P. Lear's long involvement with business aircraft and, unfortunately, another example of how well-laid plans can end up in near-disaster in markets marked by rapid changes in technology.

Chapter Six looks at the mid-sized part of the business jet market, tracing the changing postures of various manufacturers and aircraft after 1970. This chapter, like the two previous ones, shows that achieving success in the market was extraordinarily difficult because of the risks inherent in utilizing well the succession of technological opportunities. Other aspects of the market added to this general problem, however. The overall demand for business aircraft proved to be extremely sensitive to business conditions and probably to tax, environmental and product liability laws. The stock of used aircraft increased and a growing number of firms entered the business of retrofitting and renovating older models to compete with the newer ones. Additionally, the unavoidable lag between the time orders for aircraft are placed and the time the planes are delivered caused problems in pricing and in the management of periodic shortages and backlogs. The problems were further compounded by difficulties inherent in electing the appropriate interval between successive models. The strategies used in coping with the introduction of new models may have become as important to the profitability of a manufacturer as was the character of the models themselves.

Chapter Seven summarizes our conclusions and adds discussion of some new elements. While more-or-less continuous improvements were necessary for manufacturers first to obtain and then to retain and improve their market shares through the 1980s and into the 1990s, the opportunities to make truly major changes within the bounds of perceived subsonic turbojet technologies became increasingly more circumscribed. Technologically, the industry became relatively mature even while economically the markets for the products were highly volatile. The availability of new construction materials, new construction methods, and new avionics made continued Schumpeterian rivalry inevitable, but the benefits from squeezing improvements from a more niggardly technological environment were decreasing.

Some have argued that U.S. manufacturers have been fairing less well in this competitive fray than have those manufacturing abroad. The United States is the major market for business jet aircraft and yet the share of U.S. sales accounted for by aircraft manufactured abroad rose dramatically in the 1980s. During the same period and, indeed, into the 1990s, several U.S. manufacturers of business jets were acquired by other, larger enterprises, typically manufacturers of military and/or commercial planes. Other ownership consolidations have occurred. It is arguable that the changes in ownership may have adversely affected the ability of the U.S. firms to compete. It is possible, too, that differences in the technology policies of the United States and those of other nations have been of great importance. In any case, market shares in the U.S. continue to change, with the possibility emerging that only one or two aircraft types in each of the major categories of business jets can reasonably be expected to survive.

A related question dealt with in Chapter Seven concerns whether yet another major innovation in business aircraft is soon to appear. What sort of organizational form is likely to produce efforts to develop and market such innovations? Of what importance will government policies be to the directions taken by the innovators? How will this affect the balance between U.S. and foreign manufacturers? Will we see the successful development of vertical/short takeoff and landing (V/STOL) and of supersonic or hypersonic business aircraft? How can such efforts be financed? Will there be a market for the resulting products?

Through these chapters we see repeated instances showing that market structure is indeed endogenous to the competitive process when opportunities for product and process innovations abound. We suspect that any generalizations about an equilibrium structure are worse than hazardous so long as such opportunities abound. Even attempting to investigate equilibrium properties in the face of sequential and fundamental innovative opportunities reflects a failure to comprehend the truly disequilibrating properties of Schumpeterian market processes.

Notes

1. Information on *The Glasshopper* and other PPG aircraft comes from a memorandum, W. T. Branthoover to G. A. Zoghby, February 11, 1991, in response to a request from the authors.

2. "Business Flying Holds Steady Course: Up," *Aviation Week* (hereafter *AW*), March 14, 1955, p. 308.

3. "Business, Farm Flying Continue to Grow," *AW*, March 2, 1953, p. 163.

4. "Leading Turbine-powered Business Aircraft," *AW*, March 6, 1967, p. 208.

5. Schumpeter, J. A., *Capitalism, Socialism and Democracy*. New York: Harper, 1942, p. 84.

6. Schumpeter introduced the idea of "swarming" in his *The Theory of Economic Development*, translated by R. Opie, Cambridge, MA., Harvard University Press, 1934; originally published in German in 1911. According to Schumpeter, new means to combine factors of production (i.e., innovations) *"appear, if at all, discontinuously in groups or swarms"* (p. 223 italics in original). "[T]he appearance of one or a few entrepreneurs facilitates the appearance of more, in ever increasing numbers . . . [T]he carrying out of new combinations is difficult . . . However, if one or a few have advanced with success, many of the difficulties disappear" (p. 228). This occurs "up to the point of eliminating entrepreneurial profit . . . " (p. 229) Schumpeter made these comments in the context of a theory of business cycles. The content has the flavor of a "once-and-for-all" innovation, beginning and ending with conditions of equilibrium. Profits begin and end at zero.

    A review of more recent theoretical literature on "over-bidding" and appropriability appears in W. L. Baldwin and J. T. Scott, *Market Structure and Technological Change*, New York: Harwood, 1987, pp. 18-56. Most of this literature

concerns the types of market conditions and firm behavior that yield socially opti-
mal R&D and innovation for a "once-and-for-all" innovation. The existence of
zero profit equilibrium is sometimes assumed or, alternatively, tested in the various models. Baldwin and Scott conclude that, "Over the broad range of market
structures, competition can lead to too much or too little R&D investment. The
prospect of competition in the post-innovation market may erode expected returns and cause too little R&D investment, while competition in the pre-
innovation market can cause firms to invest beyond the point where marginal social gain equals marginal social cost. The net result of these offsetting effects is
not in general known, and it may be unknowable." (p.61)

See also P. Dasgupta, "The Theory of Technological Competition," in J. E.
Stiglitz and G. F. Mathewson (eds.), *New Developments in the Analysis of
Market Structure*, Cambridge, MA: MIT Press, 1986.

The theoretical models typically assume a set of firms, each of which attempts to
maximize a well-defined profit function. Such firms are a far cry from those of
Schumpeterian entrepreneurs. The latter "retire from the arena only when and because their strength is spent and they no longer feel equal to their task." Schumpeter's entrepreneur was not at all "the economic man, balancing probable results
against disutility of effort and reaching in due course a point of equilibrium beyond which he is not willing to go." *The Theory of Economic Development* (p.
92). Unlike economic man, but perhaps like those responsible for creating new
business jets, Schumpeter's entrepreneur has "the dream and the will to found a
private kingdom, . . . the will to conquer . . . the impulse to fight, to prove oneself
superior to others, to succeed for the sake, not of the fruits of success, but of success itself . . . [T]here is the joy of creating, of getting things done, or simply of
exercising one's energy and ingenuity . . . [The entrepreneur] seeks out difficulties, changes in order to change, delights in ventures."(p. 93-94)

7. Useful generalizations about the advantages and/or disadvantages of being the
    leader or follower in making innovations are lacking. There are some models, of
    course.

    See, for example, D. Futenberg, R. J. Gilbert, J. Stiglitz and J. Tirole, "Preemp-
    tion, Leapfrogging and Competition in Patent Races," *European Economic
    Review*, vol. 22, 1983; R. J. Gilbert and D. M. G. Newbery, "Preemptive Patent-
    ing and the Persistence of Monopoly," *American Economic Review*, vol. 72,
    1982; J. F. Reinganum, "Uncertain Innovation and the Persistence of Monopoly,"
    American Economic Review, vol. 74, 1984. See also the discussion of "offen-
    sive" and "defensive" innovation strategies in C. Freeman, *The Economics of In-
    dustrial Innovation*, 2nd ed., Cambridge, MA: MIT Press, 1986, pp. 169-179.

8. Baldwin and Scott, *op. cit.*, summarize the evidence as showing that, "New firms,
    or established firms entering a new market through innovation, appear to have
    made disproportionately large innovative contributions."(p. 111) In *Technology*

and Market Structure, Lexington, MA: Lexington Books, 1971, Phillips concluded that successful entry by newcomers into the production of commercial aircraft tended to exploit available technology to achieve "quantum leaps." The
incumbent firms with substantial market shares often focused on stretching existing planes rather than on major innovations. For discussion, see E. Mansfield,
The Economics of Technological Change, New York: Norton, 1968, pp. 92-93
and M. I. Kamien and N. L. Schwartz, *Market Structure and Innovation*, Cambridge: Cambridge University Press, 1982, pp. 38-42.

9. A. Phillips, *op. cit.* In addition to tracing the role of government, this book is
cast in the context of an eclectic model that partially endogenizes market structure and the R&D activities of firms. Related work includes R. R. Nelson and S.
G. Winter, "Forces Generating and Limiting Concentration Under Schumpeterian
Competition," *Bell Journal of Economics*, vol. 9, 1978, and by the same authors,
An Evolutionary Theory of Economic Change, Cambridge, MA: Harvard University Press, 1982.

See also P. P. Saviotti and J. S. Metcalfe, "Present Development and Trends in
Evolutionary Economics," in Saviotti and Metcalfe (eds.), *Evolutionary Theories
of Economics and Technological Change: Present Status and Future Prospects*,
London: Harwood Publishing, 1990; G. Dosi, C. Freeman, R. R. Nelson, L.
Soetes and G. Silverberg, *Technical Change and Economic Theory*, London:
Pinter, 1988; A. Heerrtje and Mark Perlman (eds.), *Evolving Technology and
Market Structure: Studies in Schumpeterian Economics*, Ann Arbor: University
of Michigan Press, 1990; P. Dasgupta, "The Theory of Technological Competi-
tion," in J. E. Stiglitz and G. F. Mathewson (eds.), *New Developments in the
Analysis of Market Structure*, Cambridge, MA: MIT Press, 1986.

10. The "demand-pull"/"technology-push" debate dates back to at least J.
Schmookler, "The Level of Inventive Activity," *Review of Economics and Statistics*, May, 1954. Schmookler (and others) forcefully advocated the "demand-
pull" thesis, arguing that the level of demand for an industry's output largely determined (with a lag) the amount and type of technological change in the
industry. The "technology-push" thesis, on the other hand, maintains that technological opportunities are brought to the attention of enterprises — often by their
R&D organizations — and that one or more of the firms is then successful in
innovating. One aspect of successful innovation may in fact be the creation of a
demand for the new goods that may not hitherto have existed (or, at least, have
not been well-defined). We see no reason why the (limited) acceptance of either
view necessarily suggests that the other is totally false. In fact, we find that both
demand-pull and technology-push were operative in the development of business
jets.

11. See R.R. Nelson and S.G. Winter, "In Search of a Useful Theory of Innovations,"
Research Policy, vol. 6 (January 1977); D. Sabal, *Patterns of Technological*

Innovation, New York: Addison-Wesley (1981); G. Dosi, "Technological Paradigms and Technological Trajectories: A Suggested Interpretation of the Determinants and Directions of Technological Change," *Research Policy*, vol. 11 (June 1982); G. Dosi, "Sources, Procedures, and Microeconomic Effects of Innovation," *Journal of Economic Literature*, vol. 26 (September 1988).

12. Nelson and Winter, in "Forces Generating and Limiting Concentration . . . ," and *An Evolutionary Theory* . . . , *loc. cit.*, run simulations to investigate the effects of various factors on market structure. They vary the number of firms initially in the market, the ease of making major innovations, the ease of imitating, and whether the leading firms exercise restraint (delay or curtail) in their innovative investments. Their simulations suggest that concentration tends to be greater when there is a rapid stream of technological opportunities through time, when imitation of successful innovations is difficult, when there is high variance between successful and unsuccessful outcomes, and when the larger firms do nothing to restrain their output growth.

Chapter Two

The 1950s: Pressures Build for the Introduction
of Business Jets

Aircraft Available for Business Use

In 1953, a data service defined business aircraft as planes owned by "a corporation or [other] business organization . . . , powered by at least two engines, equipped to fly day, night and [on] instruments to transport business personnel, prospects, customers, suppliers and friends in connection with the execution of business duties."[1] Using that definition, a survey showed that, as of June 30, 1953, "a total of 954 twin-engined business aircraft [were] owned by 674 U.S. firms; 517 of these firms own[ed] and operate[d] one aircraft, while 157 others operate[d] fleets." Of these planes, 46% were Beechcraft Model 18s, 20% were DC-3s, 19% were Lockheed Models 12, 14, or 18S and the remainder were assorted other types. At first glance, it appears that PPG had alternatives to buying the *The Glasshopper*, a C-47 converted to a DC-3.

Actually, there were no good alternatives for meeting PPG's needs. The Beechcraft Model 18 was, like the DC-3 and C-47, a design of the mid-1930s.[2] Improvements had been made over the years, but many of the Model 18s used by businesses in the post-World War II years were conversions of military aircraft made originally under a variety of designations between 1940 and 1945. The 1946 Model D18S was still capable of seating only six passengers, had a cruise speed of only 211 mph, and a range of 1,120 miles.[3]

The Lockheed L-12, the Electra Junior, was a scaled-down version of the Lockheed L-10 Electra.[4] The L-12 was intended for airline and executive use, although about half of those produced were actually delivered to the military. "As an executive transport, the aircraft could be fitted with more luxurious accommodation including club chairs or a sofa, table, typewriter, [and] a lavatory."[5] It could seat at most six passengers, and cruised at 213 mph.

While the plane looked good in 1936 — 39 of the initial production run were sold to U.S. businesses — production had stopped in 1942. The L-12s used by business in the 1950s were retrofitted versions of the planes produced more than a decade earlier.

The Lockheed L-14 was also a design of the mid-1930s. The plane was conceived as a "larger Lockheed Electra" and named the Super Electra. Lockheed's intention was to have a plane to compete against the DC-3. Only four L-14s were delivered to private owners, prominently including one to Howard Hughes for his 1938 record-breaking, round-the-world trip.[6] The L-14 was typically configured for 12 passengers in commercial use. In its early versions, it had a cruise speed of 215 mph and a range of 1,500 miles. Later versions and modifications offered substantial performance improvements.

Disappointing sales of the L-14 caused Lockheed to stop production of the plane in 1939, turning its attention instead to developing the Lockheed L-18 Lodestar.[7] The first production Lodestar was flown in February 1940. It was eventually produced in many models — including a military R50-3 VIP transport and a corresponding civil version — and was purchased by U.S. and foreign airlines and several foreign governments. We describe in a subsequent section the importance of this plane to William P. Lear's involvement in the business aircraft industry.

In the early 1950s, a business requiring a plane with large passenger and weight payload capabilities would have found the Beech and Lockheed aircraft distinctly poor substitutes for reconfigured DC-3s. To equal or improve on the performance characteristics of the DC-3s, a business would have had to turn to executive versions of planes such as the Martin 202/404 and the Consolidated CV-240/340, all of which were being manufactured for airline use in the late 1940s or early 1950s.

Other planes were (or shortly would be) available for business use. These included the twin-engined Aero Commander 520, the Grumman G-44 Widgeon, the Beech Model 50 Twin Bonanza and the de Havilland Dove. The Piper P-23 Apache was first delivered for business use in 1954. Converted B-26s, B-23s, B-25s and PV-1 Ventura bombers were available from a number of refitters and found considerable use among business customers. Businesses not requiring the performance of twin-engined aircraft could, of course, use planes such as the Beech Bonanza, Cessna Models 170, 190, and 195, the Piper Pacer and Tri-Pacer and the single-engined Navion.

The Growing Dissatisfaction of Businesses and Government

The Corporation Aircraft Owners Association was renamed the National Business Aircraft Association (NBAA) in 1953.[8] Data for the previous year indicated that the hours flown in business flying had reached 3,124,000, triple the number for 1946. While it was recognized that "business flying [was] here to stay," "growing pains" were also seen. Among the "major problems" was the fact that, "Present owners for the most part [were] not satisfied with their aircraft. Either they are using obsolete transport models, converted World-War-II bombers, or, as a compromise, they are operating later models that are not particularly suited for their purposes."[9] It was observed that, "A plane designed specifically for company use . . . is the dream of most business flying enthusiasts. Operators want such a plane badly, and manufacturers would very much like to produce it . . . But in the absence of a common medium through which companies can get together, define what they want in the way of specifications and present unified proposals to the manufacturers, a complete stalemate exists . . ."[10]

The perception that a common specification was needed before the production of such aircraft would be feasible probably reflected the influence of existing military and commercial airline procurement practices. Whatever its basis, it seems to have affected the willingness of manufacturers to venture into the market independently. Thus, it was stated in 1954 that, "Until definite specifications are arrived at, the multi-engine business fleet will continue to be made up of obsolescent and 'compromise' aircraft." Further, "In order to ascertain both specifications and size of the market, mutual cooperation is needed between operators and manufacturers . . . Until such a close-working, operator-manufacturer relationship is brought into being, it is considered doubtful that any type or types of multi-engine aircraft specifically designed for business flying requirements will ever get beyond the drawing boards . . . It would be a shame, observers feel, if this new and vitally important segment of aviation were allowed to deteriorate before it has a chance to reach its full potential . . . The fact remains, however, that there is an estimated multi-million dollar market among larger corporations for an efficient, high-performance, multi-engine business plane, a plane currently not in existence . . . What they want is a 1956 or 1958 design that will be capable of equaling or bettering the airline service of that day."[11]

The situation did not improve during the next year-and-a-half. In late 1955, the NBAA was "irked by what it consider[ed] the 'foot-dragging' tactics of U.S. aircraft manufacturers." The Association was "thinking of under-writing the development of a high-speed transport especially designed to fill executive needs."[12] Three hundred twenty-three corporate members of the NBAA were then operating 850 aircraft. Despite a sense that displays and mockups of new planes by North American Aviation and Fairchild Airplane were evidence of "competition for the business plane owner's dollar," the main concern still seemed to be whether any such new equipment "would leave the drawing board."[13]

The members of the NBAA were not alone in making known their de-sires for better aircraft. In early 1956, the United States Air Force expressed an interest in a small jet transport with a cruise speed of at least 400 knots (460 mph) and a range of at least 1,000 statute miles.[14] Six months later, this requirement was better defined. Two types of aircraft were specified. One was a "Light twin-jet trainer, with a range of about 1,500 nautical miles, a crew of two and passenger capacity of at least four. The aircraft [was to] have a service ceiling at design takeoff weight of 40,000 pounds; maximum cruise altitude of 45,000 feet, and cruise speed of Mach 0.76 (550 mph)."

The second plane was to be a "Medium weight four-jet utility trans-port trainer, with a normal range of 1,500 nautical miles and provisions for a crew of two and eight passengers. Primary mission [was to] be fast move-ment of critical documents and cargo. Extended range [was to] run up to 2,200 nautical miles against [a] 70-knot headwind. Service ceiling at design takeoff weight [had to] be 40,000 ft., maximum cruise altitude, 45,000 ft. Cruising speed [had to] be the same 550 mph called for in the twin-jet plane."[15]

The Air Force sent these specifications to 28 manufacturers, with notice that it was interested in as many as 1,200 to 1,800 planes. The manufacturers were asked to develop prototype aircraft at their own expense for joint commercial and military sales, with those going to the government being "off-the-shelf" versions. The Air Force was to make its selection after evaluating competing models. Fairchild, Northrop, North American, Convair, Cessna, Beech, Temco and Lockheed all expressed interest.[16]

We see here clear elements of "demand pull" that affected both the timing and the nature of entry into the production of business jets. We will consider this subject in more detail after we consider the technological environment and the development activities of the manufacturers during this period.

Developments in Jet Aircraft Technology to the Mid-1950s

The "demand pull" for the development of business jets was hardly independent of technological developments in aviation, however. Whittle described a jet engine in a thesis presented to the Royal Aircraft Establishment in 1928. Heinkel was developing a turbojet aircraft in Germany prior to World War II. Comparing Whittle with others who made major contributions to early jet propulsion technologies, Stewart concludes that Whittle's "thought was richer and earlier. His was the brain that brought together the items previously seen as independent, discrete incompatibles. His was the brain that saw the entire picture . . . Perhaps if we wish to be pedantically correct we should say that Whittle did not invent a gas turbine, he did not invent a gas propulsion system, nor yet a by-pass propulsion system or a ram jet propulsion system; he brought together certain of these items in integrated engineering productions capable of producing power and having the means of using that power in a manner suited to flying machines."[17]

Whittle's work was clearly not pulled along from the demand side. Indeed, Whittle's ideas were greeted with hostility from other engineers and technicians and he encountered grave difficulties in his attempts to raise money to support the construction of experimental engines. Only "Whittle's idealism and . . . his obstinacy" saw him through.[18] By the 1950s, military and experimental aircraft had been utilizing Whittle's ideas for a decade. This experience created a strong "technology push" and caused businesses and governments to conceive of and demand new types of jet aircraft. Business jets were among these.

The first jet airplane, the He 178, flew in Germany in August 1939. The first two-engined jet airplane, the German He 280, flew in April 1941. The Messerschmitt Me.262 was the first operational turbojet aircraft. It entered service in the Luftwaffe in July 1944. Whittle flew a plane equipped with jet engines in May 1941. The British de Havilland Vampire F.1 flew in April 1945 and entered RAF service in mid-1946. In the U.S., the Bell XP-59A flew in October 1942. Subsequent production versions were delivered to the Army Air Force in 1944 for limited use as trainers. The XP-59A used GE engines based directly on Whittle's work in England. Development of the Lockheed XP-80 (F-80), the first operational U.S. combat jet fighter began in C. L. (Kelly) Johnson's Skunk Works in early 1943. The prototype flew in January 1944 and deliveries of production models began in October of that year. Lockheed was also responsible for F-90 and F-94. Convair worked on an F-81; North American, the F-82, F-86 and F-93; Bell, the F-83; Republic, the F-84; McDonnell, the F-85 and F-88; North American, the F-86 Sabre and F-100 Super Sabre. None of these aircraft is anything like a business jet, yet experience with each gave the manufacturers knowledge that was ultimately critical to the development of business jets.[19]

Translating jet technologies into bomber aircraft was also common by the mid-1950s. Design of the Boeing B-47, the first "swept-wing jet bomber built in quantity for any air force," began in 1943.[20] In the U.S., Martin, Northrop, and Convair were also engaged in early jet bomber developments. Convair's supersonic B-58 stemmed from a 1949 Air Force design competition.[21] Again, the manufacturers derived substantial relevant technology from their experience with bombers.

Work on what was purported to be the "world's first intercity turbojet transport," the AVRO C.102, began in Canada in the spring of 1946. The design followed "the provisional specification drawn by Trans Canada Air Lines."[22] The timing is roughly coincident with the development of the Douglas DC-6B, but the C.102 cruised at 427 mph rather than at the 300-315 mph characteristic of the DC-6B. The Jetliner had a gross weight of 60,000 pounds, compared to 107,000 pounds for the DC-6B. The former could accommodate 50 passengers; the latter, typically 66, but up to 102 in a high-density seating configuration. The Jetliner, unfortunately, had a payload of only 12,700 pounds and a range of only 1,400 miles in contrast to about 25,000 pounds and 2,800 miles for the DC-6B. The day of the economical jet transport had yet to arrive.[23]

The ill-fated de Havilland Comet flew as a prototype in July 1949 and entered service for BOAC in May 1952. The Comet seated 36 passengers and cruised at 490 mph at 40,000 feet. One of the craft broke up in flight about a year after its introduction. Two more experienced the same type of structural failure within the next year. Comet 4, the commercial replacement for the first Comet, did not enter service until October 1958.[24]

In the U.S., Lockheed was among those considering an early entry into the production of jet transports. The difficulties apparent to Lockheed included an enormous financial risk — which Lockheed invited the government to assume — and the lack of reliable turbojet engines. Other problems included "1930 vintage" air traffic control rules, the need for Jet Assisted Take Off (JATO) and reverse JATO landing devices to keep the plane within the constraints of existing runways, and pressurization problems inherent in the 40,000 foot altitudes at which the plane would cruise. It was thought that "shock-mounted or spring-loaded seats" might be needed "to aid passenger comfort in the sharp, short bumps that a jet transport would take."[25] Lockheed never offered a commercial jet, settling instead for the L-188 Electra turbo-prop, a plane that itself exhibited major structural difficulties.

Boeing began work on what was to become the B-707 in May 1952. First flight was in July 1954 and first commercial operations were in October 1958.[26] Douglas did not announce plans for the DC-8 until June 1955, after the prototype of the B-707 had been flying for nearly a year. First flight of the DC-8 was in May 1958, with first commercial operations more than a year later.[27] Howard Hughes indicated that he might develop commercial jets in competition with Boeing and Douglas, but these plans apparently did not go far.[28] Convair spent years developing the Convair 880 and 990 commercial jets, only to discover that their sales potential was highly limited because of their high operating costs.[29]

The development of a business jet in the mid-1950s would have entailed enormous risks. While jet technology, in some generic sense, was clearly available, adapting and adding to that technology for the specific purpose of building a business jet would be neither easy nor inexpensive. Despite the requests of the NBAA and others for such planes, the record of successes and failures in commercial and military developments was not at the time auspicious. Each firm that postponed development faced the risk that another might beat it to the market, but "first-movers" in radical aircraft innovations had not had great records of success. Being second or even third with a successful plane would be distinctly preferable to being first with a plane that proved to be a technical and economic failure.

Efforts at Development of Business Aircraft Within the Reciprocating-Engine Technologies

At the same time that opportunities to introduce jet-powered business aircraft were beginning to appear, some saw opportunities for continued development using the traditional reciprocating engines and propellers. The Aero Commander series ranks among the most successful of these efforts.[30] The Aero Commanders were designed and produced by the Aero Design and Engineering Company, a firm organized by former employees of Douglas Aircraft who had been unable to interest Douglas in their ideas for executive aircraft. Prototypes of the late 1940s led to the Aero Commander 520, certified in 1952, and later to the 560, 560A, 680 and other variants. Subsequent versions of the Aero Commander adopted turboprop technologies and, as we see in the next chapter, the Jet Commander and, later, the Israeli Westwind and Astra series derived from this enterprise as well.

The top-of-the-line Aero Commander 680 Super/L-26C accommodated seven people, including the pilot. It had a gross weight of 7,000 pounds, and an empty weight of 4,330 pounds. Wing loading, a rough indicator of the lift-drag characteristics of a plane at high speeds, was 29 pounds per square foot, only slightly higher than that of the DC-3. The 680, however, could operate from runways as short as 1,630 feet. It had a top speed of 260 mph and a range of 1,600 miles. The 680's "fly away from factory" price was $84,500 in 1956. These characteristics, while in some respects impressive relative to the DC-3, are far from those being sought by the members of the NBAA.

The Temco Aircraft Corporation developed the Twin Navion in 1953-1954, with first deliveries in 1955.[31] Only 28 were delivered over a four-year period. This plane was built on the airframe of a Ryan/North American single-engine Navion and faced strong competition from planes such as the Piper PA-23 Apache, the Beech D18S, the Twin Bonanza and the Cessna 310.

Conversions of older aircraft often achieved notable improvements in performance. The Air Force had provided William P. Lear with a Lockheed L-18 Lodestar in connection with his work on autopilot and blind landing systems.[32] Lear began to work on the plane — changing door handles, filing rivets, redesigning the interior — and ended up with a very much improved airplane. Lear entertained a vision of 80,000 company-owned aircraft by 1960.[33] Lear, Inc. bought used Lodestars and converted them to Learstars. "The idea was to gut and strip the Lodestar down to its skin and ribs and totally rebuild it, adding new engines, Lear electro-mechanical, navigation, and communication equipment, and a luxury interior for executives. Lear wanted the Learstar to be faster, safer, and quieter than the Lodestar, and to fly a longer distance without refueling."[34] Refinements by Lear and other de-sign engineers resulted in a plane that cruised at 300 mph and had a range of 3,800 miles. These levels of performance contrast sharply with the 259 mph maximum level speed and 1,890 mile range of the original L-18 and far sur-passed the capabilities of any other twin-engined transport then in production.

Howard Aero Service converted a number of Lockheed B-34 Ventura bombers to luxurious Super Ventura executive models. These planes had "a cruise speed of over 300 mph on a 2,300-mile range carrying two crew, 14 passengers and over 1,500 pounds of luggage."[35] The On-Mark Engineering Company converted Douglas A-26/B-26 light bombers to the Marksman 450. This plane, available in the late 1950s, had a top speed of 450 mph, a cruise speed of 365 mph, seats for 8 to 12 passengers, and a range of up to 3,100 miles.[36] The Baumann Aircraft Corporation stood ready to convert Martin B-26s to the Brigadier 290 through most of the 1950s.

Theory existed to show that propeller-driven aircraft were more efficient than jets up to and even beyond the speed of sound.[37] In practice, however, the realization of better performance and efficiency proved to be elusive within the confines of propeller technologies. Cessna, for, example, "took a bold step forward in 1954 when it announced a pressurized, eight-to-ten seat business airplane powered by four engines that was intended to replace many aging postwar aircraft serving as executive transportation."[38] Design had begun in September 1953 on what was called the Cessna Model 620. The plane was pressurized and air conditioned, had a total of 1,400 shp in its four supercharged engines, had a gross weight of 13,650 pounds and a maximum speed of 282 mph at 15,000 feet.

Cessna embarked on the 620 development at the same time the editor of *Aviation Week* was issuing warnings to manufacturers about their lack of attention to the needs of the market. The editor observed that "firms have gone ahead on prototypes whose specifications and dimensions appear to be dictated by internal company conditions or ideas that have little to do with requirements of the market. Or, after work has been started, research has been launched to justify the specifications . . . The risk that such projects present is unnecessary, because they are far more likely to result in failure than to strike the peculiar combination of buyer fancies . . . Sound market research before the project ever starts — not afterward — is good business."[39]

Nearly three years passed before the Cessna 620's first flight in August, 1956. Only mild enthusiasm had been expressed for the plane even prior to first flight. While its rollout was seen as "one of the top events" of the year, NBAA officials were frank in their assessment that the 620's "design speed of 250 mph falls about 50 mph below their requirement." They also were "somewhat critical of its four-engine layout, saying they preferred a twin configuration.[40] Still, one of the critics said, "This is not the airplane I want, . . . but I wish I had one of them now."[41]

General Motors indicated an interest in a fleet of 620s. At the time of first flight, the 620 had an unofficial price of approximately $300,000. It had a range of 1,700 miles, wing loading of 40.1 pounds per square foot, and could operate from airports with runways as short as 1,800 feet. Still, its cruise speed and payload capabilities differed little from those of modified DC-3s and Beech 18s.[42]

Cessna opened a sales campaign for the 620 in September 1956. The price was raised to $375,000, with deliveries to start in late 1958. Cessna claimed that earlier performance data were conservative, that the performance of the 620 was at "the pinnacle . . . of the corporate airplane market." Sales to the military and to foreign airlines for feeder operations were foreseen. In November 1957, however, Cessna canceled the 620 project. North American had by then announced plans to develop the Sabreliner and Lockheed had said it was going ahead with its JetStar. Cessna had also found that continuing development costs were greater than had been expected, particularly if the craft was to be certified for use as a commercial transport. In addition, the timing was proving to be particularly bad. Airlines were selling older, piston-engined planes from their fleets in anticipation of the delivery of jetliners. The time for a 620, if there ever had been one, had long passed. Business jets were shortly to be on the scene in a serious way.

Government Activity Supporting the Introduction of Business Jets

The pivotal role of the government in the development of commercial jet aircraft is well documented.[43] The Boeing 707 owed much to the antecedent B-47 bomber; the DC-8, to Douglas' experience with the XB-43 and XB-42; the Convair 880 and 990, to Convair's work on the XB-46. The development of jet engines, in the U.S. and abroad, was almost entirely at the initiative and expense of the government. New construction materials and construction methods appeared because of military aircraft developments. Innovations in avionics came in large measure from military and space programs. Similarly, the National Advisory Committee on Aeronautics (NACA) and its successor, the National Aeronautics and Space Administration (NASA), were deeply involved in many avenues of research related to commercial aircraft. Today's airfoils, lift-enhancing devices, spoilers, air inlets, fuselage designs and other features owe much to basic research carried out at

NACA/NASA. Those interested in the development of business jets were in a position to benefit from the same general advances in technology.

The Lockheed T-33 was the standard jet trainer used by the U.S. Air Force through the mid-1950s. The T-33 was a modified F-80, with performance and handling characteristics much like those of the fighter from which it derived. In late 1952, the Air Force invited manufacturers to participate in a design competition for a new jet trainer. Seven manufacturers responded, proposing a total of 14 designs; Cessna's Model 318 — later to be the T-37 — won.[44] Cessna received a contract for a mockup and another for the production of several prototypes. The first of the prototypes flew in September 1955; first deliveries of T-37s to the Air Force were in 1957. Over the next twenty years, Cessna delivered nearly 1,300 T-37s. Thus, at the same time Cessna was attempting to satisfy business needs for a new plane with the 620, it was more successfully creating for the Air Force a jet trainer that had some of the characteristics business users were seeking.

The T-37 initially used two prototype Continental engines, each rated at only 920 pounds static thrust (lb st). Engines in the production models were rated at 1,025 lb st. The plane had a maximum speed of slightly over 400 mph and a cruise speed of 368 mph. It seated only two, an instructor and a student, and had a range of but 800 miles. These characteristics, while appropriate for a first-level trainer, lacked some of the essentials for businesses. We cover the reasons Cessna opted not to convert the T-37 to a business jet in Chapter Four. Note, however, that because of the competition for the USAF trainer, there were now 13 other designs for light jet airplanes on the drawing boards of other manufacturers.

The T-37 was well-suited for the training of fighter pilots, but it was not adequately advanced and lacked the configuration, weights and performance for use as a small transport and combat proficiency trainer. Thus, as already noted, the Air Research and Development Command indicated interest in a small jet transport in February 1956.[45] Perhaps as a result of the earlier competition, North American, Fairchild, Ryan, Lockheed and others already had designs for such planes. More specific requirements for a UTX (utility trainer experimental) were released six months later, August 1956. These specifications had been widely anticipated and North American announced almost immediately "that it would build a prototype of its NA-246 design to the specification."[46] The NA-246 — later the T-39 as used by the Air Force and the Sabreliner in private use — was to accommodate a two-person crew and four-to-six passengers, have a maximum speed of 595 mph at 36,000 feet, a cruise speed of 452 mph at 40,000 feet and a range of 1,725 miles. These characteristics were a far cry from those of a converted DC-3 or B-26 and radically different from those of a Beechcraft 18 or the Cessna Model 620. North American was clearly pushing the state of the art in its proposal. A prototype was ready in the spring of 1958 but the "non-availability of suitable [domestic] engines delayed the first flight until September 16, 1958." [47]

Lockheed responded to another part of the USAF request. That part specified by a larger UCX (utility cargo/transport experimental) development project was begun in Lockheed's Skunk Works under "Kelly" Johnson. The resulting CL-329 JetStar flew in September 1957, "241 days after the start of its design and nineteen months before its McDonnell competitor."[48]

The CL-329 owed much to the French SNCASE SE.210 Caravelle commercial transport. The location of engines at the sides of the rear of the fuselage and the location of the horizontal stabilizer and elevators in the lower portion of the vertical stabilizer came directly from Caravelle. Again, no suitable U.S. engines were available and the prototype used two British Orpheus engines rated at 4,850 lb st each. A later prototype used four 3,000 lb st Pratt & Whitney engines, hung in pods of two on each side. The initial version had a gross weight of 38,841 pounds, a maximum speed of 613 mph at 36,000 feet and a cruise speed of 502 mph. Production models had somewhat higher gross weight, lower maximum speeds, the same or better cruise speeds, and a greater range than the initial model.[49]

The McDonnell 119 entry into the UCX competition was also a four-engine plane. Two separate engine pods were hung beneath each wing, with the same Pratt & Whitney engines as those in the four-engine JetStar. The gross weight of the 119 was 40,298 pounds, for a wing loading of over 73 pounds per square foot. Maximum cruise speed was listed at 565 mph and the range without internal auxiliary tanks was 2,335 miles. The auxiliary tanks boosted this range to 3,000 miles. At the time, McDonnell's only successful experience with military procurement was with the XF-88 (later F-101

Voodoo) design. No 119s were ordered by the Air Force and none was produced for private sales.

Other manufacturers, buoyed by hopes of military sales, began the development of small jets. Carma Manufacturing Co., a producer of electrical
and mechanical equipment, attempted to sell its Weejet trainer to the Navy.[50]
The Temco Aircraft Co. received a Navy contract for 14 of its self-financed
Model 51 TT-1 jet trainers. The USAF performed flight tests on the Beechcraft Model 73 Jet Mentor, despite its shortcomings relative to other potential
jet trainers.[51] There must have been many other less well-recorded instances
of attempted entry into the production of small jet aircraft prompted by the
possibility of military sales.

First Efforts at Developing Business Jets

Beechcraft put its hopes for early entry into business jets not on the
Jet Mentor but rather on the Morane-Saulnier MS-760 Paris jet.[52] The
MS-760 grew from a two-seat French jet trainer, the MS-755 Fleuret, which
first flew in January 1953. The prototype MS-760 flew in July 1954, after
which date its manufacturer, Morane-Saulnier, attempted to interest both military and business customers. The plane was listed in the annual Inventory
Issue of *Aviation Week* as early as March 15, 1954.

Beech was studying jets at that time and recognized in 1955 that the
MS-760 was the "first and only twin-jet aircraft available . . . for demonstration . . . [I]t cannot be duplicated by anybody else at this time."[53] The
plane was powered by two 880 lb st Turbomeca Marbore engines, seated four
persons (including the pilot), was pressurized, had a stated long-range cruising speed of 370 mph, a stated (but unrealized) range of 1,000 miles, and a
gross weight of 7,725 pounds. At this weight, the wing loading amounted to
39.8 pounds per square foot. Takeoff speed was 105 mph and the takeoff required a runway of 4,135 feet. The original plans called for equipping the
U.S. version with Continental J69 engines, an adaptation of the French Marbore engine that was to be used on the Cessna T-37. Beech tested the MS-760
in the summer of 1955, sending it to major cities across the U.S. and Canada
for sales demonstrations.

Beech also attempted to interest the U.S Navy and the Royal Canadian Air Force in the MS-760 for use as a small transport/trainer. Beech felt that if the Navy ordered the plane, civilian orders would follow. One of Beech's distributors ordered an MS-760 in August 1955, putting down a $50,000 deposit against a delivery price of $300,000. Certification of the MS-760 for U.S. operations had not been completed by November 1956, but the continuing expressions of interest in a small jet by both the military and by NBAA continued to give hope that the plane would find American buyers.

Beech announced a "package price" of $210,000 for the MS-760 in January 1958. The package included a finished aircraft, spare parts, ground handling equipment, special tools and a course in jet aircraft maintenance. The fact that only a few fixed-base operators had the ability to maintain and service a jet was regarded as a significant obstacle to private sales. Beech listed the MS-760 in only one *Aviation Week* Inventory Issue, that of March 9, 1959.[54]

Beech discontinued distribution of the MS-760 Paris in the spring of 1961, by which time the Lockheed JetStar, the North American Sabreliner and other experimental business jets were in the air. These were far more advanced and more expensive aircraft than was the MS-760. The appearance of the JetStar and Sabreliner is probably not the reason for the lack of success of the MS-760, however. The plane Beech was offering was not the plane that businesses wanted — at any price. The first French production model MS-760 flew in early 1958, and eventually a number of them were sold to the French Air Force, the French Navy, and the Brazilian Air Force. Being first in the U.S. market with the MS-760 business jet did not pay off for Beech, however. We go into this episode in more detail in Chapter Three.

Another French Aircraft manufacturer, Avions Marcel Dassault, announced its intentions to build an executive jetliner in 1958. Dassault at the time was making the Mirage jet fighters and Mystere fighter-bombers for the French Air Force. The proposed business jet, the Mediterrane, was to be powered by two R-7 Farandole 3,000 lb st turbojet engines hung under the wings. Six-to-eight passengers were to be accommodated. *Aviation Week* listed an incredible cruise speed of 700 mph for the plane in its 1958 and 1959 Inventory Issues. The primary intended use was on flights between France and oil fields in North Africa. We have found no further record of the plane. In the following decade, however, Dassault did introduce its very successful Falcon business jets.

The Italian Cobra F.400 design of the late 1950s was a small, relatively inexpensive, four-place executive jet somewhat similar to the MS-760. The plane was to be powered by a single 880 lb st Turbomeca Marbore engine, have a maximum speed of only 360 mph, and a range of only 621 miles. There was discussion of licensing the craft for production in the U.S., but so far as we have found that idea was abandoned after 1960.[55]

Fairchild Aircraft expressed interest in business jets as early as 1955.[56] In the spring of 1956, Fairchild announced that it would "construct a prototype of a four-jet utility transport with its own funds in hopes of stimulating executive and feeder-airline purchases." This plane, the M-185F, was a follow-on from an earlier Fairchild M-225 proposal, which had been presented to the NBAA the year before in both four- and three-engine configurations.

Continental Can Co. became the first U.S. corporation to order a business jet when in 1956 it executed a letter of intent for the 1960 delivery of an M-185F. The price was something less than $1 million. Continental Can intended to use the M-185F as a replacement for its Lockheed Lodestars. On the drawing board, the M-185F cost no more to operate than the Lodestars and had significant performance advantages. The M-185F was to cruise at 540 mph and have a range of 2,200 miles (with 70 mph headwinds). The plane was to use Fairchild J-83, General Electric J-85 or Westinghouse J-34 engines depending on availability. The rear-fuselage engine mountings shown for the M-225 gave way to under-wing engine pods for the M-185F so that the larger engines and thrust reversers could be used.[57]

Enthusiasm for the M-185F was said to be high. By early 1957, Fairchild indicated that other corporations had made "definite commitments." Prospective buyers sent personnel to the Fairchild plant to inspect it. An F-27 Friendship turboprop prototype was available for demonstration flights, but only a full-scale mockup of the M-185F was on hand for the prospective purchasers. A year later, at almost the same time that Beech reduced the price of the MS-760 from $300,000 to $210,000, Fairchild announced that it was dis-continuing the M-185F project in order to concentrate on the F-27. There were, it turned out, only five options for M-185s on the books and only three buyers had made deposits. Fairchild estimated that, were it to go on, it would have to spend in excess $6 million prior to first flight in late 1957 or early 1958. With those costs, it would have taken about 100 orders to break even. Fairchild seemed for a time ready to be first, but elected not go ahead because of a lack of demonstrated demand.

Douglas Aircraft also indicated interest in business jets in this period. The Piaggio-Douglas PD-808 jet is described in the next chapter; its origins were in a design study for a six-to-ten seat executive jet undertaken at Doug-las in 1957.[58]

At the same time it was working on the Model 620, Cessna made "a number of studies of a business-plane version of its twin-jet T-37A trainer . . . Because of production know-how, [observers thought that] a civil T-37A could be marketed at attractive prices." Cessna proceeded cautiously with this idea; a mockup of its Model 407, a four-place utility jet "bearing some resem-blance to Cessna's T-37A," was displayed at the NBAA meetings in Septem-ber 1959. The plane was to be pressurized, have a cruise speed of 404 kts (464 mph), a range of about 1,580 miles and would "probably" cost about $200,000. Cessna had no intention of producing even a prototype Model 407 in the absence of signs of considerable buyer interest, however. This interest did not materialize, and Cessna never produced the plane.[59]

Cessna clearly could have produced a business jet much like the MS-760 had it chosen to do so. We will see in Chapter Four that there are a few conceptual similarities between the 407 design and that of the extremely successful Cessna Citation, a design of the late 1960s. The latter, although simple for its time, was overall quite different than the Model 407, however.

Other less well-known firms tried to develop business jets in the 1950s. The Aircraft Marine Engineering Corporation showed a mockup of its A-1 Anser as early as 1957.[60] The Anser was to be a nine-place amphibian, capable of a maximum speed of 460 mph and a range of 1,650 miles. Our re-search has uncovered no record of its having been produced. The same firm listed a 26-place A-2 Avocet in the *Aviation Week* Inventory Issues of March 1959 through March 1961. We find no record of its having been produced, either. Several American firms in addition to those already mentioned offered jet trainers to the armed forces. Some of these undoubtedly considered business jets as well. And, of course, there were many firms abroad exploring the area.

The technologies necessary to produce a business jet were there — or nearly there — by the late 1950s. Someone was going to get into the business. The only questions were who, when, and with what airplane.

Sabreliner and JetStar Get the Lead

The Air Force UTX and UCX competitions shaped the outcome of the innovation efforts of the 1950s. North American, while expressing no early "plans for commercial application of the Sabreliner," followed the Air Force idea of an "off-the-shelf " airplane. Sabreliner was to be "suitable for CAA certification." [61] The prototype flew on September 16, 1958, at which time North American had incurred as much as $8,000,000 in development costs. By November 1958, the Air Force had placed orders for seven planes, designating them as North American T-39s. Additional orders followed.

The first T-39 rolled out in the spring of 1960 and the first five were delivered to the Air Force later that year. That delivery was the first of any business-type jet aircraft in the United States. Certification by the CAA occurred in December 1959, but the Sabreliner was not offered for delivery to businesses prior to fulfilling the initial orders of the Air Force.

The much larger Lockheed JetStar, as noted, made its maiden flight in September 1957. Lockheed was looking to the business side of the market from the outset, with principal attention to buyers who might otherwise use aircraft such as the new Grumman Gulfstream turboprop or the Convair 240, 340, or 440. The early offerings were for either the two- or four-engine version with an approximate price of $1,000,000. The Air Force indicated its preference for the JetStar over the McDonnell 119 in October 1959. By that date, Lockheed reported it had firm orders from private businesses for 30 planes and that a production model would be flying by July 1960. Orders from the Air Force did not materialize until 1960.[62]

The business jet had arrived. The swarmings of new entrants and the patterns of successes and failures would now be more evident. PPG and other corporate users would soon have available the types of aircraft they had been demanding. The changing structure of the market throughout the 1960s would be told by which of them businesses found the most attractive.

Notes

1. "Business Flying Gets Data Service," *AW*, October 5, 1953,   p. 18.
2. E. H. Phillips, *Beechcraft: Staggerwing to Starship*, Egan, MN: Flying Books, 1987, p. 19ff.
3. *AW*, February 25, 1952, p. 148.
4. R. J. Francillon, *Lockheed Aircraft Since 1913*, Annapolis, MD: Naval Institute Press, 1987, p. 129ff.
5. *Ibid.*, p. 129.
6. *Ibid.*, pp. 137-143.
7. *Ibid.*, p. 188.
8. *AW*, July 6, 1953, p. 7.
9. "Multi-Million Market Goes Begging for Takers," *AW*, March 15, 1954, p. 136.
10. *Ibid.*, p. 137.
11. *Ibid.*, pp. 137-138.
12. E. J. Bulban, "NBAA May Finance Development of Modern Executive Transport," *AW*, October 17, 1955, p. 18.
13. *Ibid.*
14. *AW*, February 13, 1956, p. 32; E. J. Bulban, "Business Flying Enters 'Golden Decade,' " *AW*, March 12, 1956, pp. 270-276.
15. "USAF Asks Industry for Trainer Transports," *AW*, August 27, 1956, p. 29.
16. *Ibid.*
17. O. Stewart, *Aviation: The Creative Ideas*, New York: Praeger, 1966, p. 168. This book contains background information on the development of jet engines and many other innovations.
18. *Ibid.*, p. 163.

19. D. Ford, "Gentlemen, I Give You the Whittle Engine," *Air & Space*, October/November 1992, p. 88; "Germany's First Jet," *FI*, February 3-9, 1993, p. 45; *Jane's Encyclopaedia of Aviation*, London: Portland House, 1989; F. G. Swanborough, *United States Military Aircraft Since 1909*, New York: Putnam, 1963.

20. F. G. Swanborough, *loc. cit.*, p. 101.

21. *Ibid.*

22. W. N. Deisher, "Canada Develops Jetliners," *SAE Journal*, December 1949, pp. 17-18; "'Avro' Jetliner," *Engineering*, October 28, 1949, p. 462; "Avro Jetliner Will Fly to U.K.," *AW*, February 13, 1950, p. 16; "Jetliner Purchase by Air Force Seen Possible," *AW*, March 19, 1951, p. 16.

23. Data for the DC-6B are from R. J. Francillon, *McDonnell Douglas Aircraft Since 1920*, Vol. I, Annapolis, MD: Naval Institute Press, 1988, pp. 398-405.

24. *Jane's Encyclopaedia of Aviation*, 1989, p. 317; R. B. Hotz, "Detailed Data on Comet Revealed," *AW*, November 21, 1949, p. 16.

25. "Lockheed's Proposals for Jet Transports," *AW*, January 9, 1950, p. 13.

26. P. M. Bowers, *Boeing Aircraft Since 1916*, London: Putnam, 1966, pp. 352-358.

27. Francillon, *McDonnell Douglas . . .* , *loc. cit.*, pp. 513-516.

28. "Hughes Gives Aviation a New Jolt," *Business Week*, May 19, 1956, p. 29.

29. A. Phillips, *Technology and Market Structure: A Study of the Aircraft Industry*, Lexington, MA: Lexington Books, 1971.

30. Information on Aero Commanders is from K. Munson, *Private Aircraft: Business and General Purpose Since 1946*, London: Blandford Press, 1967, p. 145.

31. *Jane's Encyclopaedia of Aviation, loc. cit.*, p. 225.

32. R. Rashkie, *Stormy Genius: The Life of Aviation's Maverick, Bill Lear*, Boston: Houghton Mifflin, 1988, p. 169ff.

33. *AW*, May 3, 1954, p. 43: *AW*, May 10, 1954, p. 102; E. J. Bulban, "Lear Expects Commercial Sales to Overtake Military Business," *AW*, February 13, 1956, p. 89.

34. Rashkie, *op. cit.*, p. 170; "Lear Raises Lodestar Performance," *AW*, March 16, 1953, p. 51.

35. *AW*, January 16, 1956, p. 80.

36. *AW*, February 25, 1957, p. 233; *Product Engineering*, February 10, 1958, p. 22.

37. I. H. Driggs, "Why We Still Need the Propeller," *AW*, October 23, 1950, p. 28.

38. E. H. Phillips, *Wings of Cessna: Model 120 to Citation III*, Eagan, MN: Flying Books, 1986, p. 85.

39. R. H. Wood, "Research and Executive Planes," *AW*, October 18, 1954, p. 126.

40.   E. J. Bulban, "Business Flying Enters 'Golden Decade,'" *AW*, March 12, 1956, p. 273-275. Other data on the Cessna 620 come from "Cessna Completes 620 Tests, Prepares Assembly," *AW*, April 2, 1956, p. 66; *AW*, June 18, 1956, p. 115; "Cessna 620 Begins Taxi Tests to Prepare for Initial Flight," *AW*, August 6, 1956, p. 458; "Cessna Unveils Model 620 Transport," *AW*, October 1, 1956, p. 96; "Dwindling Aircraft Market Caused Production Halt of Cessna's 620," *AW*, November 11, 1957, p. 115.

41.   Bulban, "Business Flying . . . ," *loc. cit.*

42.   "Twin Beech Cruises at 245 mph," "Cruise Speed of 250 Claimed by DC-3," *AW*, July 23, 1956, p. 76; "Cessna Starts 620 Flight Tests," *AW*, August 27, 1956, p. 41.

43.   A. Phillips, *op. cit.*; N. Rosenberg and D. Mowery, "Commercial Aircraft," in R. R. Nelson (ed.), *Government and Technical Change: A Cross-Industry Analysis*, New York: Pergamon Press, 1982.

44.   E. H. Phillips, *op. cit.*, p.61; *Jane's Encyclopaedia of Aviation, loc. cit.*, p. 248; A. M. McSurely, "Cessna Jet," *AW*, January 12, 1953, p. 15; F. G. Swanborough, *op. cit.*, pp. 124-125.

45.   "USAF Wants Industry to Design Jet Executive Transport-Trainer," *AW*, February 13, 1956, p. 32.

46.   F. G. Swanborough, *op. cit.*, p. 386.

47.   *Ibid.*

48.   Francillon, *Lockheed . . .* , *loc. cit.*, pp. 394-399.

49.   *AW*, March 3, 1958, p. 247; *AW*, March 9, 1959, p. 199.

50.   *AW*, April 16, 1956, p. 34.

51.   *AW*, July 9, 1956, p. 28; E. J. Bulban, "Temco Achieves Simplicity, Economy in Jet Trainer," *AW*, October 15, 1956, p. 98.

52.   Discussion of the MS-760 is based on Munson, *op. cit.*, pp. 165-166; E. J. Bulban, "Beech to Test Jet Business Plane," *AW*, May 9, 1955, p. 22ff; *AW*, May 23, 1955, p. 7; E. J. Bulban, "Beech Should Reach Jet Decision by Fall," *AW*, June 27, 1955,   p. 44ff; *AW*, August 29, 1955, p. 7; *AW*, September 12, 1955, p. 7; *AW*, December 26, 1955, p. 42; *AW*, November 12, 1956, p. 111; *AW*, December 24, 1956, p. 73; R. L. Stanfield, "MS-760 Shows Business Plane Promise," *AW*, December 29, 1958, p. 66ff; *AW*, May 15, 1961, p. 35.

53.   Bulban, "Beech to Test . . . ," *op. cit.*

54.   *AW*, January 6, 1958, p. 88; February 10, 1958, p. 107; March 3, 1958, p. 201; March 9, 1959, p. 202.

55. D. A. Anderton, "Italian Cobra Jet Nears Maiden Flight," *AW*, February 1, 1960, p. 81.

56. *AW*, July 25, 1955, p. 16; August 15, 1955, p. 122; E. J. Bulban, "NBAA May Finance Development of Modern Executive Transport," *AW*, October 17, 1955, p. 18.

57. *AW*, April 23, 1956, p. 31. Other detail on the M-185F is from E. J. Bulban, "Fairchild Sees Market for 600 M-185Fs," *AW*, September 3, 1956, p. 100ff; E. J. Bulban, "Business Flying Shows Sharp Upswing," *AW*, February 25, 1957, p. 276; "Fairchild Drops M-185 Business Jet Transport," *AW*, January 20, 1958, p. 26; R. M. Loebelson, "What's the Outlook for Business Jets?," *Business and Commercial Aviation* (hereafter *B&CA*), March 1958, p. 19ff.

58. Francillon, *McDonnell Douglas . . .* , *loc. cit.*, p. 534.

59. *AW*, October 8, 1956, p. 117; *AW*, September 28, 1959, p. 41; *AW*, November 19, 1959, p. 143.

60. *AW*, October 7, 1957, p. 32.

61. This section relies on G. Swanborough, *North American: An Aircraft Album*, London; Ian Allen, 1973, pp. 104-107; B. Yenne, *Rockwell: The Heritage of North American*, New York: Crown Publishers, 1989, pp. 144-149; I. Stone, "Sabreliner Fits USAF Shelf Item Concept," *AW*, December 9, 1957, p. 52ff; "Sabreliner Uses J85 Engines on Initial Flight," *AW*, September 29, 1958, p. 20; *AW*, November 10, 1958, p. 23.

62. See "Lockheed JetStar 329," *B&CA*, February 1958, p. 22ff; *B&CA*, September 1958, pp. 28-29; "Lockheed JetStar Production Models Take Shape," *AW*, October 5, 1959, p. 35; "Civil Sabreliner Proposed for Late 1961," *AW*, October 12, 1959, p. 37ff; Francillon, *Lockheed . . . loc. cit.*, p. 394ff.

Chapter Three

1960-1970: The Developing Market for Business Jet Aircraft

The Debuts of the JetStar and Sabreliner

JetStar   Lockheed "gambled on the future and in November 1958 committed the [CL-329 JetStar] to quantity manufacture."[1] Sales to corporate customers had been an objective from the outset and Lockheed did not reverse its decision when the Air Force opted to buy the smaller T-39 Sabreliner for its trainer and light transport purposes. While the prototypes were developed in Burbank, California, it was decided that production models of the JetStars were to be produced at Lockheed's Marietta, Georgia, plant. Efforts to sell the craft to corporate customers began as the plane was being developed.

The lack of an acceptable, domestically-manufactured engine for the two-engine version led to the study of several four-engine versions. The second prototype was refitted with four Pratt & Whitney JT12A-6 turbojets of 3,000 lb st each and flight tested in January 1960. This prototype developed into the CL-1329 JetStar 6, the initial production version of the first U.S.-produced business jet delivered to private customers.[2]

Lockheed had orders for 31 CL-1329s by March of 1960, with 20 signed contracts and deposits on at least eleven of the planes. The U.S. Air Force did order five JetStars before mid-1960, designating them as C-140s. These orders were received during the period when the four-engine prototype was still undergoing tests and well prior to completion and FAA Type Certification of the production versions.[3] The first flight of the production model occurred in the late summer of 1960. This plane, with four others, went to the FAA in connection with the certification program. Deliveries to business customers began in mid-1961, after delays caused by compressor stall problems that occurred when the plane flew at high angles-of-attack.

A total of 204 JetStars were produced, including the prototypes, aircraft delivered to the FAA for testing, JetStar 8s (introduced in 1967), JetStar IIs (introduced in 1976), and all military versions.[4] Sixteen JetStars were delivered to U.S. business customers in 1961 and 21 more were delivered in 1962. The latter year turned out to be the record for annual deliveries. A total of only 143 JetStars had been delivered by the end of 1970, with just 109 of these being to U.S. business customers. Sales to the U.S. government for all purposes totaled only 18, with the last being in 1963. The remainder were exported to foreign governments and businesses.

Lockheed was disappointed in the sales of the JetStar almost from the beginning. The first sales efforts coincided with the 1958-59 recession. Then the Air Force chose the Sabreliner, shattering any hope that Lockheed would realize the 250 to 300 orders its had expected to get from the military. Lockheed, having projected that it would take a production run of 300 planes to break even, found that the program was not "financially satisfactory."[5] In mid-1962, when only 43 orders had been received, serious consideration was given to halting production of the aircraft.[6] Being first on the market was not a sufficient condition for success despite the NBAA's having expressed interest in such an airplane for several years.

The JetStar was a large and technologically sophisticated machine As certified, it had a gross takeoff weight of 40,921 pounds, wing loading of 75.4 pounds per square foot, a maximum speed of Mach 0.87 and a listed normal cruise speed of 500 miles per hour. The craft was 60.4 feet in length, had a wing span of 54.4 feet, and could carry up to 10 passengers (8 normal) and a crew of two over a range of more than 2,000 miles (with a 45-minute fuel reserve).[7] A JetStar received worldwide recognition in January 1964 when Najeeb Halaby, the FAA Administrator, flew it to Moscow.[8] Other distance and speed records went to the JetStar for other flights. An early flight evaluation concluded that, "For the buyer looking for high-speed, high ranges, high comfort, high prestige — and willing to pay the price — the JetStar is hard to beat."[9] The JetStar was indeed far in advance of *The Glasshopper*, PPG's converted C-47.

The 1962 "fly-away" price for the JetStar, with unfinished interior and no special avionics, was $1,366,330.[10] Finishing would have added at least $100,000, leaving a final price to the buyer of about $1,500,000. Operating costs per passenger seat mile were estimated at $0.219 in 1962.[11] The Business Jets Division of Pan Am canceled its option to buy 16 JetStars because it "found them too expensive."[12] Pan Am subsequently adopted Dassault Falcon Jets for its Business Jets division.

We will discuss the importance of price and a widespread distribution and service network in buyers' decisions after the comparable information for other aircraft has been presented. Note, however, that no new models of the JetStar were developed during the first decade of its being on the market. The JetStar 8 designation was adopted when, from the 97th production aircraft on, JT12A-8 3,300 lb st turbojets were installed. These higher-powered engines could be and often were retrofitted to the earlier versions. The last JetStar 8 was delivered in 1973, after which production was temporarily halted. Lockheed considered a three-engine JetStar configured like a Boeing 727 and a stretched twin turbofan model in 1969, but neither was moved into prototype. Thought was also given to making the JetStar into a small commercial transport.[13]

AiResearch Aviation Company, with the cooperation of Lockheed, offered JetStar 731s beginning in 1974. The 731s were conversions of JetStar 6s and 8s, using Garrett AiResearch TFE 731-1 turbofan engines, improved avionics and some aerodynamic changes. Lockheed's own JetStar II had a new airframe, many aerodynamic changes, and 3,700 lb st TFE 731-3 engines. It was not available until late 1976, however.[14] We provide more detail on the history of the JetStar during the 1970s in Chapter Six.

Sabreliner We noted in Chapter Two that North American Aviation elected not to produce commercial versions of Sabreliner until its commitments to the military had been satisfied. The first T-39 was delivered to the Air Force in January 1961 — well before Lockheed delivered its first JetStar 15. In all, 161 T-39As and derivative aircraft were delivered to the U.S. government before the end of 1963.

While North American was concerned that promoting a program for civilian Sabreliners might compromise additional sales to the military, it never lost sight of the potential of the private market. In early 1961, when 94 planes had been sold and, of these, seven had been delivered to the Air Force, North American looked carefully at the corporate market.[16] It was concluded that a green (i.e., unpainted, unequipped and without passenger accommodations) Sabreliner might sell for $700,000, while a finished aircraft would come to perhaps $900,000. North American, which never before had sold aircraft to non-military buyers, sent out sample flight plans to potential customers pointing out how a Sabreliner would "enable a management team to transact business in three cities as widely separated as New York, Minneapolis, and Shreveport, LA, in the course of a single day."[17] It was pointed out as well that the small size of the plane enabled it to operate from relatively short runways. North American began certification of the Sabreliner as an executive transport in mid-1961. No orders were taken, but a green price of $750,000 was published.[18]

Business and Commercial Aviation listed the Sabreliner as "military version only" as late as April, 1962. Yet in October of that year, North American designated Remmert-Werner, Inc. as its first distributor, established a green price of $795,000, estimated a finished price for an all-weather plane at $900,000 to $980,000, and indicated that deliveries to the distributor would begin in March 1962. Remmert-Werner immediately appointed AiResearch to be its Los Angeles representative.[19] Type certification of the NA-265-40 Sabreliner occurred on April 17, 1963. It was anticipated at that time that deliveries would begin the next month.[20] First delivery was actually on October 24, 1963, when Pet Milk accepted a Sabreliner at a completed price of $989,982.[21]

The Sabreliner was very different from the JetStar. The initial Series 40 model had a gross takeoff weight of 17,760 pounds, with a wing loading of 51.9 pounds per square foot. It had a maximum speed of 550 miles per hour (Mach 0.85 at cruise altitude) and a normal cruise speed of 495 miles per hour (Mach 0.765 at cruise altitude). The Sabreliner carried six passengers with a crew of two, and had a full-load range of 1,770 miles (45 minutes of reserve fuel). *Business and Commercial Aviation* estimated operating costs per passenger seat mile at $0.179 in 1964.[22]

North American opined in 1963 that there might "be a commercial market of about 300 aircraft during the next 8-10 years . . . and that for the next two years the Sabreliner and Lockheed's JetStar will have the field to themselves."[23]   Even then, however, it was well known that Aero Commander's Jet Commander, Dassault's Mystere 20 (later Falcon Jet), Lear Jet, and Hawker-Siddeley's HS-125 would soon be on the market. Pan Am, in fact, had by then decided to distribute the Dassault line in place of the JetStar. Atlantic Aviation and AiResearch had agreements to distribute the HS-125. There were recognized possibilities as well that there could be competition from the German HFB-320, the Piaggio-Douglas PD-808, and the Saab 105, all of which were under development. Competition from modern turboprop aircraft was also foreseen.[24] Thus, a buyer considering either the Sabreliner or the JetStar in the 1962-1964 period would almost certainly have been aware that other planes — with perhaps improved price/performance characteristics — would soon be on the market.

Sabreliner sold well during only the first years it was on the market. Three of the civil versions were delivered in the U.S. in 1963, 19 in 1964, 26 in 1965, and 31 in 1966. Deliveries to private customers fell after 1966, indicating that orders were disappointingly small as early as 1964 or 1965.[25] North American responded by announcing an "improved Sabreliner," with the higher-thrust JT12-8A engines, a slightly longer fuselage, five cabin windows on each side, improved landing and takeoff performance, higher rate-of-climb, greater reliability and increased cruise speed.[26] This model, the NA-265 Series 60 Sabreliner, received Type Certification in April 1967, although sales had begun earlier. An equity leasing plan was introduced to allow buyers to convert lease payments to down payments. The Air Force was among the early buyers.[27]

Table 3-1, on page 60 , suggests that the introduction of the Series 60 had little if any effect on sales. Rockwell-Standard and North American Aviation merged in September 1967. The new company — later called Rockwell International — then decided to buy the previously independent Remmert-Werner distributorship to bring sales under its own control. A Sabreliner 70, with 3,300 lb st engines, a deeper fuselage cross-section, square windows, and "other improvements" was certified in 1970. This plane was called the Sabre 75 after 1971. The Sabre 75A, with 4,315 lb st engines, was available for deliveries in 1973. Still, despite the new organization and the introduction of new models, deliveries never again reached the 1966 levels.[28] Additional details on the later history of the Sabre series are given in Chapter Six.

Entrants Achieving Significant Sales by 1970

Lear Jet The early moves of Lockheed and North American into the market for business jets did not deter others. Many tried to follow; some with notable success. Among the latter was William P. Lear. Lear was not concerned about first-mover advantages of the JetStar and Sabreliner. In his view, these planes were "Royal barges" with "Pentagon price tags."[29] Their presence in the market provided competitive opportunities, not barriers to entry.

Lear had been optimistic about the size of the market for business aircraft for many years. He had predicted in 1954 — prior to his converting Lodestars to Learstars — that there might be as many as 80,000 company aircraft by 1960. Lear's forecast was premised on the introduction of a number of technological developments needed to give "business flying a boost." These improvements included "Twin-engine . . . aircraft in a lower price range . . . Better instrumentation . . . [and] Automatic pilot."[30] Lear, Inc. was developing and selling aircraft instruments at the time.

By 1955, Lear, then living in Switzerland, was exploring the possibility of designing an executive jet transport with European airframe manufacturers.[31] He worked first on the idea of a pusher turboprop derived from the World War II Marvel design of Dr. August Raspet of Mississippi State University.[32] During the time the Sabreliner and JetStar were in early development, Lear presented a (drawing board) Model 59-3, an 8-place, T-tail, twin turbojet craft with engines mounted in the rear. Efforts to get Mitsubishi to enter a joint venture to produce the major parts of such a plane in Europe and assemble them in the U.S. did not succeed.

Lear's interest then turned to the P-16 Swiss fighter-bomber. This aircraft had attracted the attention of Lear's son because of its size and wing design. The plane had a dismal record at the time, with two of the four completed models having crashed into Lake Constance. Lear still found the aircraft so impressive that "he tossed all his sketches aside and hired [its designer] Hans Struder to help him convert the P-16 into a hot-rod corporate jet."[33] This work got him into so much trouble with the Board of Directors of Lear, Inc. that he formed a new company, Swiss American Aviation Corporation, to do further work on a plane that was soon called the SAAC-23. Lear planned to do the tooling and have the wings made at Flughund-Fahrzeugwerke Altenrhein in Switzerland; the fuselage and tail, at Heinkel in Germany; other parts, at various other manufacturers throughout Europe and the U.S. Assembly was to be near Zurich, where construction of prototypes soon commenced. Lear was confident that he could sell as many as 600 SAAC-23s.

Lear's European efforts did not go unnoticed in the United States. *Aviation Week* reported in October 1960 that the Swiss American Aviation Corporation had been incorporated in Delaware and gave details of the SAAC-23. The report was that the plane was a "six- to seven-passenger executive transport . . . [with] first deliveries sometime in 1963 at a retail cost of $250,000 . . . The aircraft . . . is being designed for a cruise speed of 535 mph at 30,000 ft., with a range of 1,500 miles against a 60 mi. headwind plus 45 min. holding time . . . "[34] Six months later, Lear forecast sales of 2,000 SAAC-23s over a 10-year period. He said that the plane had gone through 23 distinct designs "with the basic idea always in mind of holding down costs . . . I know that I could not go to my corporation and ask for a $900,000 airplane."[35]

Continuing friction between Lear and other directors of Lear, Inc. resulted in the 1962 merger of the firm with the Seigler Corporation. The $13 million Lear received for his Lear, Inc. shares provided additional capital for the SAAC-23.[36] By March 1962, Lear saw that attaining his sales objectives depended on "several factors, including early availability, price, reliability and relative simplicity." He said that he preferred to push the break-even quantity of sales up to 400 with a low profit margin rather than risking the lower volume of sales that might result from a higher margin. Still, the Swiss delivery price had already risen to $350,000 and it was acknowledged that it might have go as high as $450,000.[37] At that point the plane was designed to a maximum gross weight of only 11,800 pounds, a maximum speed of 588 mph, and a cruise speed of 500 mph.

Only a fiber glass mockup of the SAAC-23 was ready for the June 1962 Business Aviation Display and Forum in Reading, Pennsylvania.[38] Lear then announced that production of the SAAC-23 would be transferred to Wichita, Kansas. The plans were to produce six-to-eight planes per month. The price of a completely finished plane — now called the Lear Jet 23 — was set at $489,000.[39] By September of 1962, the first U.S. distributorship had been established.[40] Additional sales representatives in various parts of the country were named shortly thereafter.

The maiden flight of a prototype was on October 7, 1963, at which time the price was $496,500.[41] The first flight of the production model was on March 5, 1964, with delivery to the first customer occurring on October 12, 1964. The JetStar, it may be recalled, was first delivered to business customers about three years before this date and the Sabreliner, one year before.

The Lear Jet 23 used two General Electric (GE) CJ610-1 engines, each with 2,850 lb st. At the time of type certification, the Lear Jet 23 had a gross takeoff weight of 12,500 pounds. The wing area was 231.8 square feet, resulting in a wing loading of 53.9 pounds per square foot. The recommended high-speed cruise speed was 535 mph and the recommended long-range cruise speed was 485 mph. The plane had a full-load range of 1,686 miles (with 45 minutes fuel reserve). The Model 23 was only 43.3 feet long and had a wing span of 35.6 feet. Its price was raised in April 1964 to $573,500 Estimated operating costs per passenger seat mile were $0.11, about two-thirds those of the Sabreliner and half those of the JetStar.[42]

Orders for the Lear Jet were not at the level William Lear had predicted, but they far exceeded those of other planes available during the 1960s, despite a series of unexplained crashes.[43] Table 3-1 shows that three Lear Jet 23s were delivered to business customers in the United States in 1964; 68, in 1965, and 36, in 1966. Just a year after first delivery — in October 1965 — Lear announced plans to re-certify the Model 23 as a Model 24. The Model 24 incorporated improved GE CJ610-4 engines and a bird-proof windshield. Its gross takeoff weight was 13,000 pounds. The price of the Model 24 was set at $695,000, considerably above that of the Model 23.

Development of a Model 40 15-to-31 passenger Lear Liner was also announced in 1965.[44] The Model 24B (subsequently the Model 25) was announced in 1966.[45] The Model 25 was stretched version of the 23/24, with 4.3 feet added to the fuselage and with larger General Electric CJ610-6 2,950 lb st engines. Deliveries of the Model 25 began in 1968. Its price was listed in *Aviation Week* at $795,000 in March 1967 and March 1968; at $868,270 in March 1969; at $899,500 in March 1970.[46] By 1970, variations of the Lear Jet designated Models 24C, 24D, 25B, and 25C were in production.[47] By the end of 1970, 255 Lear Jet Models 23/24 and 25 had been delivered to businesses in the U.S. with another 36 going to governments and private foreign buyers.

It is doubtful that Lear Jet realized profits on the Models 23/24 and 25, despite their sales. By the time the Model 23 was certified, William Lear had spent all of the funds allocated for development, had borrowed whatever additional monies he could, and still was forced to take the company public in order to get into production. The public offering in November 1964 brought in about $5,500,000, with Lear retaining 60 percent ownership and his positions as president and chairman of the board. A considerable amount of the new cash was used to reduce existing debt, including back salaries.[48] Lear Jet was certainly not profitable for calendar 1964, during which only three planes were delivered.

Lear Jet reported a profit of $4.2 million on sales of $54.3 million in 1965. Then there was a net operating loss of $12 million in 1966, partly because of sharply reduced deliveries of the Model 23/24, but also because of monies spent in the development of the Model 40 Lear Liner, the Model 25, and other ventures. Lear was forced to sell or merge Lear Jet with another enterprise. Beech would not consider pulling "Bill Lear's chestnuts out of the fire." Cessna, too, declined to enter serious negotiations. Finally, Gates Rubber bought Lear's interests for $11.89 a share, or for more than $21 million in total. The company became Gates Learjet, and William P. Lear became a millionaire again.[49]

As we will see in Chapter Six, the family of Lear Jet (later Learjet) airplanes continued as a major factor in the market for business jets. William P. Lear was also to be instrumental in the design of the Canadair Challenger series of large business jets.

Jet Commander   The Aero Design and Engineering Corporation was formed in 1944. The company was unique in having been created for the express purpose of developing and producing executive aircraft. Its series of twin-engine, propeller-driven Aero Commanders was highly regarded through the late 1950s and into the 1960s. The Rockwell-Standard Corporation acquired Aero Design and Engineering in the late 1960 and changed the name of its new subsidiary to Aero Commander, Inc.

Aero Commander was another company apparently undeterred by the early entry of Lockheed. Studies of jet versions had begun in the mid-1950s. This research resulted in a number of drawing board models, including one with Turbomeca jet engines hung in pods under a high wing and another with General Electric or Pratt & Whitney engines buried in the aft fuselage. Yet another model was more or less like the piston-engined Aero Commander, with the wing positioned at mid-height in the fuselage. The jet engines were hung on the aft fuselage.[50] This design was announced as the Model 1121 Jet Commander in the spring of 1961. It was thought that a fully-equipped Jet Commander would sell for about $560,000. For customers preferring to provide their own interiors and avionics, a green price of $475,000 was contemplated.

Aero Commander recognized a need to act decisively on the Model 1121 if they were to realize their sales goals. Unlike William Lear, the executives at Aero Commander foresaw a limited market for business jets. They recognized that North American was poised to enter the market with the Sabreliner, a plane of about the same size. They recognized, too, that Piaggio-Douglas and a number of foreign manufacturers were considering the U.S. market. The company likened "the situation to that which existed prior to the advent of the first jet-powered U.S. airliner and point[ed] to the top-dog position achieved by Boeing as a result of chopping off the market survey processes and committing the company to a firm jetliner program in advance of its competition, then pouring funds into the program and refusing to be 'scared out' by other contenders . . . Aero Commander felt that its size and management makeup allowed it to move faster and at lower overhead costs than possible U.S. competition."[51] Contributing to the projection of lower costs and less time in development was the fact that the Jet Commander purposely borrowed many of the attributes of the earlier Aero Commanders, in order to get "the first plane built and flying as quickly as possible, with a minimum of wind tunnel research."[52]

Aero Commander also relied on its previous sales experience. Distributorships were arranged and orders taken by early 1962, a full 18 months prior to the planned date for first deliveries.[53]   Three prototype Jet Commanders were built at the company's Norman, Oklahoma, plant while a production line was being assembled at Bethany, Oklahoma. Aero Commander estimated that it would have spent more than $6 million on the program even before it began accumulating parts inventories for production. The break-even point was thought to be between 75 and 100 planes. Rollout and first flight of the first prototype occurred in January 1963, after which a strong sales program was launched. By March 1963, a total of 26 planes — more than half of the first batch committed to production — were on order.[54]

In mid-1963, the announced price of the Jet Commander was raised to $550,000, to be effective with the 51st airplane. Aero Commander still had expectations of capturing 45-50% of the total of 1,300 business jets they forecast would be sold through the next ten years. One reason for their predicting such a high share was their belief that business jets manufactured in Europe would not sell well in the United States. Then their plans went awry; unexpected delays began. By the end of 1963, major changes were made in the design. The length of the prototype was increased by 30 inches and its gross weight went up 2,000 pounds. The plane was then described as a six-to-eight, not a four-to-six passenger aircraft.[55] Deliveries of the first production model were not to be in 1963.

The certification process took the bulk of 1964, and the date for first delivery kept being pushed back. The first production model flew on October 5, 1964, and type certification was finally given on November 4, 1964. Delivery to the first customer, Timken Roller Bearing Corporation, occurred on

January 11, 1965, two years after rollout of the prototype and some 14 months after the date originally planned.[56]

The 1964 Model 1121 Jet Commander also used the GE CJ610-1, 2,850 lb st engines. It had a gross takeoff weight of 16,800 pounds, with wing loading of 55.4 pounds per square foot. While it had a maximum dive speed of Mach 0.89 (above 14,000 ft.) and was reported to have been dived at Mach 0.93, its recommended long-range cruise speed was only 400 mph. Its maximum cruise speed was about 535 mph. Range was 1,688 miles (45 minutes of reserve fuel) at the lower cruise speed and 1,296 miles at the higher cruise speed. The 1121 was 50 ft., 5.1 inches long and had a wing span of 43 ft., 3.7 inches. The wing was stiff and had a sweep of only three degrees. The lack of a pronounced sweep improved the stability of the craft at slow speeds, easing handling during landings. At the 1964-1965 price of $595,000, the Aero Commander was a relatively inexpensive plane to acquire. Still, *Business and Commercial Aviation* estimated costs per passenger seat mile with four passengers at $0.260, considerably above those of the Sabreliner and the Learjet. Costs per passenger seat mile with six or seven passengers in the 1121 would have been less, but the larger number could not be carried with adequate fuel for full range operations.[57]

There were 62 orders on hand for the Model 1121 at the time of first delivery in January 1965. Total orders, including those already delivered, amounted to 125 in January 1967. Total U.S. deliveries had reached about 90 when, in September 1967, Rockwell was required to divest itself of Aero Commander, Inc., as a condition to the Justice Department's not objecting to the acquisition by Rockwell of North American's Sabreliner operations.[58]

Jet Commander was acquired by Israeli Aircraft Industries (IAI) and production was transferred to Israel in 1968. IAI installed larger GE CJ610-5, 2,950 lb st engines on the 1121, regularly outfitted it for eight passengers rather than seven, raised the maximum takeoff weight from 16,000 to 18,500 pounds, and re-designated it the Commodore Jet Model 1121B. IAI also increased the price from $595,000 (1968 deliveries by Aero Commander) to $650,000 (1969 deliveries by IAI). By the end of 1970, worldwide deliveries of the 1121 and 1121B amounted to 141 aircraft, 125 of which were deliveries to customers in the United States. We will describe in Chapter Six the many subsequent changes IAI made in this series of aircraft. While the Model 1121 and its progeny remained important factors in the U.S. market in the following decades, it is clear that the Jet Commander was not nearly the success that its developers had anticipated. Despite their intentions and commitment, the 1121 did not reach the market as early as they had hoped. The performance of the plane did not match that of rivals, with consequent high operating costs. Further, the foreign aircraft that they had thought would not compete effectively in the U.S. turned out to compete very well, indeed.

Gulfstream II Grumman announced its Gulfstream G-159 executive turboprop in 1956. Customer deliveries of this 33,000 pound, 10-19 passenger, luxury aircraft began in 1959. It had a green price of $860,000 in 1961; over 180 G-159s had been sold by June 1966.[59] When PPG sold its first converted C-47, *The Glasshopper*, it was replaced by a G-159 turboprop.

Grumman was the last U.S. manufacturer to deliver a business jet during the 1961-1970 period. The company announced its Gulfstream II turbofan in November 1964, while sales of the G-159 were still strong. The decision to go into production of the G-II was delayed pending the receipt of at least 50 orders. The G-II was based on a lengthened version of the G-159 pressurized fuselage, but featured newly-designed swept wings and two aft-mounted Rolls Royce Spey 11,400 lb st engines. Like the G-159, the G-II was designed to be "top-of-the-line." A green price of $2.1 million was set for the initial orders for a drawing board airplane that was to weigh over 53,000 pounds, have a wing load of over 67 pounds per square foot, cruise at 580 mph, and have a range of at least 3,000 miles.[60]

Eighteen orders had been received by May 1965 when the decision was made to produce the G-II.[61] It was expected that first flight would occur in August 1966 and, "based on the fact that Grumman [saw] no aircraft for the next fifteen years to surpass its performance or economics," a long production life was forecast.[62] Materials shortages attributed to the Vietnam War delayed rollout to September 1966, at which point there were over 50 orders on hand. First flight occurred in October 1966, only two months later than had been originally scheduled.[63] Type certification was given in October 1967 and first customer delivery was in the following December. At the time, the G-II was sold out for all of 1968 and much of 1969.[64] A total of 102 G-IIs had been delivered before the end of 1970. PPG, it will be recalled, purchased its G-II, a replacement for a smaller HS-125, in the late 1960's.

As initially certified, the Model 1159 Gulfstream II had a gross take-off weight of 56,000 pounds. Re-certification in early 1968 brought this to 57,500 pounds. As re-certified, the wing load was 72.5 pounds per square foot. The listed maximum cruise speed was Mach 0.85 (about 562 mph at 40,000 ft.); the long-range cruise speed, Mach 0.75 (about 488 mph at 43,000 ft.). The plane was 79 ft., 11 inches long and had a wing span of 68 ft., 10 inches. The number of passengers depended on the configuration arranged by buyers, but typically ran 12 to 16. The 1967 price, including a Sperry automatic flight control system and basic instruments, but otherwise unfinished, was $2,525,000. The Lockheed JetStar, capable of carrying 10 passengers at a range of over 2,300 miles, could be purchased at the time for $1,590,000. No one suggested that the G-II was being offered as a low-priced, economy vehicle. Its commanding attributes were in its unmatched performance. We examine the successor G-III and G-IV, along with other "heavy iron" business jets in Chapter Five.

HS-125 The de Havilland Aircraft Company of the Hawker-Siddeley Group, Great Britain, was the first foreign company regularly to offer an executive jet aircraft in the U.S. market. The plane, first designated the DH-125, was announced in early 1961 and a batch of 10 was put into production shortly thereafter. Viper 511, 2,500 lb st engines were to be used. Plans called for starting deliveries in 1963. The plane was the 125th de Havilland design and derived directly from the 1945 design of the de Havilland Dove light transport. The manufacturer expected the Jet Dragon, as the plane was then called, to stay current for as long as 20 years.[65]

The DH-125 rolled out in July 1962. Larger Viper 520, 3,000 lb st engines, not the Viper 511s, were used. A price of $430,000 for a "standard" version (without radio and radar) was indicated. First flight of the prototype was in August 1962, after which the RAF ordered 22 of the aircraft. The certification processes of both the FAA and its British counterpart were under way by September. A study was made of providing General Electric engines for U.S. customers, but this idea was rejected because of the delay it would cause. Beech Aircraft Corporation, which until then had been attempting to sell the MS-760 Paris, entered negotiations with de Havilland to distribute the plane in the U.S. Pan Am was also considered as the U.S. distributor, particularly after it had indicated an interest in buying 40 DH-125s.

In 1963, Hawker-Siddeley announced a green price of $575,000 and a fully-equipped price of $730,000 for U.S. sales. Atlantic Aircraft Sales Corporation and AiResearch were named eastern and western U.S. sales representatives respectively. The HS-125 designation was given before the end of 1963, but first deliveries were still said to be at least seven months away.[66] FAA type certification was given in October 1964. There were then 10 orders for the plane in the U.S. and Canada. Deliveries began almost immediately, with three (including demonstrators) delivered in the U.S. in 1964, nineteen in 1965 and twenty-nine in 1966. A total of 117 had been delivered in the U.S. and 143 had been delivered elsewhere in the world by the end of 1970.[67] PPG's second DC-3 was replaced by one of the early HS-125's.

The 1964 HS-125 had a gross takeoff weight of 20,000 pounds and wing loading of 56.7 pounds per square foot. Its maximum operating speed (above 23,500 ft.) was Mach 0.725; high cruise speed, 491 mph; long-range cruise speed (at 36,000 ft.), 460 mph. Its range (45 minutes of reserve fuel) was 1,412 miles at 460 mph and 899 miles at 491 mph. The price of a fully equipped HS-125 was about $750,000 in 1964. *Business and Commercial Aviation* estimated operating costs per passenger seat mile (with six passengers) at $0.196.[68]

The 20-year forecast of the production life of the HS-125 proved to be conservative. Model after model has appeared. The HS-125-1A sold in the U.S. in 1965 had larger Viper 521, 3,115 lb st engines. The 3A of 1966 had yet larger Viper 522, 3,360 lb st engines, offering the advantage of somewhat shorter runway requirements. The 3AR of 1968 used the same engines, but aerodynamic improvements provided a bit higher cruise speed and a longer range. Beech, after 14 years of trying unsuccessfully to sell the MS-760, became the U.S. marketer (and finisher) for the HS-125 in December 1969. The first U.S. model sold by Beech was the 125-3AR, redesignated the BH-125-400. The 1970 price for a completed 400 was $1,200,000. We will see in Chapter Six that Beech later gave up this distributorship. Yet newer models of the HS-125 — renamed the BAe 125 — continued to sell quite well into the 1990's.[69]

Falcon Jet   The second foreign built business jet to be sold regularly in the United States was the Falcon Jet, a product of Avions Marcel Dassault. The Falcon Jet — called the Mystere 20 at the time — was announced by Dassault in mid-1962. Dassault had worked on the Mediterrane in 1958 and, in addition, had done some development work on a business jet in cooperation with Sud-Aviation.[70]   Dassault was one of the world's premier developers, with the rare ability to bring new and exceptionally good military aircraft to fruition on schedule and without cost overruns.   Economists studying U.S military aircraft procurement at the RAND Corporation vied with one another for trips to France, ostensibly to unravel the reasons for Dassault's efficiency.

The Mystere 20's maiden flight was in May 1963. Pratt & Whitney (PW) JT12A-8, 3,300 lb st engines were then being used. Development was aided by the near-certainty that the French government would pay for the tooling and, additionally, authorize the French Air Force to buy considerable numbers of the Mystere 20 and derivative trainer and transport aircraft. It was reported as early as June 1963 that the Business Jets Division of Pan Am was interested in becoming the U.S. representative for Dassault, with intentions to buy as many as 40 of the planes as soon as they were available. The prototype provided an impressive demonstration at the Paris Air Show in June 1963, and then was modified in a number of ways, including the installation of more powerful GE CF700-2C, 4,125 lb st turbofan engines. Two somewhat larger prototypes were made before the first production model was defined.[71]

At the urging of Pan Am, the Falcon name was adopted for the U.S. models in April 1964. The first production model flew on January 1, 1965. Type certification was given and the first Pan Am demonstrator arrived in the United States the following June. Pan Am reported that it had firm orders for 54 Falcon Jet 20s even before it had received the demonstrator. Eleven Falcons (including demonstrators) had been delivered in the U.S. before the end of the year.[72]

At the time of certification, the Fan Jet Falcon 20 had a gross takeoff weight of 25,794 pounds and a wing loading of 59 pounds per square foot. Its maximum speed was Mach 0.86 (about 570 mph at 40,000 ft) and its recommended cruise speed was Mach 0.76 (about 502 mph). The craft was 56.2 ft. in length with a wing span of 50.5 ft. It was normally outfitted for a crew of two and eight passengers, although it could accommodate up to ten passengers. Its range (45 minutes of reserve fuel) was 1,891 miles. A runway of 5,700 feet was required for full load takeoffs. The 1965 price of the Falcon 20 was $1,094,500; the 1966 price, $1,200,000.[73]

The Fan Jet Falcon — usually called the Falcon 20 — sold well right from the outset, despite its relatively high price. Thirty-four were sold in the U.S. in 1966, 38 in 1967. By the end of 1970, a total of 217 had been delivered worldwide. A smaller version of the Falcon 20, the Falcon 10, was announced in 1970. It had seats for four-to-seven passengers, weighed only 13,500 pounds gross, and was to sell for $900,000 rather than the $1,650,000 then being asked for the Falcon 20. The Falcon 20 itself was already available in five configurations — the standard and the 20C, 20D, 20E and 20F. Pan Am, in addition to acting as the U.S. representative for sales and service, pressured Dassault to improve the Falcon 20 and to move quickly to a new generation of aircraft. Other models, the Falcon 50, in particular, were under development by 1970 and introduced a few years later.[74] These and later Falcons are discussed in Chapters Five and Six.

Some Early Entrants That Failed

The manufacturers and planes that found their way into regular sales in the U.S. market were far outnumbered by others that tried and failed. We noted in Chapter Two that well-known U.S. companies such as Fairchild, Ryan, Douglas and McDonnell considered but elected not to enter. Some foreign manufacturers were in this set as well. Morane-Saulnier, we saw, did try to enter. Its MS-760, the first business jet available for sale in the United States, provides a fascinating example of an unsuccessful attempt at innovation.

MS-760 Paris Morane-Saulnier sold at least 80 of the MS-760 Paris I to the French and Brazilian armed forces in the 1958-1960 period. The plane did not make "much of a dent in the executive aircraft market," however.[75]

The MS-760 was a tiny airplane. It had a gross weight of only 7,725 pounds and wing loading of 39.8 pounds per square foot. There were seats for a pilot and three passengers. Two Turbomeca Marbore 880 lb st engines were located in the wing roots. The maximum speed of the plane was 415 mph; the normal cruise speed, somewhere between 335 and 370 mph. Its range was 700 miles (45 minutes reserve fuel). The price in September 1958 was $210,000.[76] It is not clear that Beech made strenuous efforts to sell the airplane after it became the U.S. distributor in 1955. We have found records of only two sales of new MS-760s in the U.S. during the 14-year period Beech was distributing the plane.

A 760B Paris II was developed in 1960-1961. It was essentially the same as the Paris I except for larger Marbore 1,058 lb st engines and greater fuel capacity. Again, the French government, other governments and some foreign businesses bought the plane. Apparently no one in the U.S. bought a new Paris II. A larger, six passenger MS-861 was considered but apparently never built.

A total of 219 Paris Is and Paris IIs were built (including 76 built under license in Argentina). Morane-Saulnier filed for bankruptcy in late 1962 and its operations were taken over by Establissements Henri Potez. Beech decided at about this time to drop the MS-760. The Potez group then developed the 760C Paris III, an enlarged version of the earlier plane, with six seats (including crew), and improved cabin layout and access. A prototype of the 760C flew in February 1964. The plane was to go into production in 1966. *Aviation Week and Space Technology* reported in late 1965 that a "group headed by F. William Carr of Corpus Christi, Tex., [had] production rights for the Morane-Saulnier MS 760C Paris III, and [hoped] to make the aircraft in the United States from French-made components. Price of the 4-6 passenger jet will be about $325,000."[77]

By early 1966, Potez had yet to decide whether to put the Paris III into production. Henri Potez held out hopes for a "substantial order" . . . "a possible order for 500 aircraft" from the United States. The Paris III was listed among the "Leading International Aircraft" in the Inventory Issues of *Aviation Week and Space Technology* for 1965, 1966, 1967 and 1968. Thereafter, it and Establissement Potez disappear from the listings.[78] Eighteen Paris Jets were registered in the United States as late as 1988.[79]

Hansa HFB 320 Work began in West Germany on the HFB 320 in March 1961 in a joint venture among Hamburger Flugzeugbau, C.A.S.A. (Spain), Fokker, General Electric, Hispano Suiza and Napier. The design drew on an experimental Junkers bomber of World War II and incorporated forward-swept wings — unusual, to say the least.[80] The development of the HFB 320 was announced nearly simultaneously with and, one may suspect, not independent of an announcement by the Bundestag that it was canceling an order for 12 Lockheed JetStars. The 320, which was announced as "a 6-to-14 place twin-jet transport . . . roughly in the same category as the 12-place JetStar," was at that time scheduled for first flight in late 1963.[81] The possibility of "overbidding" by the several manufacturers of business jets was recognized at the time the 320 was announced. The danger of the "executive jet arena" being "already crowded" was explicitly seen by the developers. Their market survey showed nonetheless that as many as 100 320s might be sold in Europe and that there was hope for a "substantial market" in the United States.[82] The West German government was, it seems, still the prime potential customer.

Page Airways was named the first U.S. sales representative in September 1963 and orders were received from U.S. customers well prior to first flight. An estimated $4 million had been spent on development at the time of first flight on April 24, 1964. The second prototype flew in October 1964 and a U.S. demonstration tour for the plane was set up for the following January.[83]

Subsequent events marked the HFB 320 project for failure. The first prototype crashed in May 1965, killing the American test pilot. This accident further delayed FAA type certification and raised questions about the stall characteristics of T-tail jets, in general, and the HFB 320, in particular. Significant modifications had to be made in the production models.[84] By March 1966, when the growth in the U.S. market was already waning, the HFB 320 was still said to be a year away from delivery. The German air force, nonetheless, selected the plane to replace its old C-47s. A U.S. distributor for the HFB 320 was killed in the crash of a Jet Commander in October 1966 while FAA type certification was still pending. German type certification was given in March 1967; the FAA's, two months later. A special computer-based stall prevention system had been adopted for the craft and over 750 test stalls had been performed prior to certification.[85] The mere requirement for such extensive testing — however satisfactory the technical results — must have dampened sales.

The HFB 320 of 1967 could be configured for up to eleven passengers. A nine-passenger setup was typical. The certified version of the 320 had gross takeoff weight of 19,400 pounds and wing loading of 59.8 pounds per square foot. GE CJ610-1, 2,850 lb st engines were used. Maximum speed was Mach 0.83 (550 mph at 40,000 ft) and cruise speed was Mach 0.76 (500 mph at 40,000 ft). The plane had a range 1,660 miles (45 minutes of reserve fuel). The 1968 green price was $700,000. The standard avionics package and interior brought this to about $940,000. Three HFB 320s were delivered to U.S. customers in 1968; four in 1969; two in 1970.[86] A few more, but only a few more, were sold in the U.S. after 1970. Sales outside of the U.S., including those to the German government, amounted to three in 1967, five in 1968, ten in 1969, and two in 1970. Again, a few more were sold after 1970.

Piaggio-Douglas 808   Douglas Aircraft Company began a design study of a business jet in 1957, at about the same time North American and Lockheed first considered such planes. At the time, Douglas was pressing hard to complete the DC-8 in time to fend off the loss of its historic share of the commercial transport market to Boeing's 707. Douglas' concept for a business jet was of a six-to-ten seat plane with two turbojet engines set into the sides of the aft fuselage. Douglas did little with this design until 1961 when it reached an agreement with an Italian company, Rinaldo Piaggio Spa, for further development. Piaggio was to finish the design and development work, with Douglas working in an advisory capacity. Douglas retained rights to produce and/or distribute the PD-808 in the United States.

The 1961 "paper airplane" showed a gross weight of 15,000 pounds and a wing loading of 66.7 pounds per square foot. The developers were aiming for a maximum cruise speed of 520 mph, the ability to fly for 4 hours without landing, and a takeoff runway requirement of no more than 3,900 feet. There were distinctive "bug-eye" cockpit windows and tip-mounted fuel tanks. The horizontal tail was set low on the vertical fin to minimize stall and other control problems. It was thought that the Vespa-Jet, as the plane was first called, would sell for about $450,000 green and $500,000 with interior and basic avionics.[87]

When work began in Italy, the PD-808 was scheduled to be available for deliveries in 1963. Both *Aviation Week* and *Business and Commercial Aviation* listed the plane under the Douglas name in their 1962 Business Aircraft Directories. "[S]trikes at Piaggio and supplier plants," however, led to a 1963 announcement that first flight date was "indefinite."[88] The date was pushed back to early 1964, then to later in the year. First flight finally occurred on August 29, 1964, but then the second PD-808 did not fly until June 14, 1966. In March 1966 it was said that the 808 might be "nearing the production stage" in 1967.[89]

A distributor for sales of the PD-808 in the Western Hemisphere was appointed in 1966 as FAA certification was getting underway. The Italian air force ordered 25 and assisted the "company to get the PD-808 into the world market." The demonstrator flown to the U.S. was an Italian air force plane. Rinaldo Piaggio was quoted as saying, "We know we are entering the [U.S.] market later than our major competitors, the Hawker-Siddeley HS-125 and the Lear Jets, but we are determined to concentrate on the United States first, where we have achieved a good reputation with the Piaggio 166 [propeller-driven] series."[90]

The PD-808 of 1967 was quite different from the 1961 design. It had a gross weight of 18,300 pounds, wing loading of 81.3 pounds per square foot, a maximum speed of Mach 0.85 and a recommended long-range cruise speed of 380 mph. Its range was about 1,300 miles (45 minutes of reserve fuel). Bristol-Siddeley Viper 526, 3,330 lb st engines were used. The green price was $715,000. Only 29 PD-808s were produced; the two prototypes, 25 aircraft sold to the Italian air force and two purchased by private parties. None was delivered new in the United States despite Piaggio's clear objectives. The plane went out of production in 1973.

IAI B-301C   Israeli Aircraft Industries started to develop a business
jet prior to its acquisition of the Jet Commander line. The B-301C design had
reached full mockup by early 1961. First flight was planned for 1962. The
six-to-nine place B-301C would have had a gross takeoff weight of 12,500
pounds, wing loading of 52 pounds per square foot, top speed of 510 mph,
economical cruise speed of 400 mph, and a range of 1,520 miles. The estimated price was $350,000.[97]

IAI halted development of the B-301C in October 1961, citing a need
to improve the speed and range of the plane in order to compete effectively.
Development resumed in mid-1962, but it was acknowledged that both
funding and lack of qualified personnel were creating problems.[92] We have
found no record of the B-301C after 1962.

Heinkel-Potez CM-191   The CM-191 was developed by the Fouga
company in France as a competitor to the MS-760. After the French Air
Force selected the MS-760, Fouga merged with Potez and, later, Potez and
Heinkel joined to propose the CM-191 to the West German air force. The
West German government provided funds for a prototype. First flight occurred in the spring of 1962. The CM-191 had a V-shaped rudder-elevator
tail, swept wings, tip tanks and, like the MS-760, was powered by two 880 lb
st Turbomeca Marbore Mk. 2 engines set into the fuselage at the wing roots.
Gross weight of the CM-191 was only 9,780 pounds and it had a maximum
speed of 438 mph. Civilian models were to be sold at $220,000. An A and B
version were listed by Heinkel for training/liaison purposes in the 1963
through 1969 *Aviation Week and Space Technology* Inventory Issues. We
have found no evidence of the plane's having been sold as an executive jet.[93]

Saab 105   The Saab 105 was another effort at a small, inexpensive
business jet. It was developed first as a trainer for the Swedish air force. The
four-to-five seat plane had gross takeoff weight of 6,609 pounds, wing loading of 37.8 pounds, maximum speed of 500 mph, maximum cruise speed of
450 mph, normal cruise speed of 400 mph, and range of 1,450 miles. The design featured a T-tail, high swept wings with negative dihedral and two Turbomeca turbofan 1,540 lb st engines hung below the wings near the fuselage.
A price of $210,000 was indicated in 1961. The Swedish air force committed
to buying 100 of the 105s if flight trials of the prototype were satisfactory.

The prototype flew on June 29, 1963. Seven production models were sold to the Swedish air force. A price of $260,000 was quoted for an executive version in 1965, but no civilian orders had as yet been received. Military versions of the 105 were listed in *Aviation Week and Space Technology* through the 1960s, but there is no record of the plane ever having been sold to private buyers.[94]

Hispano Aviacion HA-230   Spain's HA-230 also developed from a military trainer. The design was for a six-place executive transport with gross weight of 8,378 pounds, cruise speed of 420 mph and range of more than 1,600 miles. The plane was listed in the 1962 Inventory Issue of *Aviation Week and Space Technology*, but not in subsequent issues.[95]

Macchi MB.330   Another Italian firm, Aeronautica Macchi, proposed a low-priced, six place executive jet in 1963. This plane was to compete with the PD-808.   The early plans were to sell a finished MB.330 at about $380,000, $120,000 below the price announced for the PD-808.   Models showed the 330 with wings at mid-fuselage, a horizontal tail located at the top of the fuselage, and two engines mounted on the sides of the aft fuselage. A maximum speed of 516 mph and cruise speed of 435 mph were planned. The project was canceled in September 1963 because of a "lack of support by the Italian government."[96]

ME.P-308   Messerschmitt announced entry into the light end of the executive jet market in 1963. Its ME.P-308 Jet Taifu was to be a five-to-six place plane using two Turbomeca 860 lb st engines. The principal market was to be "air forces throughout the world." We believe the project was aborted shortly after announcement.[97]

Aero Star Model 2000   Ted R. Smith was one of the leading designers of the Aero Commanders and the Jet Commander when he was employed at Aero Design and Engineering. He established Ted Smith Aircraft Co. in 1964 and, among other planes, proposed to build a twin-turbojet Model 2000 plane with top speeds "over 550 kt. [632 mph]."   The price was to be "under $400,000." Smith also proposed developing a "five-to-six passenger supersonic business aircraft which he believe[d] could be marketed for $750,000-$1,250,000."   Rockwell Standard, the producer of the Jet

Commander at the time Smith left, held first option on all Ted Smith products. If unexercised, Rockwell's options expired 30 days after any of Smith's planes were certified. The Model 2000 was not certified, and Ted R. Smith Co. was acquired by American Cement Corporation for $9 million in stock in 1968.[98]

Century Miles Aviation and Transport, of Great Britain, listed a Century six-to-eight passenger executive jet in the 1967 and 1968 inventory issues of *Aviation Week and Space Technology*. The plane was to have a gross weight of 9,000 pounds and a maximum speed of 450 mph. We know nothing else about this project.

Other Projects of the 1960s

As the DC-9, Boeing 727 and Boeing 737 found their way into the fleets of commercial air carriers, their manufacturers offered executive versions. For businesses considering an executive jet as large and expensive as the Gulfstream II, such planes might well be realistic alternatives. They were also options considered by private buyers who for one reason or another wanted the size and performance that only executive versions of commercial jets could provide.

Aerospatiale announced the SN600 Corvette executive jet in 1968. We will discuss this venture in Chapter Four. Beech and Hawker-Siddeley considered collaborating in the development, production and marketing of business jets in 1969. Beech was also considering introducing a tri-jet on its own.[99]

The event of the late 1960s that was to have a major impact on the market of the 1970s was Cessna's decision to enter with its Citation. Cessna's announcement was made in September 1968, when the market for business jets was decidedly soft. Cessna opted to try the low end of the market, with a plane that was much closer to turboprops than to the better-selling business jets in terms of both performance and price.[100] The failure of the MS-760 and other similar ventures caused many to think that Cessna had little chance of success.[101]

Observations on the Formation of the Market

Table 3-1 provides data on U.S. deliveries of business jets during the decade following customer acceptance of the first JetStar. Sales to the U.S. government as well as sales to business customers are included. The inability of North American and Lockheed to hold their initial market positions is clear. So, too, is the market penetration of Lear, Hawker-Siddeley, Dassault, and Grumman, all secondary swarmers in the Schumpeterian sense. Table 3-1 also shows the volatility of the total market. Deliveries grew fairly steadily until 1966 and then fell. In 1970, total deliveries were less than half of the level reached in 1966. This decrease reflects two principal factors: the working-off of backorders accumulated prior to first deliveries of the later entrants and the 1969-1970 recession.

The rivalry stemming from new entrants and new models had pro-found effects on the structure of the market. As shown in Table 3-2, five companies (or separate divisions of companies) delivered new business jets to U.S. customers in 1964. A total of 64 planes (including military versions) were shipped that year, and Sabreliner accounted for 51 (80%) of them. Lockheed was next with six JetStars (9%). Expressed in terms of approxi-mate market values, Sabreliner shipments were 80% and JetStar shipments were 14% of a total of roughly $70,000,000. By any conventional measures, the market was highly concentrated.

In 1970, eight firms delivered 87 new business jets (including military versions) to U.S. customers. These planes had a total market value of about $131,200,000. The market was still concentrated, but the relative positions of the sellers had undergone a radical change. Lear accounted for 38% of unit sales and about 29% of the value of shipments. The 14 Gulfstream IIs ac-counted for only 16% of the units, but led all others with 33% of the total value of shipments. The HS-125 was second in unit sales (17%) and third in the value of aircraft delivered (14%). Only 12 Sabreliners and two JetStars were delivered in 1970. The market was still concentrated, but there was a radical shift of market leaders during the six-year period.

Table 3-1

Total U.S. Deliveries of Business Jets, 1960-1970

Manufacturer	1960	1961	1962	1963	1964	1965	1966	1967	1968	1969	1970	Total
North American/Rockwell	5	33	56	67	51	28	31	16	25	14	12	338
Lockheed	—	13	17	8	6	17	21	17	17	7	2	125
Lear Jet/Gates Learjet	—	—	—	—	3	68	36	26	39	51	33	256
Aero Commander/IAI	—	—	—	—	1	30	48	25	9	9	3	125
Hawker-Siddeley	—	—	—	—	3	19	29	12	18	21	15	117
Dassault	—	—	—	—	—	11	34	38	25	20	6	134
Grumman	—	—	—	—	—	—	—	2	39	36	14	91
Hamburger Flugzeugbau	—	—	—	—	—	—	—	—	3	4	2	9
TOTAL	5	46	73	75	64	173	199	136	175	162	87	1195

Source: AvData, Inc.

Table 3-2
U.S. Market Shares, 1964 and 1970[1]

Manufacturer	1964				1970			
	Units		Value		Units		Value	
	Number	Percent	Dollars (millions)	Percent	Number	Percent	Dollars (millions)	Percent
North American/Rockwell	51	79.7%	$56.10	80.1%	12	13.8%	$14.40	11.0%
Lockheed	6	9.3%	$9.60	13.7%	2	2.3%	$3.80	2.9%
Lear Jet/Gates Learjet	3	4.7%	$1.50	2.1%	33	37.9%	$37.80	28.8%
Aero Commander/IAI	1	1.6%	$0.60	0.9%	3	3.4%	$2.30	1.8%
Hawker-Siddeley	3	4.7%	$2.20	3.1%	15	17.2%	$18.00	13.7%
Dassault	—	—	—	—	6	6.9%	$9.90	7.5%
Grumman	—	—	—	—	14	16.1%	$43.40	33.0%
Hamburger Flugzeugbau	—	—	—	—	2	2.3%	$1.60	1.2%
TOTAL	64	100.0%	$70.0	100.0%	87	100.0%	$131.20	100.0%

[1] Includes military sales

Source: *Aviation Week* and *Aviation Week and Space Technology* Inventory Issues, 1958-1970; and *Business and Commercial Aviation* Planning and Purchasing Handbook Issues (various years).

The structure of the market was decidedly unstable as the decade of the 1970s began. Losses and weak earnings by some of the firms portended probable exits and mergers. Cessna and others were planning to enter. Existing manufacturers were considering new models, some of which would strengthen market positions and some of which would do just the opposite. The market positions of even the more successful firms would be insecure, not because of direct price competition from firms producing near-substitutes but rather from the threat of improved performance from new and different airplanes. It was already clear that to hold market position — much less to gain share — a competitor had to improve the performance of its offerings almost continually. Thus market structure, while apparently concentrated at any point in time, was actually in a state of dynamic disequilibrium.

Table 3-3 presents summary data on the characteristics and prices of the business jets available on the U.S. market through 1970. The planes are listed by year of availability. The characteristics are those as of the date of U.S. certification. Price data relate to the year of first U.S. sale (or offer of sale), adjusted to 1970 price levels.

Comparisons of the planes and records of the manufacturers in Tables 3-1, 3-2 and 3-3 provide the basis for some preliminary observations. It is clear that "being first" conferred no obvious advantage. Indeed, the very concept of "being first" is not unambiguous. It can be debated whether the distinction should go to the MS-760 or to the JetStar. The MS 760 was, of course, available in the U.S. several years before the JetStar and it was powered by jet engines. But in most respects it was not much of an innovation. The MS-760 had only four seats, including that for the pilot. Many other planes were available — not jets, of course — that were considerably larger. The MS-760 had a range of only 700 miles; other planes — not jets — had longer ranges. The price of the MS-760 was well above that of many conventionally-powered planes. While the cruise speed of the MS-760 was above that of most propeller aircraft, it was not so much higher that, on trips within the range limitations of the MS-760, the difference in speeds resulted in appreciable time saving.

Table 3-3
Business Jet Aircraft Available in the United States Through 1970

Model	First Year Available	Number of Pass.	Wingspan (ft)	Length (ft)	Gross Takeoff Weight (pounds)	Number of Eng.	Power (thrust/lbs)	Max Cruise (mph)	Long Range Cruise (mph)	Max Full Load Range (miles)	Approx. Price Fully Equipped
Paris MS-760	1958	2-3	33.3	32.9	7,725	2	880	415	370	700	$210,000
JetStar 6	1961	8-10	54.4	60.4	40,921	4	3,000	565	520	2,000	$1,500,000
Sabreliner 40	1963	6	44.4	40.0	17,760	2	3,000	550	495	1,770	$990,000
Lear Jet 23	1964	6	35.6	43.3	12,500	2	2,850	535	485	1,686	$573,500
HS-125	1964	6-8	47.0	47.4	20,000	2	3,050	491	415	1,760	$750,000
Jet Commander 1121	1965	6-7	50.4	43.3	16,800	2	2,850	515	400	1,688	$595,000
Falcon 20	1965	8-10	50.5	56.2	25,794	2	4,125	555	490	1,891	$1,094,500
HS-125-1A	1965	8	47.0	47.4	20,000	2	3,115	491	415	1,720	$775,000
HS-125-3A	1966	8	47.0	47.4	21,000	2	3,360	535	477	1,590	$780,000
Learjet 24	1967	6	35.9	43.3	13,000	2	2,850	526	485	1,600	$649,000
JetStar 8	1967	8-10	54.4	60.4	42,500	4	3,300	565	520	2,370	$1,650,000
Sabreliner 80	1967	8	44.4	46.9	20,000	2	3,300	550	518	1,700	$1,300,000
P-D 808	1967	5-6	43.3	42.2	18,300	2	3,330	550	488	1,400	$870,000
Hansa HFB-320	1967	7-11	47.5	54.4	19,400	2	2,850	540	490	1,650	$940,000
Gulfstream II	1967	12-16	68.8	79.9	57,500	2	11,400	550	485	3,800	$2,825,000
Learjet 25	1968	6-8	35.6	47.6	15,000	2	2,950	526	485	1,510	$795,000
BH-125-400	1968	8	47.0	47.4	22,700	2	3,360	535	470	1,800	$820,000
Commodore Jet 1121B	1969	8	50.4	43.3	18,500	2	2,950	535	470	1,450	$650,000

Source: *Aviation Week* and *Aviation Week and Space Technology* Inventory Issues, 1958-1970; and *Business and Commercial Aviation* Planning and Purchasing Handbook Issues (various years). Data on speeds vary from year to year and listed cruise speeds often exceed those normally used.

Moreover, few locations were available to service or even provide fuel for jets at the time the MS-760 was introduced. In short, unless one simply wanted the notoriety of owning a jet, there were no real reasons to buy the MS-760 in 1958-1961. And few did.

The JetStar presents quite a different picture. With the notable exception of the Grumman's turboprop Gulfstream, the JetStar could accommodate as many passengers as even the largest of other new airplanes. It offered the safety of a two-person crew. Except for commercial jets, no other airplane came close to its speed. Again, except for the turboprop Gulfstream, its 2,000-mile range outdid any other plane of its size. By 1961, there were enough commercial jets in service that obtaining fuel and finding service personnel were not critical problems. That the JetStar had relatively high operating costs was not of much consequence to the business buyer who wanted to move people from place to place in a hurry. In 1961, there was no alternative. Until there was, the JetStar sold well. When other planes with superior price-performance characteristics were introduced, JetStar quickly lost its market position.

The appearance of the Sabreliner on the private market in 1963-1964 cut into the sales of the JetStar. Buyers not requiring so large an airplane could get the speed and nearly the range from the Sabreliner. And the costs of operating a Saberliner were considerably less than those of the JetStar. Lear may have exaggerated in referring to the JetStar and Sabreliner as "royal barges." He was not wrong, however, in the conclusion that a less expensive plane with equivalent (or better) performance characteristics could be sold in quantity in the U.S. market. The Lear Jet 23 was just such a plane. The Model 23 flew with only 2,083 gross pounds per seat, in contrast to the 2,960 pounds of the Sabreliner and the 5,115 pounds of the JetStar. The operating costs per passenger seat mile were thus appreciably below those of the other planes, without sacrifices in performance. Then Lear went ahead immediately to bring out new versions, fashioning different aircraft for different customer needs. Lear recognized that a single model would not suffice for all buyers, and that no manufacturer would survive for long if improvements in existing models were not made on a fairly continuous basis.

The Jet Commander sold well for only a brief period. Its introduction was delayed and, consequently, the brief window of opportunity prior to the introduction of the Lear Jet and the Falcon was missed. Even when the Jet Commander came out, it could be used for long-range flights only at the expense of reduced carrying capacity. And an expense it was. Long trips required intermediate stops and extra time. Further, if only four passengers were carried to achieve a long-range, the cost per seat mile of the Jet Commander was higher than those of the JetStar operating with its normal eight passengers. Gross weight per passenger was but 2,285 pounds when there were seven aboard; weight per passenger reached 4000 pounds with only four aboard. Despite this and other shortcomings, little was done to improve the Model 1121 in its early years. Only nine were delivered in 1968; nine, in 1969; three in 1970. By then, of course, ownership and production had shifted to IAI in Israel.

The introduction of the Gulfstream II brought a new class of business jet to the market. The JetStar had some of the "big iron" flavor, but the G-II was much larger, was equipped with state-of-the-art avionics, had far superior performance and, consequently, commanded a much higher price. Gulfstream (under various owners) has remained strong in this end of the market by making improvement after improvement in its airplanes. These improvements will be treated in Chapter Five.

The distinctive features of the HS-125 are not apparent from Table 3-2. It flew no further, cruised no faster and, in standard configuration, carried no more passengers than the Lear Jet and Sabreliner. The HS-125 never commanded a large market share, either. It did offer far more passenger comfort, however, in a larger cabin, more window area, improved lavatory, larger wardrobe and baggage areas, and folding worktables. The HS-125 could be configured for up to eight passengers if the customer wished. As will be discussed in Chapter Six, the HS-125 (later the BAe 125) was also upgraded frequently throughout the 1970s and 1980s.

In addition to being a state-of-the-art airplane, the Falcon Jet 20 was marketed strenuously by Pan Am, with a strong service organization. Its range and passenger capacity were less than those of the Gulfstream II, but it outperformed other business jets in other important dimensions. Its cabin was nearly five feet longer than that of the HS-125, providing adequate space for the normal eight passenger seats. Falcon moved quickly to introduce the smaller Falcon 10 and thereafter pushed into the heavy end of the market as well. In short, Dassault provided a good plane and followed that with agg-ressive product development and aggressive selling and service.

Neither the PD-808 nor the HFB-320 had outstanding performance at-tributes. Each lacked a strong sales and service organization in the U.S. Crashes of the prototypes raised questions about design safety. If there had been no Lear Jet and no Sabreliner — and there had been none when the first designs of these planes were laid down — and if sales and service efforts had been expanded, either or both might have been more successful. Many things can go wrong when attempts are made to commercialize new technologies, as the records of these planes amply demonstrate.

It is difficult to be conclusive about tendencies for overbidding on the basis of the first ten years of market experience. Note, however, that none of the manufacturers realized anything close to the sales levels they had forecast. Indeed, most failed to reach what they had announced as break-even levels. If it were typical that a sales volume of, say, 150 was needed to break even, the sum of the profits of all of the firms that tried to enter the market up to 1970 must have been negative.

The lack of profitability of existing firms probably plays a weak role in deterring entry in a market such as this one. An entrepreneur with ideas for a new product may foresee the probability of successful entry despite the fact that many of those who have attempted to do the same thing in the past have failed. Recall that the Schumpeterian entrepreneur is not driven solely — or even primarily — by the expectation of profit. As long as visionaries who want to "do something different" — for whatever reason — have access to technology and can command the necessary financial resources (usually not their own), innovation will continue. From what we have already seen, these entrepreneurs can operate in the form of corporations or, indeed, as groups or individuals within corporations. We will explore these points further in the next chapters.

Notes

1. Francillon, *Lockheed Aircraft Since 1913, loc. cit.*, p. 395.

2. *Ibid.*, pp. 395-396.

3. *AW*, March 7, 1960, p. 271; March 21, 1960, p. 33; September 5, 1960, p. 79.

4. Francillon, *op.cit.*, p. 534.

5. *Ibid*, p.34; H. D. Kysor, "JetStar," *B&CA*, June 1962, p. 36.

6. *Ibid.*

7. *Ibid.*, pp. 32-33.

8. *AWST*, January 6, 1964, p. 34.

9. Kysor, *op. cit.*

10. *B&CA*, April 1962, p. 23.

11. Kysor, *op. cit.*, p. 33.

12. K. Munson, *op. cit.*, p. 169.

13. *AWST*, January 6, 1969, p. 13; September 29, 1969, p. 24; January 5, 1970, p. 20.

14. Francillon, *op. cit.*, p. 397.

15. B. Yenne, *op. cit.*, p. 144.

16. R. Hawkes, "North American Studies Civil T-39 Market," *AW*, February 6, 1961, pp. 102-108.

17. *Ibid.*, p. 108.

18. W. S. Reid, "Sabreliner Shows Fighter-Like Handling, Performance," *AW*, June 6, 1961, pp. 54-57.

19. *AWST*, October 8, 1962, p. 30.

20. Yenne, *op. cit.*, pp. 144, 148; *AWST*, May 6, 1963, p. 108.

21. Yenne, *op. cit.*, p. 148.

22. H. D. Kysor, "Sabreliner," *B&CA*, January 1964, p. 57.

23. D. A. Brown, "Plans Aim at Future Executive Markets," *AWST*, September 23, 1963, p. 108.

24. *Ibid.*, pp. 103-111.

25. The order backlog was for about six planes in March 1964. *AWST*, March 16, 1964, p. 255. A year later North American reported that the sales outlook was promising, that there had been no decrease in orders. *AWST*, March 15, 1965, p. 257.

26. *AWST*, October 18, 1965, p. 19; *AWST*, April 25, 1966, p. 114; September 12, 1966, p. 68; October 3, 1966, p. 23.

27. G. Swanborough, *North American: An Aircraft Album*, London: Ian Allen, 1973, p. 106.

28. *Ibid.*

29. Rashke, *op. cit.*, pp. 219-220.

30. *AW*, May 3, 1954, pp. 27-28.

31. *AW*, August 22, 1955, p. 7.

32. This section relies heavily on Rashke, *op. cit.*

33. *Ibid.*, p. 219.

34. *AW*, October 3, 1960, p. 47.

35. *AW*, March 6, 1961, pp. 87, 89.

36. *AW*, February 9, 1962, p. 34.

37. C. Brownlow, "SAAC Success Depends on Price, Early Availability," *AWST*, March 26, 1962, p. 78.

38. *AWST*, April 23, 1962, p. 105.

39. *AWST*, June 11, 1962, p. 30.

40. *AWST*, September 3, 1962, p. 27.

41. Munson, *op. cit.*, p. 167; *AWST*, September 16, 1963, p. 89.

42. *AWST*, April 20, 1964, p. 113; H. D. Kysor and D. J. Wodraska, "Lear Jet Model 23," *B&CA*, January 1965, p. 57ff.

43. *AWST*, November 1, 1965, p. 23; November 22, 1965, p. 30; January 17, 1966, p. 39; March 14, 1966, p. 32; May 2, 1966, p. 30; May 16, 1966, p. 37; November 14, 1966, p. 129.

44. *AWST*, October 18, 1965, p. 19.

45. *AWST*, June 13, 1966, p. 66; August 15, 1966, p. 47; September 26, 1966, p. 19.

46. Inventory Issues, *AWST*, 1962-1970.

47. *AWST*, September 29, 1969, p. 25.

48. Rashke, *op. cit.*, p. 253.

49. *Ibid.*, pp. 287-293.

50. E. J. Bulban, "Aero Commander Building Executive Jet," *AW*, May 8, 1961, p. 92ff.

51. *Ibid.*, p. 93.

52. *Ibid.*, p. 95.

53. *AWST*, March 5, 1962, p. 15.

54. *AWST*, January 7, 1963, p. 85; January 21, 1963, p. 43; E. J. Bulban, "Twin-Engine Jet Commander Begins Flight Test Program," *AWST*, February 4, 1963, p. 90; D. A. Brown, "Jet Commander Purchase Plan Detailed," *AWST*, March 4, 1963, p. 82.

55. *AWST*, May 20, 1963, p. 35; D. A. Brown, "Plans Aim at Future Executive Market," *AWST*, September 23, 1963, p. 103; *AWST*, September 30, 1963, p. 34.

56. *AWST*, January 6, 1964, p. 29; March 16, 1964, p. 253; March 30, 1964, p. 68; D. A. Brown, "Jet Commander Provides Solid Handling," *AWST*, May 11, 1964, p. 98; *AWST*, June 8, 1964, p. 99; *AWST*, July 27, 1964, p. 20; *AWST*, October 12, 1964, p. 24; *AWST*, January 25, 1965, p. 28.

57. Brown, "Jet Commander Provides Solid Handling," *loc. cit.*; "Jet Commander," *B&CA*, August 1964, p. 55ff.; Munson, *op. cit.*, pp. 166-167.

58. *AWST*, January 25, 1965, p. 28; *AWST*, October 3, 1966, p. 29; June 5, 1967, p. 35; Munson, *op. cit.*, p. 166-167.

59. Munson, *op. cit.*, p. 158; *B&CA*, April 1961, pp. 36-37.

60. *AWST*, November 29, 1964, p. 39; December 14, 1964, p. 13.

61. *AWST*, May 10, 1965, p. 43; May 24, 1965, p. 31; May 31, 1965, p. 93.

62. D. A. Brown, "Grumman Gulfstream 2 Aimed at Ease of Maintenance," *AWST*, April 29, 1965, p. 82ff.

63. *AWST*, September 19, 1966, p. 37; September 26, 1966, p. 107; October 10, 1966, p. 33.

64. *AWST*, May 22, 1967, p. 87; August 21, 1967, p. 114; D. A. Brown, "Corporate Experience Aids Gulfstream 2," *AWST*, October 9, 1967, p. 56ff; *AWST*, October 16, 1967, p. 33; October 23, 1967, p. 34; March 18, 1968, p. 306.

65. Munson, *op. cit.*, pp. 168-169; *AW*, February 27, 1961, p. 34; April 17, 1961, p. 33; H. J. Coleman, "de Havilland Modifies Engine for DH.125 Executive Jet," *AW*, May 29, 1961, p. 74ff.

66. *AWST*, June 11, 1962, p. 63; H. J. Coleman, "DH-125 Faces U.S., French Competition," *AWST*, July 23, 1962, p. 68; *AWST*, August 6, 1962, p. 23; September 10, 1962, pp. 26-27; II. J. Coleman, "More Range, Power Planned for DH-125," *AWST*, December 3, 1962, p. 110ff.; *AWST*, December 10, 1962, p. 43; March 11, 1963, p. 270; September 2, 1963, p. 58; September 9, 1963, p. 27.

67. *AWST*, September 7, 1964, p. 149.

68. H. D. Kysor and D. J. Wodraska, "DH-125," *B&CA*, May 1964, p. 31ff.

69. E. H. Phillips, *Beechcraft: Staggerwing to Starship*, *loc. cit.*, p. 8; Inventory Issues, *AWST*, 1965-1970.

70. *AW*, January 6, 1958, p. 88; February 10, 1958, p. 107; *AWST*, July 23, 1962, p. 77; Munson, *op. cit.* , p. 170.

71. *Ibid.*, *AWST*, March 11, 1963, p. 27; March 25, 1963, p. 36; April 29, 1963, p. 35; May 13, 1963, p. 39; June 10, 1963, pp. 90-93; H. J. Coleman, "Flying Demonstrations Cap Paris Air Show," *AWST*, June 24, 1963, pp. 30, 32; H. J. Coleman, "Jets Top Business Plane Display at Paris," *AWST*, July 8, 1963, p. 55ff.; *AWST*, August 5, 1868, p. 21 (editorial), p. 30, p. 55ff.; September 23, 1963, p. 108; October 10, 1963, p. 37; H. J. Coleman, "Modification Improves Mystere 20 Stall," *AWST*, February 10, 1964, p. 100ff.

72. *AWST*, April 6, 1964, p. 106; July 13, 1964, p. 75; August 10, 1964, p. 28; October 5, 1964, p. 35; January 11, 1965, p. 26; January 18, 1965, p. 90; March 15, 1965, p. 260; April 5, 1965, p. 36; May 17, 1965, p. 19; H. J. Coleman, "Dassault Plans Mystere 20 Production Increase . . . ," *AWST*, June 14, 1965, p. 260ff.; "Mockups Pave Way for Falcon Arrivals," *B&CA*, May 1965, p. 62ff.

73. *AWST*, March 7, 1966, p. 201.

74. D. A. Brown, "Pan Am Prepares for Next Business Jet," *AWST*, July 31, 1967, p. 81; *AWST*, August 26, 1968, p. 24; September 2, 1968, p. 52; February 23, 1970, p. 21.

75. *Jane's Encyclopaedia of Aviation*, *loc. cit.*, p. 687; *AW*, May 16, 1960, p. 38.

76. *B&CA*, September 1958, pp. 26-27.

77. *AWST*, December 25, 1961, p. 23; January 14, 1963, p. 27; March 11, 1963, p. 272; July 5, 1965, p. 77; November 22, 1965, p. 30.

78. *AWST*, March 7, 1966, pp. 296-297; April 11, 1966, pp. 114, 119.

79. *'89 Jet and Propjet Corporate Directory*, Wichita, KS; AvCom International, 1989, p. 281.

80. Munson, *op. cit.*, pp. 170-171; *Jane's Encyclopaedia of Aviation*, *loc. cit.*, p. 639.

81. *AWST*, April 13, 1962, p. 22; May 14, 1962, p. 127; August 6, 1962, p. 109.

82. "HFB 320 Hansa," *B&CA*, May 1964, p. 43ff.

83. *AWST*, March 11, 1963, p. 271; W. C. Wetmore, "HFB.320 Modified to Boost Performance," *AWST*, June 17, 1963, p. 99; *AWST*, September 23, 1963, p. 108; September 30, 1963, p. 34; March 16, 1964, p. 259; May 30, 1964, p. 22; May 4, 1964, p. 23; July 27, 1964, p. 20; October 26, 1964, p. 36; H. D. Kysor and D. J. Wodraska, "HFB 320 Hansa," *B&CA*, October 1964, p.62ff.

84. *AWST*, May 17, 1965, p. 37; June 14, 1965, p. 295.

85. D. A. Brown, "Booming Jet Sales Growth Stabilizing," *AWST*, March 7, 1966, pp. 267, 269; *AWST*, March 7, 1966, pp.267, 269; April 11, 1966, p. 86; October 3, 1966, p. 33; March 20, 1967, p. 107; H. J. Coleman, "Hansa Jet Enters Business Aircraft Fleet," *AWST*, May 29, 1967, p. 351.

86. *AWST*, August 5, 1968, p. 121; April 7, 1969, p. 90.

87. Francillon, *McDonnell Douglas, loc. cit.*, pp. 534-535; *Jane's Encyclopaedia of Aviation, loc. cit.*, p. 723; *AWST*, October 2, 1961, p. 85; October 16, 1961, p. 77; December 25, 1961, p. 75; April 23, 1962, p. 107.

88. *AWST*, March 11, 1963, p. 272.

89. Francillon, *McDonnell Douglas, loc. cit.*; *AWST*, March 7, 1966, p. 270.

90. H. J. Coleman, "Italian PD-808 Handles Like Light Twin," *AWST*, September 26, 1966, pp. 97, 99.

91. E. J. Bulban, "Israeli Aircraft Surveying B-101C Market," *AW*, April 10, 1961, p. 108.

92. A. Sherman, "Israeli Aircraft Considers Private Financing for B-101C Development," *AWST*, July 23, 1962, p. 68.

93. *AW*, May 8, 1961, p. 93; *AWST*, April 23, 1962, p. 103; H. J. Coleman, "Hanover Features CM-191 Demonstration," *AWST*, May 14, 1962, p. 105; H. J. Coleman, "CM-191 Provides Easy Transition to Jets," *AWST*, May 28, 1962, pp. 19, 103.

94. *AW*, June 19, 1961, p. 118; E. Walford, "Saab Reveals Entry into Twin-Jet Market," *AW*, July 3, 1961, p. 79; *AWST*, March 12, 1962, p. 267; March 15, 1965, p. 261.

95. *AWST*, November 13, 1961, p. 115.

96. *AWST*, January 14, 1963, p. 89; September 23, 1963, p. 108.

97. *AWST*, July 8, 1963, p. 59.

98. *AWST*, February 14, 1966, p. 1233; October 3, 1966, p. 99; June 10, 1968, p. 24.

99. *AWST*, December 15, 1969, p. 26; December 29, 1969, p. 17.

100. D. A. Brown, "Cessna Readies Sales Drive for New Jet," *AWST*, October 14, 1968, p. 110; *AWST*, September 16, 1968, p. 31.

101. E. J. Bulban, "Cessna Girds for Sluggish Market," *AWST*, December 22, 1969, p. 46; *AWST*, December 29, 1969, p. 17.

Chapter Four

Cessna Opens the Lower End of the Market

Background

Cessna's decision to enter the market in 1971 with a small, modestly-performing, low-priced business jet was a very risky one. As we have seen, a number of other companies had tried to market a low-priced business jet, and none had come close to success. The MS-760 Paris was available in the U.S. prior to any other business jet, yet it (and subsequent versions of it) found few customers.

Lear had a similar goal when he developed the SAAC (Lear Jet) 23 in the early 1960s. The original idea was to develop a small, relatively high-performance aircraft that would sell for $250,000 — a fraction of the prices of the Sabreliner and the JetStar. Lear did not fully achieve this objective. The price of the first Lear Jet 23s was about twice that initially announced, and it was not clear that development and production costs could be covered even at the higher price.

The Italian Cobra F. 400, another low-cost, modest performance proposal, never reached the production stage. The same is true of the IAI B-301C. The Heinkel-Potez CM-191, while announced for sale at only $220,000 in 1962-1963, found no market. The Saab 105 ($210,000, 1961), the Macchi MB-330 ($380,000, 1963) and the Hispano Aviacion HA-230 were welcomed in much the same way.

Cessna itself had failed utterly with its four-engined Model 620 in the mid-1950s. Nonetheless, Cessna had some important advantages as it considered the low end of the market for business jets in the 1960s. One of these was its long record of successful small aircraft and the business reputation that came with that record. Clyde Vernon Cessna began dabbling with airplanes in 1911.[1] In the following years, he designed, built and flew a series of innovative craft. Cessna, with Walter Beech and Lloyd Stearman, was a

73

founder of the Travel Air Manufacturing Company in 1925. That company was responsible for several well-known planes, including some monoplanes with semi-cantilever wings. Cessna left the Travel Air venture because he, unlike Beech and Stearman, thought that design efforts should focus on full-cantilever monoplanes.

The Cessna Aircraft Company was formed in 1927 in Wichita, Kansas. It produced some 250 planes between then and the end of 1931. While the company was profitable in these early years, the depression forced a temporary closing of the plant. Clyde Cessna became discouraged and turned the company over to his nephews, Dwane and Dwight Wallace, in 1933. The factory was re-opened in 1934 and a stream of successful aircraft have come from the Wichita plant ever since. Among these were 5,399 twin-engined advanced trainers built for the U.S. Army Air Force between 1941 and 1944. After World War II, Cessna introduced a series of two-to-four place, single-engine monoplanes and, in the 1950's, a series of four-to-five place, twin-engined planes. It also produced some training and light observation aircraft for the military.

Among the military trainers designed and produced by Cessna was the Model 318/T-37 "Tweety-Bird." The Model 318 proposal was entered against 13 other models offered by six other manufacturers in the 1952-1953 U.S. Air Force competition for a twin jet trainer.[2] Cessna received a contract to develop the XT-37 in April 1953 and immediately set to work on prototypes of the airplane. Apparently few difficulties were encountered. Schedules for first flights were announced in August 1954, and shortly thereafter the Air Force ordered eleven "pre-production" versions of the T-37A. First flight took place in October 1954 and the first T-37A was delivered to the Air Force in June 1956. Orders for production model T-37s were received and the first batch of 270 planes — jet planes — was in production in 1956-1958. First delivery of a production model was in 1957.[3]

A total of 1,272 T-37s were built before production ended in 1977. Cessna was engaged in modification programs for the T-37s for years after that. In addition, over 600 A-37A and A-37B attack aircraft based on the T-37 were manufactured.[4]

Table 4-1 shows that the T-37 was remarkably similar to the MS-760. Cessna studied the possibility of producing a business version of the T-37 but elected not to do so.[5] While we do not know why Cessna rejected this opportunity, certain factors must have entered into its deliberations. First, of course, is the fact that the MS-760 did not attract corporate buyers and, at least as it was offered to the U.S. Air Force, the T-37 had no clear advantages over the MS-760. Second, Cessna was trying to push the larger, more comfortable — albeit slower — 620 for the first few years of T-37 development. Third, Cessna at the time had a full range of successful small planes and no compelling need for a business version of the T-37 in its marketing program. This situation continued into the mid-1960s.

Development of the Cessna Fan Jet 500 Citation

Cessna studied the executive jet market for 10 years after the first deliveries of production T-37s before it announced the Fan Jet 500.[6] Cessna's Wichita neighbor, Beech Aircraft Corporation, was in large measure responsible for Cessna's entering the market at this time and with this particular design. Beech had worked briefly on a Model 120 executive turboprop transport in 1961. By 1963, this concept had evolved to the Model 90 King Air. The Model 90, the first of many versions of the King Air, provided for a crew of two and up to nine passengers. It was powered by two Pratt & Whitney 550 shaft horsepower (shp) engines, had a pressurized cabin (though to only a 4.6 psi differential), could operate from relatively small airports, and had a range of 1,560 mi. With a top speed of 280 mph and a cruise speed of 260 mph, the Model 90 was an instant success. Beech sold 112 Model 90 King Airs between 1964 and 1966, and then introduced the improved and equally popular Model A90.[7] The Model 90 sold for $320,000 in 1965 and the Model A90 was announced at $407,000 in 1966.[8]

In view of the King Air's success, Cessna's objective became not the development of a business jet that could compete against the Sabreliner, Lear Jet and JetStar, but rather one that would compete against the King Air and similar turboprops.[9] A plane that could carry only two or three passengers would not accomplish this purpose. A design considerably larger than the T-37 was needed. An immediate difficulty was the lack of a suitable engine.

Table 4-1 Comparisons of the MS-760 and the T-37		
Item	MS-760	T-37
First Flight Date	29 July 1954	12 October 1954
Wing Span	33 ft, 3 in	33 ft, 9 in
Length	33 ft, 0 in	29 ft, 3 in
Height	8 ft, 7 in	8 ft, 10 in
Wing Area	194 sq ft	184 sq ft
Wing Load	38.4 lb/sq ft	35.7 lb/sq ft
Gross Takeoff Weight	7,440 lb	6,600 lb
Number of Seats (including pilots)	4	2
Max. Level Speed	404 mph	425 mph
Cruise Speed	335 mph	368 mph
Range	700 mi	800 mi
Engines	2 @ 880 lb st (in wing root)	2 @ 1,025 lb st (in wing root)

Source: Swanborough, *United States Military Aircraft Since 1909*; *Jane's Encyclopaedia of Aviation*; Phillips, *Wings of Cessna*.

The jet engines then available were appropriate at one extreme for high-performance Lear Jets, Sabreliners and Gulfstreams or, at the other extreme, for T-37s or MS-760s. There was no engine in the power range Cessna needed for its Fan Jet 500. This problem was ultimately resolved when Pratt & Whitney agreed to develop non-exclusively the 2,200 lb st JT15D-1 turbofan. Then Cessna moved quickly to get its business jet onto the market.

Table 4-2 provides some of the specifications of the Fan Jet 500 as announced in October 1968 and of the Cessna Citation at the time of its certification in September 1971. The Table repeats comparable specifications for the T-37. Two things are obvious: First, the Fan Jet 500 was quite different from the T-37 in most dimensions. Second, the Citation as certified was much like the announced (and pre-flight) Fan Jet 500, indicating that few changes were required during the last two years of development.

The Citation name was adopted just prior to first flight of the prototype on September 15, 1969. Cessna began tooling for a production rate of 96 Citations per year, a very high rate compared to other business jets then in production.[10] Cessna also stressed marketing and facilities for maintenance and service. Factory service centers were planned for Wichita and on the East and West coasts of the U.S. Technical representatives were trained and stationed in the field. Training of the pilots of purchasing companies was included in the purchase price, along with standard radios, radar, instruments, automatic flight control, ice prevention and interiors. The Citation airframes were given three-year warranties; the engines, two-year warranties; various components, one-year warranties. An interactive computerized database was set up to assist owners in scheduled maintenance and to provide notices of modifications.[11]

First flight of the Citation prototype was on September 15, 1969, almost exactly on the original schedule. Flight testing in the next year presented no major problems. The first production Citation rolled out in early June 1971. Provisional type certification was given under commercial air transport FAR 25 standards in early July and the first production model was flown shortly thereafter. FAA certification was given in mid-September. Although the single-pilot certification sought by Cessna was not given at that time, Cessna was ready to begin deliveries.[12]

Table 4-2
Comparisons of the T-37, the (Announced) Fan Jet 500
and the (Production) Cessna Citation

Specification	1957 T-37	1969 Fan Jet 500	1971 Citation
Wingspan	33 ft, 9 in	44 ft	43.75 ft
Length	29 ft, 3 in	43 ft	46.50 ft
Height	8 ft, 10 in	13 ft	14.33 ft
Empty Weight	n.a.	5,290 lb	5,939 lb
Max.Takeoff Weight	6,600 lb	9,500 lb	10,350 lb
Normal Cruise Speed	368 mph	402 mph	400 mph
Max Speed	425 mph	413 mph	400 mph
Wing Area	184 sq ft	n.a.	260 sq ft
Range	800 mi	1,580 mi	1,322 mi
FAA Takeoff Distance	n.a.	3,350 ft	3,035 ft
Number of Seats (including Pilots)	2	8	8
Engines	2 @ 1,025 lb (wing roots)	2 @ 2,200 lb (sides,rear)	2 @ 2,200 lb (sides,rear)

Source: *Aviation Week and Space Technology*, Inventory Issues, March 10, 1969, March 13, 1972; C. E. Schneider, "Cessna Aims Citation at Turboprop Market," *AW*, March 15, 1971, p. 46; E. H. Phillips, *Wings of Cessna, loc. cit.* Slightly different specifications can be found in other sources.The price of the basic airplane was quoted at $595,000 in 1969 for 1971 deliveries. The price with standard equipment — the way Cessna sold most of the Citations — was $695,000. The Beech B90 King Air was selling at $465,000 in 1969 and the King Air 100 was priced at $605,000 in 1971.

It turned out that Cessna's timing was not ideal. The market for general aviation aircraft — and for business jets, in particular — had been in a slump since 1968-1969. Total shipments of business jets to U.S. business customers fell from 170 in 1968 and 161 in 1969 to 82 in 1970 and 45 in 1971. Despite Cessna's best efforts, the Citations coming off its production line in late 1971 found their way only to the ramps around the factory. The first delivery did not occur until December, and only two Citations were delivered in that month.[13]

Pundits familiar with the popular Learjets dubbed the Citation the "Near Jet." Jokes circulated that the Citation had a "calendar instead of an airspeed indicator" and that it was the "first business jet certified for bird-strikes up the tailpipe."[14] The jesting was short-lived, however. Business conditions improved in 1972 and 1973. The recession of 1974-1975 had little effect on business flying. Overall, sales of general aircraft rose fairly steadily from 1972 into 1981. The Citations sitting on the ramps at Wichita were quickly sold and order backlogs soon appeared.[15] The production rate of the aircraft rose from four per month for the first nine months of 1972, to five per month up to March 1973, then to six per month from March to August of 1973, then to seven per month until December 1973 and to ten per month following that date. The Citation was a hit at the Paris Air Show of June 1973. Plans for a stretched version were announced. Between 128 and 140 Citations were scheduled for delivery during Cessna's 1974 fiscal year. Deliveries in the U.S. amounted to 35 in calendar 1972, 52 in 1973, 54 in 1974, 54 in 1975, and 37 in 1976. Worldwide deliveries were 52, 81, 85, 69, and 54 in the same years. In terms of units sold — not dollar sales — the Citation became far and away the best-selling business jet in the world.

There were apparently no important cost overruns and the 1971 price of the Citation was, as announced, $695,000, including "complete interior, dual IFR avionics with radar, transponder, flight director and autopilot, training for 2 pilots and mechanics; computerized maintenance program" and the warranties.[16] The price went up to $725,000 in 1974, and $795,000 in 1975. *Business and Commercial Aviation* estimated that a typically-equipped Citation would have cost about $825,900 in 1975.[17]

Follow-On Citation Models

The popularity of the Citation 500 did not cause Cessna to lose sight of the need to upgrade its product offerings in order to retain its market position. There were continuing improvements in the turboprops against which the Citation was designed to compete. By 1976, the Beech 200 Super King Air could accommodate 6-to-14 passengers and cruise at 333 mph over a range in excess of 2,000 miles. Other manufacturers of business jets had been attracted to the low end of the market, as well. By 1975, the Falcon 10, although higher-priced (and higher-performing), was viewed as an alternative to the Citation. It appeared that the Aerospatiale SN 601 would become another. Cessna recognized as early as 1973 that some of the corporate buyers introduced to jets on its Citations were turning to other manufacturers for replacements or for second airplanes. It felt compelled to develop new versions of the Citation because it "did not go into the high-volume Citation program to develop a new market for competitors when owners . . . wanted to add or move up to a high performance airplane."[18]

The Cessna Model 501 Citation I was developed between 1974 and 1977. Cessna was working on a number of concepts in these years, including the Model 550 Citation II and a Model 700 tri-jet with supercritical airfoils. The latter, with redesign, became the Model 650 Citation III.[19] The Citation I incorporated major improvements on the original Citation, but was in no sense an effort to move into a different class of airplane. The wingspan of the original Model 500 was increased by 3 feet, 2 inches, the cabin pressurization differential was increased from 7.6 to 8.5 psi and the range was increased to over 1,500 miles with full load. The Citation I was also certified in a single-pilot, Citation I/SP version. The Pratt & Whitney JT150-1A engines incorporated minor improvements but remained at 2,200 lb st. The Citation I was usually configured for six or seven passengers; the Citation I/SP typically had seven or eight passenger seats. The 1977 price of the new plane, equipped with standard avionics and interior, was $945,000.[20]

Again, Cessna appears to have encountered few difficulties in the development of the Citation I and I/SP. FAA certification testing of improved Citations began around June 1975 and the Citation I began to replace the Citation on the production line for deliveries in 1977.[21] The first U.S.

delivery of a Citation I/SP occurred in January 1977; of a Citation I, in February 1977. A total of 48 Citation I and I/SPs were delivered in the U.S. during that year. The last U.S. delivery of a new Citation Model 500 was in February 1977. The market for used Citations was active, too; 36 sales of previously-owned Model 500s took place in the U.S. in 1977. Independent companies began to offer modifications for the used Citations. With these retrofits, the older versions rivaled the new planes that Cessna was putting out.[22]

Cessna announced its Models 550/551 Citation II and II/SP in 1976, a year before first delivery of the Citation I and I/SP. The Citation II was considerably different from the I. The wings of the II were 3 feet, 7 inches longer, had a different aspect ratio and leading edge design and provided for 150 additional gallons of fuel. The fuselage of the II was 42 inches longer so that two additional passengers could be carried. Gross takeoff weight of the Citation II was 13,300 pounds, compared to 12,000 for the Citation I. Pressurization was increased to an 8.7 psi differential. The engines of the Citation II delivered 2,500 lb st. Its range was about 500 miles greater than that of the Citation I, with somewhat higher long-range cruise speeds. In 1977, *Business and Commercial Aviation* estimated the typically-equipped price of the yet-to-be-delivered Citation II at $1,363,000 and, of the Citation I, $1,116,625.

Table 4-3 shows the remarkable market penetration achieved by Cessna with its first series of business jets. From 1972 through 1981, Cessna delivered more business jets in the U.S. than did any other manufacturer. All of these were variants of the Citation I and Citation II aircraft. Cessna continued to deliver far more business jets than any other manufacturer after 1981. We cover successors to the Citation 560, Citation I and Citation II later in this chapter. In addition to its offerings in the lower end of the market, Cessna introduced the high-performance Citation III in 1982 and, more recently, it has announced the larger, more sophisticated Citation X.

Cessna's achievements with the first series of Citations were truly remarkable. These airplanes were hardly state-of-the-art as they came onto the market. Still, Cessna produced a total of 352 Citation 500s between 1971 and 1977 when the improved Citation I was introduced.

Table 4-3
Unit and Dollar Value of Cessna Business Jets and
Total Business Jets Delivered to U.S. Customers,
1971-1981

Year	Units			Approximate Dollar Value (in millions)		
	Cessna	Total*	Percent	Cessna	Total*	Percent
1971	2	41	4.9 %	$1,390	$68,016	2.0 %
1972	35	134	26.1 %	$24,325	$180,321	13.5 %
1973	52	179	29.1 %	$37,700	$233,525	16.1 %
1974	54	172	31.4 %	$39,479	$247,381	16.0 %
1975	54	174	3.0 %	$44,599	$287,991	15.5 %
1976	37	173	21.4 %	$33,962	$334,063	10.2 %
1977	54	238	22.7 %	$60,299	$526,631	11.5 %
1978	51	217	23.5 %	$74,178	$558,047	13.3 %
1979	94	265	35.5 %	$177,620	$694,486	25.6 %
1980	87	292	29.8 %	$188,344	$1,004,951	18.7 %
1981	147	393	37.4 %	$340,526	$1,611,587	21.1 %

*Excludes B-707, B-727, B-720, BAC 1-11, Convair 880 and 990, F-28, DC-9,
and SUD Caravelle aircraft sold to businesses.

Source: AvData Inc.; *Business and Commercial Aviation; Aviation Week and
Space Technology.*

Then more than 345 Citation Is were produced between 1977 and the disconti-nuation of its production in 1985.[23] The Citation II and II/SP aircraft have been equally popular.

The factors underlying Cessna's success with these planes are ob-vious: First, they were relatively inexpensive to own and operate. Costs per seat mile for the Citation were estimated at only $0.165 in 1971, with 600 hours of annual use, average stage lengths of 750 miles, and fuel at $0.34 per gallon.[24] Costs per seat mile were estimated at $0.14 in 1973, based on 600 hours of use, stage lengths of 575 miles, and fuel at $0.42 per gallon.[25] For comparison, the costs per seat mile of the Sabreliner 40A were estimated at $0.25 in 1972, based on six seats, 500 hours of operation and fuel at $0.45 per gallon.[26] Citations became renowned as great "utility" airplanes — they can get in and out of airports with runways as short as 2,900 feet. They are highly reliable and easy to fly. Cessna provided excellent warranties on the air-frames, engines and avionics, and service was available at convenient loca-tions. Little prestige might be associated with a CEO's use of a Citation, but many corporations found them extraordinarily productive vehicles for use in everyday business matters. And Cessna realized substantial profits from having them in the product line.[27]

Challenges to the Citation

Other manufacturers were not oblivious to the possibility of garnering some part of the low end of the market. Success, however, proved difficult to achieve.

Aerospatiale SN-600/601 Corvette   Aerospatiale announced its SN-600 Corvette in 1968, roughly coincident with Cessna's announcement of the Citation 500. As shown in Table 4-4, the two planes were quite similar in many respects. While the Corvette had swept wings, was larger, and could carry more passengers, it was designed to sell for less than $1 million for 1974 deliveries and to compete against the Citation and upscale business tur-boprop aircraft. In addition to anticipated sales of 60 or more planes to the French military, Aerospatiale sought to sell at least 400 in the worldwide market. Aerospatiale forecast that the total sales for this class of aircraft might reach as high as 2,800 planes between 1974 and 1980.[28] Arrangements

Table 4-4		
Comparison of SN-600 Corvette and Citation 500		
Item	1971 Prototype SN-600 Corvette	1971 Citation 500
Wingspan	42.0 ft[a]	43.75 ft
Length	44.8 ft[b]	46.50 ft
Height	13.0 ft	14.33 ft
Empty Weight	7,076 lb[c]	5,939 lb
Max. T.O. Weight	13,500 lb[d]	10,350 lb
Normal Cruise Speed	403 mph[e]	400 mph
Wing Area	237 sq ft	260 sq ft
Crew/Passengers	2/6-12[f]	2/6
Range: 6 pass	1,490 mi	1,322 mi
Engines	2 JT15D-1 @ 2,200 lb[g]	2 JT15D-1 @ 2,200 lb

a. 45.2 ft in 1975 production model with wingtip tanks.

b. 45.4 ft in 1975 production model.

c. 8,540 lb in 1975 production model.

d. 14,660 in 1975 production model.

e. Production model normal cruise listed as 500 mph in 1972 - 1974 Inventory Issues of *Aviation Week and Space Technology* and at 472 mph in subsequent years. *Business and Commercial Aviation* lists long-range cruise speed at 350 mph.

f. *Business and Commercial Aviation* lists as 2/7.

g. JT15D-4 @ 2,500 lb st in 1975 production model.

Source: *Aviation Week and Space Technology*, March 8, 1971, p. 99; D. E. Fink, "SN-600 Design Stresses Simplicity," *Aviation Week and Space Technology*, April 12, 1971, p. 53ff.; *Business and Commercial Aviation,* April 1975, pp.60-61.

were made first with LTV and then with Piper for distribution in the U.S.[29]

Aerospatiale encountered serious problems after only a few flights of the prototype. In March 1971, the first Corvette mysteriously fell out of the air in a nose-down position while undergoing stall tests at 20,000 ft. After investigation, the crash was attributed to the combination of a 45-degree flap setting and an improperly trimmed elevator. The resulting "aerodynamic anomaly" caused the plane to pitch down even though flying at 20 kt above normal stall speed. Recovery from the stall was impossible. While these problems were said to be easily corrected, some potential buyers began to question the general airworthiness of the craft.[30]

Production began on a "slightly refined" production version of the Corvette in October 1971. Further refinements occurred thereafter. The nature of the changes is indicated in the footnotes to Table 4-4. No new prototype, as such, was made. The new model was designated the SN-601, and first flight was scheduled for late 1972. Actual first flight occurred on December 20, 1972, after a pilot escape hatch had been installed. Flight tests continued to show troublesome stall and slow-speed pitching behavior. The Corvette was by then three years behind the Citation 500 even though the two planes had been announced at about the same time.[31]

A new sales and aircraft completion organization, U.S. Corvette, Inc., was established in Atlanta in 1973. Plans called for deliveries of 10 units in 1974, 25 in 1975, and 35 in 1976. The price for 1974 deliveries was set at $1,295,000, including a choice of two interiors and standard avionics.[32] At that time, the price of a completed Citation was $725,000. A completed Learjet 24D sold for only $883,000. Despite these lower-priced rivals, U.S. Corvette reported orders for 70 planes by mid-1973.[33] Deliveries were to begin in March 1974, even though continuing flight tests showed needs for further modifications.[34]

The French government was skeptical of the Corvette program and considered shutting it down in 1973. A go-ahead decision was finally issued, however, after the contract with U.S. Corvette was canceled and the Air Center of Oklahoma City was named as the new U.S. finisher and distributor. The French government later installed a new management at Aerospatiale, apparently because of cost overruns in both the Concorde and Corvette programs.[35]

A French airworthiness type certificate was awarded to the Corvette in May 1974, but deliveries were pushed back to early 1975, in part because of a strike at United Aircraft of Canada, the manufacturer of the engines. The Air Center of Oklahoma City then sued Aerospatiale for non-performance, noting that it had contracted for the delivery of 70 planes by May 1974 and that only one demonstrator model had been delivered. There had been no deliveries of FAA certified planes. The contract with the Air Center was subsequently amended to reflect anticipated deliveries of only eight SN-601s in 1975. The price was increased to $1,450,000.[36]

In fact, while at least six Corvettes reached Oklahoma for completion, there were no outright sales of new Corvettes to U.S. customers in 1975 or, indeed, at any time thereafter. Aerospatiale terminated the U.S. marketing program in March 1976. The entire program was abandoned in late 1977 after completion of the 40th plane.[37] Up to early 1977, four Corvettes had been sold under firm contract, with 14 more assigned to leasing companies "with the understanding that Aerospatiale would take back the aircraft and repay the losses . . . in case of default by their clients . . . Additionally, 13 other aircraft were rented 'under more or less precarious conditions.'"[38]

A study by the French Cours des Comptes concluded that losses from the program would come to $190 million, or 66% of Aerospatiale's total deficits from 1972 to 1975. The study commented that:

> This failure shows, in effect, that an aeronautical program of secondary importance . . . can nevertheless place [an] enterprise in a very difficult financial situation.

> [T]he competitive risks [were] singularly underestimated in this very disputed market slot where Avion Marcel Dassault had already launched the Falcon 20 and were preparing the Falcon 10 version, and where several British and American companies were equally in the ranks.

> [I]t is certain that the Corvette program is, and will remain, a major commercial and financial failure . . . This program [was] launched entirely under the responsibility of the

management of the company, against the contrary advice of the interested administrations, and in particular the ministry of [transport], which has never accepted the several market studies presented by the manufacturer and has always refused to provide any financial aid whatever to the program.[39]

It was not just poor market research and the competitive strength of rival manufacturers that led to the demise of the Corvette program. There were major cost overruns associated with recurrent modifications and the consequent time delays. But these factors, in turn, were the result of inadequate design and production planning. The plane incorporated wing and power designs that were incompatible with the safe accomplishment of any single flight mission. The power load of the Corvette SN-601 was 2.93 lb st per pound of gross takeoff weight. The same figure for the Citation was 2.35, while that of the Learjet 24D was 2.29. The wing load of the SN-601 was 62 lb per sq ft; that of the Citation, 39.8 lb per sq ft and, of the Learjet 24D, 58 lb per sq ft. Thus, the power loading of the Corvette was relatively high — it had low total thrust compared to its weight. On the other hand, the Corvette had small wings relative to its weight. It had to be pushed along at a good speed in order to fly. The consequence was a plane that used a lot of runway, had a high stall speed and a low range.[40] This left the Corvette an airplane with no defined flight mission it was capable of performing better than another aircraft. At the same time, the Citation was selling for slightly more than half of the price of the Corvette and the Learjet 24D, at about two-thirds the price of the Corvette. Price/performance superiority in some dimension is essential for any business jet, and the Corvette appears to have had none.

Other Early Efforts to Compete with the Citation Cessna's effort with the Citation was paralleled and imitated by other manufacturers. Turbomeca, a French engine manufacturer, experimented in 1971 with the use of two of its 1,570 lb st Astafan 2 engines on a highly-modified Hawk Commander airframe. The jet-equipped model had a maximum cruise speed of 340 mph, a normal cruise speed of 325 mph. Plans to go ahead with other versions with more power and on other airframes were apparently aborted.[41] Piper Aircraft and Swearingen considered joining forces to develop a Merlin 5 light business jet to compete with the Citation, the Falcon 10 and the low-end of Learjet offerings, but they also abandoned their efforts at the early stages.[42] Ted R. Smith proposed a twin jet Superstar 3000 version of the Aerostar design. The plan was for a six-passenger, 8,500 pound plane that would cruise at 460 mph over a range of 2,000 miles and sell for only $500,000. While this offering was listed in *Aviation Week and Space Technology* Inventory Issues in the early 1970s, no production models were ever built.[43] Rockwell also began the design of a twin jet executive plane to compete with the Citation, but it too cut short its efforts in this direction.[44] Beech was seemingly engaged in an "on again-off again" search for a plane to use in competition against the Citation throughout the 1970s.[45]

The Foxjet program was a more serious and longer-lasting effort to get into the Citation segment of the market. Foxjet International was a subsidiary of Tony Team Industries, Inc. The parent company was owned privately by Tony Fox, a designer and inventor of waste compactors, electrical hand trucks and rocket-powered race cars. The 1977 ST-600 Foxjet design was based on two Wright Research 570 lb st turbofan engines that were derivatives of the engines used in Tomahawk cruise missiles.

The ST-600 Foxjet had features reminiscent of the 1954 MS-760 Paris. The original plan called for four seats, gross weight of 4,181 pounds, maximum speed of 376 mph, cruise speed of 330 mph, range of 1,400 mi., and a takeoff distance (over 50 ft obstacle) of 2,220 ft. A 1978 price of $695,000 was announced. At that time, the much larger Citation I was listed at $1,050,000.

William P. Lear was among those consulted on the ST-600 design. Flight tests of the sleek prototype were set for June 1978. Trijet and six-place versions were also considered. Arrangements were made at one point to have the plane produced at the Aeronca plant in Middletown, Ohio. Then a site in Phoenix was considered, but the final decision was to produce in Minneapolis. The first flight date slipped from June 1978 to mid-1979, with deliveries promised for 1980. The power of the engines was raised to 800 lb st and the price was increased to $795,000. By March 1980, forecasts of first flight dates were no longer made. The work force was down to only nine engineers and it was reported that only 70% of the paper engineering work was completed. The last listing of the ST-600 Foxjet by *Aviation Week and Space*

Technology was in the March 1981 Inventory Issue. The entry attempt had failed.[46]

   Later Challenges to the Citation   Gulfstream American, the resulting firm responsible for the "heavy iron" Gulfstreams after corporate reorganizations that occurred in 1978, purchased the General Aviation Division of Rockwell International in 1981. That division was then producing the Commander line of turboprops for business customers. The Jet American group of Gulfstream American had a flying model of the Hustler 500 under development at the time. The Hustler design had a small turboprop in the front of the fuselage and a small jet pusher engine in the tail. With the Commander line in hand, Gulfstream tried to modify the Hustler into a small, twin turbofan business plane to be called the Peregrine 2. The Peregrine name was adopted from a two-seat, military jet trainer Gulfstream American was developing and which was also a derivative of the Hustler.[47]

   Gulfstream changed the design and the name of the plane shortly after the project began. The twin-engine project remained as a turboprop development, the Gulfstream Aerospace Commander 1200. The turbofan project was the single-engine Gulfstream Aerospace Commander Fanjet Model 1500, a more direct derivative of the Hustler.

   A prototype of the Model 1500 made its first flight on January 14, 1983. The engine was the Pratt & Whitney JT15D-1 used in the Citation 500, but plans called for a larger JT15D-5 in the production model. The air inlets for the engine were on the upper fuselage, with the engine itself in the center of the aft fuselage. Wings, tail sections and other parts were taken from the Peregrine trainer. The aim was for a six-place plane with gross takeoff weight of 7,500 pounds, a cruise speed of 416 mph and a range of 1,200 miles. The prototype was taken to the June 1983 Paris Air Show, where it was indicated that the plane would be certified in time for 1986 deliveries. The name was subsequently changed back to the Peregrine and Gulfstream said it would develop a production model for 1986 deliveries when had received 50 orders.[48]

   By early 1984, Gulfstream had apparently decided to go ahead with a production version. Three prototypes were flying and another was being used for fatigue tests. The plane had grown larger and now was listed at a gross weight of 9,400 pounds. The engine was changed to a 3,500 lb st Garrett TFE731-2. The range was increased to 1,500 miles, and the normal cruise speed went to 436 mph. The contract price for 1987 deliveries was set at $1.6 million (1984 dollars). The plane was to have six or seven seats, yet the maximum payload was only 680 pounds. Gulfstream later reduced the price to $1.4 million (1984 dollars), but orders were apparently few.[49] The plane was never listed as a production offering in any *Aviation Week and Space Technology* Inventory Issue. Another attempted entry into the field of the Citation had failed.

Gulfstream did not give up the idea of having a small business jet with the end of the Peregrine program. Its subsequent efforts centered around a brief joint venture with Swearingen Engineering and Technologies, Inc. and the Swearingen SA-30 business jet.

The SA-30 was designed by Ed Swearingen, designer of the Lockheed JetStar II, the Merlin series of turboprops, the Fairchild Metro and the Piper Twin Comanche. As announced in 1986, the SA-30 was to be a six to seven place twin with a range of about 2,500 miles at most economical cruise speeds. The maximum cruise speed was to be over 500 mph with fuel consumption some 30% less than comparable jets. The engines were to be the new Williams International FJ44 turbofans with 1,800 lb st.

The development of the SA-30 appears to have gone smoothly through wind tunnel model tests in 1987. Some businesses expressed interest in placing orders but, given adequate financing from other sources, Swearingen elected not to accept orders at that point. By late 1988, design work was 80% completed and it was decided to go ahead with production. First flight was scheduled for the third quarter of 1989, and arrangements had been concluded to have Gulfstream do the marketing.

The SA-30 was to sell for less than $2 million — $1 million less than the King Air 200 turboprop and $2.5 million less than the Citation SII against which it was to compete. A two-year flight test program was foreseen and it was anticipated that sales for 1,000 planes might be realized over the life of the design. Swearingen was convinced that business jets up to that time were designed to be "propelled by brute force," with excessively powerful and excessively expensive engines and operating costs because of inadequate attention to aerodynamic improvements. He saw no need to turn to "uncertain methods" and "exotic materials" (e.g., composites) to improve on the other planes. Rather, the key Swearingen saw was to have "every decision . . . driven by economics" and, as an example, to have a "careful matching of the wing to the chosen engine and the latest flap technology." He thought that more attention should be given to the technologies employed in the design and production of commercial aircraft since most business jets of the late 1980s "are less efficient than was the Boeing 707 when it was introduced" in the late 1950s.[50]

It was announced in May 1989 that the SA-30 would be designated the Gulfjet, "a crisp concise new name . . . [which] will have appeal . . . " Specifications then were for a maximum cruise of Mach 0.78, a VFR range of about 2,500 miles and a gross takeoff weight of 9,250 pounds. A manufacturing site and a production schedule had yet to be determined. Then, for unannounced reasons but after it had been acquired by Chrysler, Gulfstream withdrew from the program effective September 1, 1989. A prototype SA-30 was then in production. Swearingen quickly got support from the Jaffe Group to continue the work and redesignated the plane as the SJ30. At that time, Swearingen was "looking farther down the road to certification and production and focusing on a total schedule."[51] The specifications were for a length of 42.3 feet, wingspan of 36.3 feet, maximum takeoff weight of 9,850 pounds and aim IFR range of 1,990 miles. The fuselage had a chemically milled aluminum skin and was constructed for pressurization to a 10 psi differential. No stringers were used in fuselage construction. Instead, the skin was milled to 0.040 inches except for the areas where stringers would otherwise have been. In these areas, the thickness was 0.090 inches, the dimension of the stock from which the skin was crafted.

Delays in the scheduled first flight of the SJ30 occurred in late 1990 due to late parts deliveries. First flight took place in February 1991 and eight distribution and service centers were appointed. Certification was expected in late 1992.

By February 1992, the prototype had accumulated 150 hours of flying. It was decided that the fuselage of the production model would be a bit longer than that of the prototype. Five or six passengers could be accommodated. The William-Rolls Royce FJ44 engines were then rated at 1,900 lb st and a runway of only 3,300 feet was adequate for takeoff. The plane was extremely smooth, with no air scoops or inlets on the fuselage. Even antennae were flush with the skin.

The Marquandt Manufacturing Company was to selected construct the fuselage. By mid-1992, Swearingen had begun construction of a plant in Dover, Delaware. Distributors were appointed in Canada, Germany, France, the United Kingdom, Austria, Switzerland, Mexico and other countries. A few months later, work on the Dover facility was terminated. Swearingen cited "political and financial problems." Before the end of the year, a West Virginia location had been chosen as the production site. The expected date for certification of the SJ30 was pushed back to April 1994. Despite the delays, Swearingen claimed orders in excess of $170 million.

A second SJ30 was in production in 1993. Certification was scheduled for the summer of 1994. Rumors were then circulating that Bombardier — already the owner of the Challenger and Learjet lines — might acquire the SJ30 also.[52]

Others continued to search for ways to enter the low end of the market despite the generally depressed condition of the industry and Cessna's strong position. JetCraft USA announced the Executive Mark 1, a six-place business jet in early 1985. The Mark 1 used the wings and twin-boom tail assembly of the old de Havilland Vampire fighter. JetCraft, Ltd., a prior organization, had done a good deal of work on this design in the 1968-1977 period, but went out of business before completing it. The Mark 1 was to be powered by a single GE CF700-2D2 engine of 4,500 lb st and have a maximum cruise speed of 541 mph. JetCraft was asking for deposits of $50,000 on orders stipulating a $895,000 price. Certification was to occur by 1988. A somewhat larger Mark 3 was also on the drawing board.

JetCraft was forced to move its facilities in late 1985 because it was several months behind in the rent at its first site. Its chairman, who had served two jail terms because of certain of the securities transactions of JetCraft, Ltd., planned to raise $10 million through the sale of convertible debentures. The absence of a subsequent record suggests that his plans were not successful.[53]

Ian Chichester-Miles, who had previously served a chief research engineer for British Aerospace, began work on his CMC Leopard business jet in 1979. The Leopard, like the Foxjet, also had similarities to the MS-760 design. Indeed the Leopard was even smaller than the Foxjet, having provisional specifications for four places, a length of 23 feet, span of 23 feet, maximum weight of 3,750 pounds, Mach 0.76 cruise, and range of 1,725 miles. The target price was £270,000, or about $472,000. Appropriate engines were being sought as late as 1986.

A prototype Leopard was completed in late 1986 using Noel Penny NPT 301 engines with 300 lb st. Engines with 700 or 750 lb st were planned for the production models. The wings were "mirror-smooth," supercritical, laminar flow, with a 35-degree sweep. First flight was in December 1988 and for certification was scheduled for 1989. The Noel Penny engines were apparently unsatisfactory. Further development was delayed until Chichester-Miles began discussions with Williams International in 1992. The second version of the Leopard was apparently to use modified Williams F107 engines with 1,600 lb st. A price of $900,000 for deliveries in 1995 was announced.[54]

Still others were in the wings. Honda began flying its UA-5 in 1993. While Honda indicated that this small, twin-engine plane was being used to develop advanced aerospace materials for automobile designs, it has the potential of becoming a light business jet.[55] Another firm, Advanced Aerodynamics and Structures, in North Hollywood, California, was considering production of its Stratocruzer 1250-ER, using the Williams FJ44 engines. The 1250-ER design calls for a gross takeoff weight of 12,500 pounds and seats for up to 12 passengers.[56]

Beech became increasingly concerned during the mid-1980s about not having a business jet in its line as it saw that "60% of operators who sold their King Airs purchased a small to mid-sized jet aircraft."[57] Beech, with Burt Rutan, initiated research on a light, cabin-class twin jet. This project, using two Williams FJ44 engines, achieved first flight in 1988, but was abandoned thereafter. Eventually, as we will discuss in Chapter Six, Beech elected to buy the Mitsubishi Diamond 1 line. Williams International, the manufacturer of the FJ44 engines, itself announced a six-place craft with forward swept-wings, but this, too, did not go far.[58]

Cessna's Success in Holding Its Position in the Market

It was not just the unique price/performance attributes of the original Citation that gave Cessna its ability to retain its position in the market. We have pointed out that Cessna followed the Citation 500 with the improved Citation I, and I/SP and then the Citation II, II/SP and SII. The SII was certi-fied in 1984 with the improved JT15D-4B engines and other modest changes.

The acquisition of Cessna by General Dynamics in 1985 afforded the financial resources to proceed on this path even in the face of depressed sales at that time. At the low end, the Citation V was announced in 1987 and certi-fied in 1988. The Citation V is a stretched version of the Citation SII, and re-tains the same general performance attributes as its predecessors. It is powered by JT15D-5, 2,900 lb st engines and has a gross takeoff weight nearly 2,000 pounds greater than that of the Citation II. The cruise speed and range of the V are considerably higher than those of the Citation II. The equipped price of the Citation V was about $3,840,000 in 1988. This price had gone up to about $5,130,000 by 1993.

The Model 525 CitationJet project, announced in 1989, is a smaller, four-to-six passenger, entry-level plane intended to replace the original Citation and Citation I in the product line. The CitationJet was certified in October 1992 following a year and a half of flight testing. Deliveries began in 1993. The Williams-Rolls Royce FJ44 engine is used. The wings incorpo-rate a new NASA laminar flow technology that yields significant improve-ments in performance. The CitationJet accommodates five or six passengers, has a long-range cruise speed of about 435 mph and a range of about 1,700 miles. When the first CitationJet was delivered, Cessna had orders for deliv-eries through 1994. The equipped price was about $2,620,000 in 1992 and $2,890,000 in 1993. Over 2,000 Citations had been delivered by June 1993. The original civilian Citation, it will be recalled, grew from Cessna 's ex-perience with the T-37 military jet trainer. In 1993, Cessna based its proposal for the U.S. Air Force/Navy Joint Primary Aircraft Training System (JPATS) on the civilian CitationJet design.[59] At the same time Cessna was so actively improving its offerings at the low end, it was searching for improved market position at the higher end of the performance spectrum with the Citation VII and, most recently, the Citation X. These planes are discussed in Chapter Six.

There is, of course, no assurance that a company actively attempting successive improvements in its aircraft will thereby achieve its goals. There are always risks that any development will be technically unsuccessful — entailing cost and time overruns and, often, the consequent losses in reputation before the craft reaches the delivery stage. There is also obvious economic risk in replacing one's own planes with newer models with improved price/performance characteristics. The replacement may come at the wrong time in the product cycle, at the wrong point in the business cycle, and may have the wrong degree of differentiation from the predecessor models. On the other hand, markets such as those for business jets make clear an opposite risk; if a company does not act to improve and, to some extent, displace its own successful models, it is probable that another will. Whether any company can eventually attain profits in this kind of a market remains a question — although Cessna clearly did through at least the late 1980s.

Cessna, as we have pointed out, faced threats of entry throughout the period covered here. That none of them was particularly successful was not because Cessna had in any way preempted any relevant technology, skill or resource. The problem faced by the entrants was not that means could not be found for, say, producing a cheaper or a faster plane. Some of the proposed aircraft were cheaper, both to buy and, ostensibly, to operate. Some others were faster, some were slower; some had shorter range, some longer; some utilized more recent, state-of-the-art technologies, others less recent techniques. Similarly, the problem faced by entrants was not that they lacked experience or, in the reverse, that they were stultified by whatever previous experience they may have had. Some of the entering firms — like Aerospatiale, Beech and Gulfstream — had vast experience with several types of aircraft, including very successful ones. Others — like Foxjet and JetCraft USA — were far less experienced and surely willing to experiment with unconventional approaches to aircraft development.

In assessing the fact that these other manufacturers did not attain a market position anywhere near that of Cessna, it is critical to remember that there are literally thousands of technically defined variables and parameters that go into the design of an airplane. These variables and parameters end up interacting with one another in different ways in different parts of the performance envelope of the airplane. Aeronautical and related sciences have progressed to the point that proposed designs can be "flown" in computer simulations. Wind tunnel and other tests help in ferreting out difficulties early in the development process. Computer-aided design and manufacturing methods can be used. Still, unanticipated and even unexplainable problems crop up. These difficulties may not be apparent until well into the development process or, less happily, well into flight experience with the airplane. These sheer technical uncertainties, piled on top of the financial, marketing and organizational problems facing any business, make it inevitable that some firms will fail while others do well in the maelstrom of Schumpeterian competition.[60]

Cessna faced competition from sources other than the potential entrants, of course. Buyers of business jets have widely varying mission requirements for their aircraft, with the result that alternate craft against which a Cessna might be compared by one would be different from the alternates used for comparison by another. The Citation and the Citation I were designed to compete primarily against Beech's King Airs, and they did. But they also competed against the Rockwell Commanders, Piper Cheyennes and, indeed, Cessna's own Conquest turboprops. Very importantly, Citations and Citation Is were in strong competition with used Citations and Citation Is. In 1978, for example, there were only 32 new Citation Is and I/SPs delivered in the U.S. In the same year, 45 used Citations and Citation I/SPs were sold. The used planes were often modified in ways that made them in some respects better than they were when new.[61]

The Citation Is were, of course, sometimes compared against other jets, too — the Learjet 24E, Learjet 24F, Learjet 25F and Falcon 10, for example.[62] The Citation IIs were even more frequently compared to other business jets. The seven-passenger Learjet 25D, Learjet 28, and Learjet 35A were among the alternatives. The effect of all of this is to put enormous pressure on any producer, no matter how successful to that point, to search for ways to withstand the "perennial gale of creative destruction." To think of Cessna as being unrivaled because of the success of the Citations is to miss the nature of Schumpeterian competition entirely.

Notes

1. This section draws generally on E. H. Phillips, *Cessna: A Master's Expression*, Eagin, MN: Flying Books, 1985, and, by the same author, *Wings of Cessna: Model 120 to Citation III*, Eagin MN: Flying Books, 1986.

2. A. M. Surely, "Cessna Jet," *AW*, January 12, 1953, p. 15.

3. *AW*, February 15, 1954, p. 24; August 9, 1954, p. 11; August 23, 1954, p. 7; October 18, 1954, p. 15; June 18, 1956, p. 119.

4. E. H. Phillips, *op. cit.*

5. *AW*, October 8, 1956, p. 117.

6. E. H. Phillips, *Wings of Cessna, loc. cit.*, p. 84.

7. E. H. Phillips, *Beechcraft: Staggerwing to Starship*, Eagin, MN: Flying Books, 1987.

8. *AWST*, Inventory Issue, March 15, 1965; March 7, 1966.

9. C. E. Schneider, "Cessna Aims Citation at Turboprop Market," *AWST*, March 15, 1971, p. 44.

10. *AWST*, September 28, 1970, p. 16.

11. C. E. Schneider, "Cessna Citation Marketing Emphasizes Aircraft Utility," *AWST*, February 22, 1971, p. 60; R. Piper, "Cessna Citation: First of the Mini-Fans," *B&CA*, March 1971, p. 42.

12. *Flight International (FI)*, October 2, 1969, p. 521; *AWST*, February 22, 1971, p. 7; June 7, 1971, p. 52; July 12, 1971, p. 59; September 20, 1971, p. 56; *B&CA*, May, 1971, p. 30; June 1971, p. 23; October 1971, p. 29.

13. *AWST*, December 13, 1971, p. 17.

14. N. Moll, "Citation X is a 10," *Flying*, June 1991, p. 106.

15. *AWST*, September 18, 1972, p. 12; March 19, 1973, p. 84; March 15, 1976, p. 185; D. M. North, "Growth Climate 'Best' in Years," *AWST*, September 11, 1978, p. 48; "General Aviation Deliveries Hit Peak," *AWST*, September 18, 1978, p. 17; "Corporate Orders Set Records," *AWST*, September 24, 1979, p. 36; "Demand for Aircraft Unabated," *AWST*, October 1, 1979, p. 14; "Gates Presses

Series 50 Certification," *AWST*, April 14, 1980, p. 60 (reporting depressed sales and layoffs).

16. *B&CA*, April, 1971, p. 47.

17. *B&CA*, April, 1975, p. 60.

18. *AWST*, March 19, 1973, p. 87.

19. E. H. Phillips, *Wings of Cessna, loc. cit.*; *AWST*, August 21, 1972, p. 9; September 17, 1973, p. 23; April 15, 1974, p. 77; September 23, 1974, p. 48; November 4, 1974, p. 20; November 18, 1974, p. 64; June 16, 1975, p. 71; E. J. Bulban, "NBAA Show Stresses New Technology," *AWST*, September 20, 1976, p. 78.

20. E. H. Phillips, *Wings of Cessna, loc. cit.*; *FI*, October 2, 1976, p. 1012.

21. *AWST*, June 16, 1975, p. 71; January 3, 1977, p. 23.

22. E. J. Bulban, "Modifications Developed for Citation," *AWST*, October 10, 1977, p. 41.

23. E. H. Phillips, *Wings of Cessna, loc. cit.*

24. R. Piper, *op. cit.*

25. *B&CA*, June 1973, p. 108.

26. *B&CA*, February 1972, p. 34.

27. Profits reported by Cessna Aircraft Corportation include those arising from civilian sales other than business jets as well as those from military contracts. See, nonetheless, *Wall Street Journal,* January 16, 1975, p. 16; December 1, 1975, p. 25; January 19, 1976, p. 28; April 14, 1977, p. 37; October 19, 1978, p. 38; December 12, 1979, p. 32; December 10, 1980, p. 40; October 22, 1981, p. 40; October 21, 1982, p. 22 (loss reported); *AWST*, October 31, 1983, p. 26 (loss for 1983); *Wall Street Journal*, September 17, 1985, p. 4 (General Dynamics began a tender offer for Cessna shares after operating problems resulted in lowered ratings on Cessna bonds).

28. D. E. Fink, "SN-600 Design Stresses Simplicity," *AWST*, April 12, 1971, p. 53; "Maker Strives to Regain SN-600 Pace," *AWST*, May 31, 1971, p. 220; J. Holahan, "Corvette SN 600: Second of the Mini-Fans," *B&CA*, May 1971, p. 42.

29. *AWST*, May 31, 1971, p. 220; June 21, 1971, p. 51.

30. *AWST*, March 29, 1971, p. 18; May 31, 1971, p. 220.

31. *AWST*, October 18, 1971, p. 127; June 12, 1972, p. 51; October 16, 1972, p. 19; January 1, 1973, p. 15; H. Field, "Aerospatiale Corvette," *FI*, January 31, 1974, p. 147; *B&CA*, February 1973, p. 24.

32. E. J. Bulban, "French Pushing U.S. Sales of Corvette," *AWST*, May 21, 1973, p. 65.

33. *AWST*, May 28, 1973, p. 28.

34. *AWST*, June 25, 1973, p. 67.

35. *AWST*, September 10, 1973, p. 17; August 12, 1974, p. 20.

36. *AWST*, November 4, 1974, p. 20; June 16, 1975, p. 66; *FI*, June 13, 1974, p. 767.

37. *FI*, November 20, 1975, p. 755; *AWST*, March 29, 1976, p. 21; April 19, 1976, p. 25; July 12, 1976, p. 14; August 22, 1977, p. 22; February 13, 1978, p. 9.

38. *AWST*, August 22, 1977, p. 22; *FI*, July 9, 1977, p. 120.

39. *AWST*, August 22, 1977, p. 22; February 13, 1978, p. 9. An effort was made in 1979 to sell used but "overhauled to zero time" Corvettes. See *B&CA*, June 1979, p. 91.

40. *B&CA*, June 1974, p. 44.

41. *AWST*, May 31, 1971, p. 212.

42. E.J. Bulban, "Piper, Swearingen Study Link; Later Developing Business Jet," *AWST*, July 26, 1971, p. 19; *B&CA*, November 1972, p. 51.

43. *AWST*, August 16, 1971, p. 59 and various *AWST* Inventory Issues.

44. *AWST*, June 18, 1973, p. 11.

45. For example, *AWST*, November 14, 1977, p. 19; June 26, 1978, p. 63.

46. *AWST*, April 4, 1977, p. 9; May 16, 1977, p. 57; September 26, 1977, p. 51; October 3, 1977, p. 19; January 23, 1978, p. 18; February 13, 1978, p. 23; August 14, 1978, p. 18; September 11, 1978, p. 46; October 23, 1978, p. 20; January 15, 1979, p. 67; February 5, 1979, p. 5; March 3, 1980, p. 213; April 14, 1980, p. 13; *FI*, May 21, 1977, p. 1402.

47. *AWST*, September 11, 1978, p. 26; February 9, 1981, p. 32; *Jane's Encyclopaedia of Aviation* (1989), p. 455.

48. *AWST*, January 24, 1983, p. 25; July 4, 1983, p. 56; October 3, 1983, p. 114; *B&CA*, April 1983, p. 78; April 1984, p. 80.

49. *AWST*, February 27, 1984, p. 73; *B&CA*, April 1985, p. 104; *FI*, February 5, 1983, p. 306.

50. *AWST*, November 10, 1986, p. 32; September 28, 1987; November 14, 1988, p. 83; quotes are from *FI*, April 16, 1988, pp. 19-21.

51. *AWST*, September 25, 1989, p. 24.

52. *Flying*, May 1989, p. 17; May 1991, p. 16; *AWST*, October 8, 1990, p. 78; R. B. Parke, "Swearingen's SJ30," *B&CA*, April 1990, p. 52; *B&CA*, May 1991, p. 13; J. W. Olcott, "Swearingen SJ30," *B&CA*, February 1992, p. 42; *B&CA*, April 1992, p. 30; May 1992, p. 18; June 1992, p. 22; October 1992, p. 22; November 1992, p. 26; *FI*, April 14-20, 1993, p. 12; J. Flint, "If at First . . .," *Forbes*, July 6, 1992, p. 88.

53. *AWST*, March 25, 1985, p. 28; August 12, 1985, p. 26; January 13, 1986, p. 27; *B&CA*, April 1991, p. 42.

54. *FI*, Februry 13, 1986, p. 341; July 5, 1986, p. 15; December 27, 1986, p. 12; *AWST*, September 8, 1986, p. 107; *B&CA*, October 1992, p. 26; K. Sarsfield, "Rich Pickings, Poor Market," *FI*, September 16, 1992, p. 55.

55. *B&CA*, October 1992, p. 26; May 1993, p. 119.

56. *B&CA*, May 1993, p. 114.

57. *AWST*, October 7, 1985, p. 79.

58. *AWST*, September 30, 1985, p. 16; July 18, 1988, p. 24; H. J. Coleman, "Williams International Builds Mockup of Forward Swept-Wing Business Jet," *AWST*, September 23, 1985, p. 28.

59. *AWST*, September 23, 1985, p. 25; June 29, 1987, p. 29; August 17, 1987, p. 31; E. H. Phillips, "New Derivative Aircraft Enhance Upbeat Atmosphere at Exhibit" and "Cessna Foresees Large Market for New $2.4 Million Jet," *AWST*, October 9, 1986, pp. 36, 38; E. H. Phillips, "Cessna Begins Developmental Tests on Citation Prototype After First Flight," *AWST*, May 13, 1991, p. 100; R. N. Aarons, "Cessna's Citation II and SII in Head-to-Head Competition," *B&CA*, October 1986, p. 50 and "Cessna's New Citation V," *B&CA*, May 1988, p. 52 and "Cessna's Citation V," July 1989, p. 49; *FI*, October 8, 1988, p. 21; E. H. Phillips, "CitationJet Nears Certification; Prototype Citation 10 to Fly Next Year," *AWST*, September 21, 1992, p. 45; *AWST*, October 26, 1992, p. 15; *FI*, October 2- November 3, 1992; p. 22; *B&CA*, September 1992, p. 34; December 1992, p. 24; F. George, "Cessna Citation V," *B&CA*, January 1993, p. 46; *B&CA*, April 1993, p. 24; D. M. North, "Cessna Gambling on Low Cost JPATS Entry," *AWST*, April 19, 1993, p. 65; D.M. North, "Single-Pilot CitationJet Primed for Competition," *AWST*, May 3, 1993, p. 38; F. George and R. N. Aarons, "Cessna Citation-Jet," *B&CA*, June 1993, p. 59.

60. See H. C. Smith, *The Illustrated Guide to Aerodynamics*, 2nd ed., Blue Ridge Summit, PA: Tab Books, 1992, especially chapters 8-10.

61. For example, E. J. Bulban, "Modifications Developed for Citation," *AWST*, October 10, 1977, p. 41; *AWST*, February 7, 1983, p. 80; *B&CA*, May 1993, pp. 97-98, 111-113.

62. The Falcon 10 was designed to compete at the low end of the market. The Falcon 10 is discussed in Chapter Six, not in this chapter, because in most respects it was not a "mini-fan." The Falcon 10 was capable of speeds as high as Mach 0.85 in level flight, weighed in excess of 18,000 pounds, and was priced (green) at $1.15 million in 1971. See G. Eremea, "Dassault Falcon 10," *B&CA*, September 1971, p. 56.

[T]he competitive risks [were] singularly underestimated in this very disputed market slot where Avion Marcel Dassault had already launched the Falcon 20 and were preparing the Falcon 10 version, and where several British and American companies were equally in the ranks.

Chapter Five

The "Heavy Iron" Business Jets: Gulfstream, Dassault and Canadair

Grumman's History in Military and Business Aircraft

Grumman Aircraft Corporation was established in 1929. The company has a distinguished record in the development and sale of sophisticated military aircraft. Grumman's first planes were the carrier-based, single-seat FF-1, F2F and F3F biplanes. The F4F Wildcat was developed and produced under a 1931 contract with the U.S. Navy. The Wildcat was followed by, among others, the F6F Hellcat (1942), the F7F Tigercat (1945), the F8F Bearcat (1945), the F9F Panther jet (1948), the F9F Cougar jet (1954) and the extremely well-known F-14 Tomcat (1972). Grumman was also responsible for the TB Avenger (1942), the AF Guardian (1950), the S-2 Tracker (1953), the OV-1 Mohawk (1959), the E-1B Tracer (1960), the A-6 Intruder (1963), the C-2A Greyhound (1966) and the EA-6B Prowler (1971). Above all else, Grumman was recognized as the producer of state-of-the-art naval aircraft.[1]

Grumman produced a series of amphibians at the same time it was developing carrier-based aircraft. It was from its experience with the amphibian line that Grumman became interested in the possibilities of the business side of the market. The Grumman JF/2F Duck was introduced into Navy and Coast Guard service in 1933. Over 600 were built. The twin-engined G-21A Goose (1937) was then built expressly for the private market. More than 300 orders were received, but most of the first run went to the Navy and Coast Guard during the military buildup prior to U.S. entry into World War II. The JRF versions of the Goose followed, with some being designated OA-9s for the Army Air Force. The principal uses of these amphibians was for photography, target towing and navigational training. Production of the Goose was stopped in 1945, but many of them were later converted for private use by McKinnon Enterprises. The conversions included the G-21C, D and G Turbo-Goose (1966), a 12,500 pound plane with up to 12 seats (including

103

crew) that was capable of a 243 mph maximum cruise speed and a range of 1,600 miles.

The G-44 Widgeon went into military service as the Model J4F in 1941. McKinnon also converted many of these to Super Widgeons after the war. Then Grumman developed the Mallard (1946), the Albatross (1949) and, later, training and small private craft such as the T-Cat, the Lynx, the Cheetah, the Tiger, and an agricultural sprayer-duster, the G-164 Ag-Cat.

Grumman's turboprop G-159 Gulfstream was announced in 1956 — the year Cessna was promoting its Model 620 piston-powered executive plane and Beech was trying to sell the MS-760. The G-159 claimed many firsts — "the first 'heavy' twin-engined executive design to appear, the first to be designed for turbine power and the first to be certified for cruising flight at a 30,000 ft (9,140 mi.) altitude."[2] The inaugural flight of the prototype was in August 1958 and FAA certification occurred in May 1959. First customer deliveries began in June 1959. The G-159 had a gross weight of 33,600 pounds, a wing span of 78.6 ft, a normal cruise speed of 350 mph and a range of 2,400 miles. It was typically configured for 10-14 passengers. The initially announced price was $700,000, but this was increased to a $860,000 green price by 1960.[3] About 200 G-159s were produced before construction was halted in 1969. PPG bought a G-159 when it sold *The Glasshopper* in 1960.

The G-159 design invited modifications and extensions. A stretched commuter-feeder liner version of the plane was certified in 1962. In 1974, Grumman announced that it was designing another stretch, this time with turbofan engines, to be called the G-159A, for use as a commuter liner and 20-25 seat executive aircraft.[4] A twin-turboprop, 32-38 seat commuter liner version of the G-159 was explored as late as 1978.

Gulfstream G-II

Design work on the G-1159 Gulfstream II began at Grumman at least as early as 1965. In announcements made that year, the G-II was described as a 54,000 pound fanjet capable of carrying 10 passengers (and baggage) with a full load of fuel. Up to 19 passengers could be accommodated. Less than a full fuel load could be carried, however, when more than 10 passengers were on board. Powered by Rolls Royce RB163-25 11,400 lb st Spey engines, the G-II was to have a long-range cruise speed of Mach 0.75, an "optimum cruise speed" (maximum) of Mach 0.83, and a full-load range against 90 kt head-winds in excess of 3,000 miles. The wings of the G-II were swept to 25 degrees and the engines were mounted on the aft fuselage. The price was first set at $2,100,000 green, with the costs of avionics and interiors estimated at an additional $200,000. Grumman was "counting heavily on the still growing number of satisfied Gulfstream I operators" for sales.[5]

Development of the G-II was apparently marked by few unanticipated problems. First flight was scheduled for August 1966, and occurred on October 2, 1966. A large volume of orders had been placed prior to first flight. By May 1967, four G-IIs had been completed and the FAA had granted type certification.[6] No major changes were required as a result of flight testing. The gross weight had, however, increased to 58,000 pounds by late 1967, when the first two G-IIs were delivered to customers. New orders slowed during the winter of 1967-68 due to the Vietnam War but, by March 1968, deliveries were sold out well into 1969.[7] The average green price of the G-IIs delivered in 1968 came to $2,550,000, or about $3,000,000 when fully equipped. Some thought that prices this high were a major reason for the slowing of sales.[8] Nonetheless, an improved version of the G-II, with better instrumentation, increased fuel capacity, longer range and higher weights, was put into production in 1969. In 1970, further improvements raised the gross weight to 62,000 pounds, effective with the 97th aircraft. As these versions were delivered in 1972, the green price had risen to $3,200,000. This was increased to $3,500,000 in 1974, $3,775,000 in 1975, and $4,400,000 in 1976.[9]

An extended-range G-II/TT was produced after 1977. This version had strengthened wings and wingtip tanks for 3,120 pounds of additional fuel. The gross weight was increased to 66,000 pounds and range was increased by about 350 miles with these changes. G-IIs were equipped with "hush kit" noise suppressers from airframe 166 onward in order to meet increasingly stringent FAR Part 36 noise regulations. Grumman offered all of these changes as retrofits on previously produced aircraft.[10]

The numbers of new Gulfstream IIs delivered to U.S. customers during the period it was in production are given in Table 5-1. The initial popularity of the G-II grew in part from the experience owners had with the G-I turboprop. Suggestions from pilots of the G-I had been solicited in the design

Table 5-1	
Deliveries of Gulfstream II Aircraft to U.S. Customers	
Year	Number Delivered in U.S.
1967	2
1968	35
1969	35
1970	16
1971	11
1972	13
1973	14
1974	11
1975	10
1976	15
1977	13
1978	15
1979	14

Source: AvData, Inc.

of the G-II. Through 1972, 96% of the buyers of G-IIs, with PPG among them, owned a G-I at the time of purchase. Procter & Gamble — an extreme example — operated two G-Is and three G-IIs in 1972.[11]   The G-I was itself so popular that in 1974 consideration was given to retrofitting it with turbofan engines.[12]

Gulfstream G-III

Derivatives of the G-II were being studied by Grumman as early as the spring of 1971.[13] The path to the G-III, however, was far from smooth. By 1974, design efforts for the improved "Gulfstream X" focused on a three- or four-engine, 12-20 passenger plane with a range of 4,140-4,600 miles and a cruise speed of Mach 0.80-0.85.[14] These were ambitious objectives. A General Electric and two different Rolls Royce engines were being considered for the plane. One design showed a three-engine configuration akin to that of the Boeing 727, but ultimately the two-engine configuration of the G-II was retained. Accommodations for up to 19 passengers and a three-person crew were planned. First flight was projected for 1979, with deliveries beginning as early as 1980.[15]

Unlike the G-II, the G-III was to use the supercritical wing technology developed in the late 1960s by Richard Whitcomb at NASA. Supercritical wings will enter our discussion at a number of places. Adapting the technology to business jets presented development problems for the manufacturers and a short explanation is in order.

The velocity of the air over the upper surface of an airfoil is greater than the velocity of the airplane itself. As the velocity of the airplane increases, the velocity of the air over the top wing surface will at some point reach Mach 1.0, the speed of sound. The velocity of the airplane when this occurs is defined as the "critical Mach number." The critical Mach number might be, say, 0.80 with a particular wing design. At speeds in excess of the critical Mach number, shock waves develop when the air moving at supersonic speeds slows to subsonic speeds as it flows aft towards the trailing edge of the wing. These shock waves greatly increase drag and, consequently, fuel consumption as the aircraft's speed is increased. The NASA supercritical wing has an upper surface with a shallow curvature that permits an aircraft to fly at speeds approaching Mach 1.0 before reaching the critical Mach number. Even at speeds in excess of the critical Mach number, drag increases less rapidly than is the case with the earlier wings.[16]

Grumman created a separate division, Grumman American, in 1975. The Gulfstream work was within that organization. A contract with Grumman

American's sister company, Grumman Aerospace, was arranged to help in the design of the G-III's new airfoil. Grumman American also decided to add winglets at the tips. The winglets were also based on ideas originating with Richard Whitcomb at NASA. The forward part of the winglets turned downward to reduce drag stemming from the outward flow of air from the under side of the wing. The rear of the winglets was turned up to correct drag from upper-surface air flows.

The demand for large business jets was strong in the first part of 1977. Grumman American said in March that it expected to deliver 21 G-IIs in the course of the year, eight or nine of which would be exports. The company also had 47 letters of intent, each accompanied by a $100,000 deposit, for sales of the G-III. It was expected that the Board of Directors would give a final go-ahead decision at their June meeting.[17] The G-III then under development had a maximum gross weight of 67,400 pounds, a wingspan of 84.75 ft, a length of 87.33 ft, and a wing loading of about 81 pounds per square ft. Based on use of the supercritical wing, its maximum speed was to be Mach 0.88 and its normal cruise speed, Mach 0.84. A range of 5,075 miles was contemplated, much more than that of the G-II because of the greater fuel efficiency the wing would induce. The two engines on the G-III were to be the same Rolls Royce Spey Mark 511 11,400 lb st engines as those on the G-II. The improved aerodynamics were to permit takeoffs using only 9,000 lb st in order to mitigate noise problems.[18]

In May, a month prior to the meeting of the Board, Grumman American aborted the G-III program. Development costs associated with the advanced technologies greatly exceeded estimates and new environmental and noise standards required modifications to (or replacement of) the Spey engines. The cost overruns were apparently massive. In the fall of 1976, Grumman American had planned a green price of $6.4 million for the G-III; the intervening cost increases would have required a $12 million green price. Grumman American elected to cancel outstanding orders and return the deposits, with interest.[19]

June 1977 saw deliveries of the G-II passing the 200 number and the shutdown of the G-I production line. Grumman American then decided to make improvements in the G-II based on the work that had been done on the

G-III. It was hoped that the decrease in demand for the G-II resulting from the planned introduction of the G-III could be reversed. The recently certified E-R (extended range) G-II, with wingtip fuel tanks, helped. Studies were also made of ways to modify the Spey engines to reduce emissions and noise. The G-II "hush kit" came from this effort.[20]

A new G-III was announced in the spring of 1978. It was substantially different from the G-III planned just the year before. Rather than using the NASA supercritical wing that had been initially proposed, the redesigned G-III was to use a modified G-II wing. The span was nine feet longer, the leading edge was changed, and the chord was moved forward. Winglets were used, but the downward extension planned for the first G-III was eliminated. The G-II fuselage was altered by adding a two-foot plug in the passenger section, a smoother, longer radome in the nose and a wrap-around windshield. A cockpit voice recorder, three VHF radios, dual VHF navigation systems, dual automatic direction finders, dual transponders and dual distance measuring equipment were included in the standard avionics package. Customers were offered a choice of a Sperry or Collins automatic flight director system and of a Collins, Bendix or RCA weather radar system. The G-III used the Spey engines that had been on the G-II and its initial gross weight, 66,000 pounds, was the same as that of the G-II.

The performance of the new G-III was also quite different from that of the proposed first G-III. The range (with 45 minutes reserve fuel) was now to be 4,460 miles (not 5,060 miles), long-range cruise speed was Mach 0.75 (not Mach 0.85), operating altitude was 45,000 ft (not 51,000 ft) and the take-off field length was to be 5,500 ft (not 5,900 ft). G-IIs had already been sold through airframe number 247 in March 1978 and it was planned that the G-III would start with airframe number 253. Grumman went back to the corporations that had put down deposits on the first G-III, offering them the same places in the production line of the new G-III. First flight was scheduled for late 1979 and first delivery, spring of 1980. The projected green price was $7.5-$8.0 million. With typical interior finish and optional equipment, the 1980 delivered price was estimated at about $9 million.[21]

American Jet Industries acquired the Grumman American division of Grumman in August 1978. The arrangements called for Grumman to continue the G-III development and marketing program under contract to American Jet. Grumman American was renamed Gulfstream American Corporation. Allen Paulson, the President of American Jet, said at the time that, among other projects, he was considering further improvements to the G-II.[22]

The new G-III had its own problems. By May 1979, the G-II run had been extended to the 256th airframe. First flight of the 257th — the first G-III — was planned for late October and first deliveries were to occur in January or February 1980. First flight was delayed until December 2, 1979. Certification test flights began in January 1980 and FAA certification was then expected in June 1980.[23] The flight tests showed some undesirable characteristics, however. The G-III exhibited tendencies to roll in straight and level flight at very high cruise speeds and to roll off in high altitude stalls. Vortex generators were added to correct for the rolling tendency and various fences, stall strips and stick pusher arrangements were tried to correct for the stall problems.[24]

Gulfstream American was experiencing other problems during the G-III certification period. The company agreed in principle to be acquired by Tesoro Petroleum in January 1980. The agreement was terminated the following month. Gulfstream American was simultaneously trying to sell its piston-engine operations and to arrange joint ventures for the Peregrine jet trainer and Hustler turboprop/turbofan light business aircraft programs. The stretched G-I for commuter airlines was under development. There were concerns that Gulfstream American was experiencing cash flow difficulties. While there were 60 orders for G-IIIs in hand, with deposits, by March 1980, no new cash would be generated by the G-III until customer deliveries began.

FAA type certification was finally granted for the G-III on September 22, 1980. The gross weight of the production model had grown to 68,200 pounds. A few G-IIIs were already at completion centers and deliveries began almost immediately. The green price in late 1980 was $9.75 million, plus an 8% per year escalation factor based on the January 1979 price.[25] In March 1981, the green price was changed to $9.85 million with escalation from January 1981. There were 80 firm orders at that time. The first available delivery date was October 1983.[26] The G-III was at last a going venture.

As the G-IIIs began rolling off the line, Gulfstream American began work on the Gulfstream IIB project. The G-IIB is a G-II retrofitted with G-III wings and all other changes made since the date of manufacture. The 1981 price for these modifications was $2.298 million. The price was increased to $2.565 million effective with the 19th order. A G-IIB has much the same performance as a G-III, including the substantially improved fuel efficiency, better airport characteristics, faster cruise speeds and longer range.[27]

U.S deliveries of the G-III and the G-IIB are shown in Table 5-2. The data include three standard G-IIIs shipped to the U.S Air Force under lease in 1983-1984 and eight more purchased by the Air Force in 1986-1987. These planes are designated as C-20As and were replacements for Lockheed C-140s, the military version of the old JetStars. In all, 202 G-IIIs had been put into production when the line was closed to new orders in late 1986. PPG was among those buying a G-III. More than half of the G-IIIs were delivered to foreign customers, with 120 in government service in 32 countries by 1986.[28]

Gulfstream G-IV

Gulfstream American began discussing a G-IV and a G-V in June 1982, 21 months after FAA certification of the G-III. Certifications of the G-III in France and the United Kingdom were still pending and modifications to the G-III were still being made. The latter included incorporation of a digital flight management system, with the same ring laser gyros as those going onto new Boeing 757 and 767 airliners. Preliminary specifications of the G-IV showed a four-engined derivative of the G-III with a longer range, increased cruise speeds and lower noise levels. The G-V was described as a two-engine, 34,600-pound plane with a long-range cruise speed of Mach 0.75 and a range of about 2,900 miles.[29]

Gulfstream American was renamed Gulfstream Aerospace in October 1982. Marketing of the G-IV began in early 1983. The plane then was shown as a two-engine, not a four-engine, upgrade of the G-III. Development costs were estimated at $50 million and a green price of about $13.5 million (1983 dollars) was forecast. New Rolls Royce Tay engines were selected, with Gulfstream committing to buy at least 200 of them. Rolls Royce estimated that development of the 12,420 lb st, high bypass ratio engine would cost between $75 and $90 million. With the new engines, the G-IV would be 15% more fuel efficient than the G-III and meet the new FAR Part 36 Stage 3 noise requirements. A cruise speed of Mach 0.80 and a range of 4,600 miles were planned. Certification and first deliveries were expected to occur in late 1986.[30]

Table 5-2 Deliveries of Gulfsteam III Aircraft to U.S. Customers	
Year	Number Delivered in U.S.
1980	10 (includes test models)
1981	20
1982	22
1983	22
1984	25
1985	12 (plus 4 G-IIBs)
1986	8 (plus 1 G-IIBs)
1987	1 (plus 5 G-IIBs)
1988	2 (plus 3 G-IIBs)
1989	0 (plus 2 G-IIBs)

Source: AvData Inc.

Design efforts on the smaller G-V languished after the first announcement. This airplane never materialized. Development of the G-IV, however, continued at full speed. The simultaneous development of the Falcon 900 and the Canadair Challenger CL-601 presented Gulfstream with direct competition that it had not previously faced. This was not so much price competition — though these other planes surely constrained Gulfstream in its pricing — but rather competition in the mix of performance characteristics that buyers were increasingly demanding. The wing of the G-IV was changed to a supercritical design as a result of further extensive computer and wind tunnel tests. Better fuel efficiency and a longer range resulted. The fuselage was lengthened by 4.5 feet. Improved aerodynamics and greater passenger comfort resulted. Composites were used in the rudder, ailerons, spoilers, trim tabs, trailing edge panels, cabin doors and pressure bulkheads. More efficient manufacturing and improved structural integrity resulted. The cockpit was designed with state-of-the-art, digital electronics, including laser inertial reference systems and six large CRT displays. Greater safety and more accurate navigation resulted. The new engines offered better fuel economy and less noise. All of these were necessary for Gulfstream to retain its reputation as the producer of premier business jets. Despite a major contraction in the overall demand for business jets from 1982 onward, orders for the G-IV were strong.[31]

Rollout of the first G-IV was on September 11, 1985. First flight occurred on September 19, 1985. Performance seemed so good that thought was given to stretching it into a 24-26 passenger, all first class, commercial version. It was reported that the development schedule was advanced by several months because of the lack of problems. Chrysler Corporation optimistically acquired all of the shares of Gulfstream Aerospace in June 1985 for $637 million as a means of diversifying Chrysler's activities. Allen Paulson owned 71% of the shares tendered to Chrysler and remained as President and CEO after the acquisition.[32]

Flight tests continued through all of 1986 and some problems did appear. "Electronic gremlins" had to be eliminated from the avionics. Modifications in the wing had to be made in late 1986 to correct slow-speed flight and stall problems. Type certification, anticipated in early 1986 to occur in September of that year, was moved back, first to March and then to April 1987. When certification was given on April 22, 1987, the G-IV had undergone 1,412 hours of test flying. Fifteen G-IVs were then at completion centers and deliveries began soon after certification. Gulfstream Aerospace had over 100 orders for the craft at that time. Six weeks later, a G-IV with Allen Paulson in command left Paris for a round-the-world flight. The trip took 45 hours 25 minutes 10 seconds, with an average ground speed of 503.9 mph.[33] No civilian aircraft bettered this record until 1992, when an Air France Concorde SST cut two hours from this time.

Business and Commercial Aviation estimated the price of a typically-equipped G-IV at $15.8 million in 1987. This figure rose to $17.8 million in 1988, $21.0 million in 1989, $23.5 million in 1990, and $24.0 million in 1991. The 1991 model was, of course, different from the 1987 version. The Rolls Royce Tay engines had been improved. In 1991, each produced 13,850 lb st rather than the original 12,240 lb st. The new engines are also quieter. Maximum takeoff weight was increased from 71,700 pounds to 73,200 pounds. Modifications were made in the avionics, as well. The flight management system of 1991 provided for minimal pilot intervention, contained worldwide navigation and flight manual performance data in its computer memory, and could be programmed prior to engine start. Consistent with long-standing policies, the new engines and the G-IV wings were to be made available for retrofits on the G-IIBs and G-IIIs. Corrosion inspection and corrosion inhibiting actions were developed for all older Gulfstreams. And a Free Turbine Noise Suppressor was devised to quiet the Spey engines of the G-IIs, G-IIBs and G-IIIs while simultaneously increasing thrust and fuel efficiency.[34] Gulfstream's retrofit policies eliminated much of the owners' risk of technological obsolescence, albeit for a price. There was much more covered in buying a Gulfstream than the simple acquisition of an airplane.

More Recent Gulfstreams

Chrysler sold Gulfstream Aerospace to Forstman Little Company and Allen E. Paulson in 1989. A heavy debt load was imposed on the company by the buyout. Two years later, Gulfstream reintroduced the G-V nomenclature. Rather than representing a smaller craft as it did in the announcement of June 1982, the G-V discussed in 1991 was to be a follow-on version of the G-IV. Preliminary concepts called for a gross takeoff weight of 80,460 pounds, a cruise speed of Mach 0.80, upgraded Rolls Royce Tay engines with 18,000 lb st, and a range (with eight passengers) of 5,750 miles. First flight was foreseen in 1994.[35]

Forstman Little bought Allen Paulson's 31% share of Gulfstream Aerospace in 1992. After his retirement from Gulfstream, Paulson became active in breeding race horses. The repeated ownership reorganizations appear not to have dampened Gulfstream's quest for continued improvements of the airplanes in its line. It was announced in 1992 that the G-IV was to be improved to the G-IV/SP. Here the SP stood for "special performance." The IV/SP incorporated modified wings, fuselage, empennage and landing gear. It was designed to a gross takeoff weight of 74,600 pounds. The green price of the plane was about $23.5 million and the equipped price was around $27 million in 1992. The prototype G-IV/SP was flying by March 1993 at which time Gulfstream stopped taking orders for the G-IV.[36]

The introduction of the IV/SP permitted Gulfstream to spend more time further refining the Gulfstream V. Reevaluations showed that the up-graded Rolls Royce Tay engines would not yield the performance Gulfstream wanted in the G-V. New engines suggested by Allison, Pratt & Whitney and General Electric were considered. The BR710-44, 14,700 lb st engine pro-posed by Rolls Royce and BMW was eventually selected. With this engine, the planned gross takeoff weight of the G-V grew from 80,460 pounds to 85,100 pounds. The G-V was to be about eight feet longer than the IV/SP. The wingspan was increased by over 13 feet. A full-fuel (not full-payload) range of over 7,200 miles was predicted. Deliveries of the G-V were sched-uled to begin in 1996 at a green price of $29.5 million (1993 dollars).[37]

Gulfstream also indicated in 1991 that it was looking again at a smaller Gulfstream, the Gulfstream XT. The XT was described as a plane with dimensions similar to those of the G-II, but somewhat lighter and faster. A gross weight of about 50,000 pounds is envisioned. Plans call for engines with 13,700 lb st, upgradeable to 22,000 lb st, a cruise speed of Mach 0.85 and range of 3,450 miles.[38]

Looking even further into the future, Gulfstream entered an agreement of understanding in 1988 with Sukhoi of what was then the U.S.S.R. to devel-op a supersonic business jet (SSBJ). This venture is discussed in the final chapter.

Competition from Dassault

We noted in Chapters Three and Four that Dassault recognized the need to offer new and improved aircraft early in the life of the successful Falcon 20. One variant of the expanded line was a smaller plane, the Falcon

10, a 0.7 scale model of the Falcon 20 with an improved wing. Other variants represented improvements in the Falcon 20 itself — the 20C, 20D, 20E and 20F. At the same time, however, Dassault began probing into the development of a larger version of the Falcon.[39]

The first move by Dassault towards the "heavy iron" end of the business jet market was in the 20T program. The Falcon 20, it should be recalled, was itself a relatively large plane, with the 20F, for example, capable of seating up to ten passengers and having a gross takeoff weight of 28,660 pounds. The Falcon 20T was to have a fuselage 3.7 feet longer, a wing span 0.8 ft longer and a width 12.5 inches greater than the 20D. The 20T was to accommodate up to 25 passengers. The "T" in the designation came from "transport," but an 8-15 passenger executive configuration was included in the planning. At one point, the 20T was called the Mystere 30, but this was later changed to Falcon 30. A prototype Falcon 30 flew in 1973. That model was seen primarily as a small commuter transport.[40]

The Falcon 50

The Falcon 30 was never offered. A survey by Dassault showed that business customers and airline passengers preferred the safety of three engines, particularly when flying over water. In addition, regulations restricted twin-engined planes to over-water routes that were within one-hour's flying time of an airport. These considerations led Dassault to the development of the Falcon 30T, a three-engined jet configured like the Boeing 727. The Falcon 30T project was later divided into two separate developments. One was for the Falcon 40 commuter transport. The other was for a Falcon 25 three-engined business jet.

Dassault gave the go-ahead for development of the Falcon 25 in June 1974. At the same time the plane was redesignated the Falcon 50. The engines for the new plane were to be Garrett TFE 731-3 turbofans with 3,700 lb st each. The gross weight of the Falcon 50 was put at 36,375 pounds. The plane was to be configured for 8-10 passengers with a range of 3,100 miles (with six passengers) at a Mach 0.75 cruise speed. Aerospatiale, which was then working on the Corvette SN-600, joined Dassault in the development of the Falcon 50. What proved to be a temporary refusal by the French government to provide financial support threatened the project for a time. Orders for 38 Falcon 50s had been received by December 1974. Dassault then said that the Falcon 50 would be produced if the flight tests of the prototype were successful. $30 million was committed to the program. The first flight was scheduled for eleven months later, November 1975.[41]

Dassault, despite its reputation for keeping development projects on schedule and within budgets, was overly optimistic on the Falcon 50 project. Significant design changes were necessary. The Falcon 50 was at first to use the basic Falcon 20 wing, but computer tests indicated that a very different design was needed. The wing adopted at this stage was similar to the NASA supercritical airfoil that Gulfstream had attempted to use in the first version of the G-III. The fuselage section between the engine pods had to be redesigned to reduce drag. The fuselage was also shortened and the cross section changed to afford more headroom. The tail plane was given an anhedral to correct for instability at low speeds. The design of the S-shaped air inlet duct for the tail engine was troublesome. The required changes brought the gross weight to 37,480 pounds, but at these weights the Falcon 50 could carry only four passengers with a full load of fuel.

First flight was delayed by a year. Rollout occurred on September 4, 1976, and first flight was on November 7, 1976.[42] Ten years had passed since rollout of the G-II. In comparison with the G-II and the Canadair Challenger then under development, *Business and Commercial Aviation* rated the Falcon 50 below average in cabin volume per seat, baggage volume per seat, payload with maximum fuel, and range. It was ranked above average only in length of required runway.

Dassault was confident in early 1977 that its 1977-1978 flight test program would permit deliveries to begin in February 1979. A green price of $4.85 million was set for U.S. customers, with the typical long-range avionics package estimated at another $700,000. With interiors and painting, a delivered price in the neighborhood of $6.0 million appeared probable. Dassault expected worldwide sales to exceed 300 units and thought they might be as high as 500 over the life of the aircraft.

Flight tests during 1977 showed that the supercritical wing had to be abandoned. Thus, a third wing design was tried. This wing permitted added fuel capacity and the maximum takeoff weight rose to 38,800 pounds. A range of 3,170 miles was realized at a cruise speed of Mach 0.75 at 41,000 ft with eight passengers. A reviewer in September 1978 observed that "the aerodynamics of the Falcon 50 represent a tour de force in computer-aided deign. The entire airflow around the wing, fuselage and empennage, as well as through the S-duct . . . has been analyzed and optimized by computer-aided design techniques. The Falcon 50 may have 'lost' its supercritical wing, but the aircraft continues to be an outstanding example of advanced technology among the new breed of business jets." By the end of 1978, the green price had escalated to $5.175 million (1977 dollars).[43]

Annheuser-Busch took the first U.S. delivery of a Falcon 50 in the early spring of 1980. The typically-equipped plane then ran at about $8.4 million. A total of 12 were in the fleets of business customers in Europe by June 30, 1981. *Business and Commercial Aviation* listed $8.75 million as the typical-equipped price at that time.[44] Table 5-3 gives total U.S. deliveries through 1989. Considering that Dassault had invested in excess of $150 million on R&D alone, sales of the Falcon 50 proved to be very disappointing.

The Falcon 900

Falcon announced a larger and improved Falcon 50 — the Falcon 900 — in May 1983. The new version, Falcon indicated, was necessary to compete effectively against the recently announced Gulfstream IV and the Challenger 601.[45]

Significant changes had occurred in the market for heavy business jets during the six years that elapsed between Dassault's decision to develop the Falcon 50 and the time it was ready for customer deliveries. The Canadair Challenger was unknown by that name in 1975. The Gulfstream G-II had been flying for nearly ten years by 1975, but the G-III was still a paper airplane in the early phases of development. By 1980-81 the G-III was flying. A year later the G-IV was under development. As we see in the next section of this chapter, the original Challenger 600 program was in trouble by 1980-81, but an improved Challenger 601 was in the offing.

Table 5-3 U.S. Deliveries of New Falcon 50 Aircraft, 1980 - 1989	
Year	Number Delivered in U.S.
1980	9
1981	16
1982	36
1983	17
1984	11
1985	6
1986	5
1987	5
1988	6
1989	3

Source: AvData Inc.

Dassault had little choice but to improve the 50 if it was to sell heavy business jets into the coming decades.

Table 5-4 compares a few of the characteristics of the Falcon 50 and Falcon 900. It is easy to see that the changes were not just cosmetic. In addition to the obvious physical differences, the Falcon 900 used considerably more carbon fibre and Kevlar composites. The avionics package in the 900 was a state-of-the-art digital system, including a Honeywell laser gyro inertial reference system.

The 900 fell into place quickly. The prototype flew on September 21, 1984. A second prototype flew on August 30, 1985 and a month later flew nonstop from Paris to Little Rock, Arkansas, a distance of 4,954 miles against headwinds. FAA Type Certificate was given in March 1986. Two of the planes were delivered in the U.S. in December of the same year. Twelve Falcon 900s were delivered in the U.S. in 1987, 20 in 1988, and 5 in 1989. The equipped price for a Falcon 900 was about $17.5 million in 1988.

Dassault introduced a Falcon 900B in 1991. The 900B is a 900 with 4,750 lb st Garrett TFE731-5BA turbofans. Recognizing that its reputation for service did not match that of Gulfstream and several other manufacturers, Dassault also introduced a more comprehensive warranty and service policy in 1991. The price of an equipped 900B was about $22.35 million that year. A total of 129 Falcon 900s (including 900Bs) had been delivered worldwide by the end of 1991. By then Gulfstream had the G-V, the G-XT and, less definitively, a supersonic business jet under development. Survival in the high end of the market would not be achieved without continuing and heavy R&D by Dassault. Yet it is probably true that the company had to that point in time done little better than break-even on the Falcon 50/900 projects.[46]

Table 5-4		
Selected Characteristics of the Falcon 50 and Falcon 900		
Characteristic	Falcon 50	Falcon 900
Wing span	61 ft, 10.5 in	63 ft, 5 in
Length	57 ft, 11 in	66 ft, 3.75 in
Wing area	504.1 sq ft	527.75 sq ft
Gross takeoff weight	38,800 lb	45,400 lb
Cabin and baggage volume	822.5 cubic ft	1,522 cubic ft
Passengers accommodated	Up to 12	Up to 19
Engines	3 Garrett 731-3 @ 3,700 lb st	3 Garrett 731-5A @ 4,500 lb st

Source: *Jane's All the World's Aircraft: 1987-88,* pp. 81-82.

Dassault was working on an improved Falcon 20 — the Falcon 2000 — during this period. The 2000 is discussed in the next chapter. By 1992, Dassault announced that it hoped to add the Falcon 9000. International partners to share in production and in the financial risks were being sought. Preliminary plans were for an aircraft weighing some 12,500 pounds more than the Falcon 900B.[47]

Canadair Enters the Fray

William P. Lear signed a five-year noncompetition agreement with Gates when the latter bought Lear Jet. When that agreement expired in 1974, Lear — at age 73 and in failing health — decided to build another airplane. The project grew from the idea of retrofitting the many Learjets then flying with supercritical wings based on the NASA design. That limited project was abandoned when Lear became convinced that he could instead use his own version of a "super wing" on a unique, new business jet that would outperform any then on the market.[48] Lear worked with an aerodynamic engineer, Larry Heuberger, and came up with several designs. One was for a Lear Avia Cavalier 600, a 14-place turbofan craft with a 600 mph cruise speed and a range of 3,600 miles. This plane was to be priced at $1.5 million, in contrast to the $3.5 million green price of the G-II with which it was to compete. The Cavalier 600 design was subsequently called the LearStar 600. In later designs, the plane was to accommodate 10 passengers with seats set at a 40-inch pitch, or up to 20 passengers with higher density seating. The 10-passenger design showed a gross takeoff weight of only 20,000 pounds and supercritical wings with a 25 degree sweep. The plane was to be capable of Mach 0.85-0.90 cruise speeds. It was a "widebody," with an interior maximum cabin width of 80 inches and cabin height of 75 inches. These dimensions were to provide "walk-around comfort features . . . in tune with transcontinental and transoceanic nonstop flight planning." Lear expected to have a prototype flying by August 1976 and to begin deliveries 6-9 months later. Variations of the LearStar 600 were to be available for cargo or as a 30-passenger commercial commuter aircraft.[49]

Lear tried unsuccessfully to get financing for production of the LearStar. Then he turned to firms like Gates Learjet, Vought, Boeing, Beech and Cessna, but none of them was interested in joining him in the production of the plane. By the end of 1975, it was announced that engineering on the LearStar was 50% complete and that Learjet parts had been designed into the plane to reduce costs. It was at this time that William Lear was diagnosed as having hydrocephalus due to injuries from a fall. He elected not to have surgery at that time, but did undergo a series of operations to correct the condition in 1977.

The Canadair CL-600

The Canadian government purchased Canadair Limited from General Dynamics in January 1976 for $39 million. Canadair was to be used to "revitalize the Canadian aerospace industry." Representatives of Canadair were introduced to William Lear shortly after the government's acquisition and both realized that the LearStar 600 might be a project that would contribute to that revitalization. Agreement was reached in April 1976 for Canadair to pay Lear $375,000 for an option. If the option were exercised, Canadair would pay Lear $1.5 million, plus $3.0 million when the 600 was certified and an additional $2.4 million a year later. Lear was to serve as a consultant during construction of a prototype.[50]

At the time Canadair took the option, the LearStar 600 was described as a 14-passenger, long-range business jet. Very high-level performance goals were set. Two pilots and a flight attendant were envisioned. The plane was to have a range of 5,000 miles, a maximum cruise speed of Mach 0.91-0.95 and a normal cruise speed of Mach 0.85-0.90. The fuselage was to be 88 inches in outside diameter. Two 6,500 lb st Avro Lycoming ALF 502D turbofan engines were positioned on the aft fuselage, with their exhaust flowing directly over tailplanes set on the fuselage behind the engines. The low-set tail planes and their distinct anhedral were intended to mitigate the stall problems then being encountered on many T-tail, swept-wing business jets.

Lear saw a market for 2,500 aircraft over a ten year period and thought that production rates of the LearStar 600 could reach ten per month. A price in the neighborhood of $3-4 million was indicated. James Taylor, who had earlier been with Falcon Jet, resigned from Cessna to head the marketing efforts. Sandor Kvassey left Gates Learjet to work with Taylor. Lear was not alone in thinking that the LearStar 600 would be a commercial success.

Canadair invited 40 corporate pilots and aviation department managers to a briefing in Montreal in July 1976. By then a decision had been reached to use a larger, yet-to-be-produced 7,500 lb st version of the Avro Lycoming ALF 502 turbofans. The alternative GE CF34 engines were rejected because of their higher price. The potential buyers were assured of adequate warranty and after-warranty service and were told that the price for serial numbers 1 through 50 would be US$4.4 million. Deliveries, it was said, might begin in 1979.[51]

Canadair wanted 50 firm orders before it exercised its option with William Lear and committed to production. While Lear had an obvious economic interest in getting Canadair to move ahead quickly, he exhibited what Canadair saw as a stubborn, proprietary interest in his preliminary design concepts. This perception, whether or not correct, led to acrimony between Lear and his design team, on the one hand, and the engineers and marketing personnel at Canadair, on the other. The Canadair group, for example, decided that a "widebody" should be just that, and wanted to increase the fuselage diameter from the 88 inches Lear had specified to a full 106 inches. The change would permit four-abreast seating in a commuter version. When Lear learned of this, he publicly dubbed the Canadair version as "Fat Albert." He was sure that the larger fuselage would destroy his clean aerodynamics, add weight, and reduce the range.

The preliminary specifications released by Canadair in July 1976 retained the LearStar 600 designation, but were different in many respects from Lear's earlier ideas. The anhedral on the tail planes was no longer incorporated. Lear's unique wing root was redesigned. The gross takeoff weight was raised to 32,500 pounds. The fuselage diameter was 106 inches. Without fuel, the craft would weigh 24,400 pounds. With maximum fuel, the payload was only 940 pounds — less than the equivalent of five passengers with baggage. The maximum operating speed was listed as Mach 0.90, with the maximum cruise set at Mach 0.88, normal cruise at Mach 0.85, and long-range cruise at Mach 0.80. Startup costs were expected to exceed $50 million, with what proved to be an overly optimistic development schedule. Canadair, if it elected to go ahead, would build three prototypes, get certification by February or March of 1979, and begin deliveries before the end of 1979.

Canadair exercised its option in November 1976. A design competition between Lear's group and Canadair's design team was organized ostensibly to develop the 106 inch diameter airplane in more detail. Relations between the two groups did not improve, however, and Lear ended up with plans for yet another airplane, the Allegra. Lear announced publicly that the

Allegra was better than the LearStar 600 — lighter, faster, and more fuel efficient. Canadair rejected the Allegra design, angry that customers were getting confused and that sales were being jeopardized. The name of the LearStar 600 was changed to the Challenger 600 at that point. Lear then absented himself from the 600, and turned his attention to the last plane associated with his name, the Lear Fan, an unorthodox design with all-composite construction and twin "pusher" turboprop engines. A year later, on May 14, 1978, William P. Lear, the "stormy genius," died of leukemia.[52]

Canadair was busy redesigning the Challenger 600 throughout the controversies with Lear. Wind tunnel tests indicated in early 1977 that the tail configuration would have to be changed. A T-tail was adopted. The fuselage was lengthened and the wing span was increased. Canadair had 70 orders by March 1977, with nine or ten more under negotiation. Canadair — still looking for first deliveries by the middle of 1979 — was guaranteeing delivery dates to within 60 days. It also was guaranteeing the performance of the CL-600, assuring buyers that their deposits would be refunded if its range proved to be less than 4,620 miles, if its operating costs exceeded $0.73 per mile, if its high cruise speed did not reach 554 mph, or its long-range cruise speed did not reach 527 mph. Canadair claimed that the plane would take off from a 5,000-foot runway at gross weight and fly 4,000 miles at Mach 0.80 with a 1,700-pound payload. For shorter runs, it was claimed that the Challenger would sprint 1,700 miles at Mach 0.86 with a payload of 400 pounds. At the same time, Canadair had begun efforts to have certain FAA regulations modified since they "affect CL-600 weight and systems design excessively." The order backlog had reached 102 by July 1977. At that time, first flight of the first of the prototypes was still scheduled for early 1978. Canadair thought that it could sell 400 CL-600s in five years.[53]

Pre-flight testing continued into 1978, and the date of first flight was pushed back. A "late spring" date was indicated in February 1978. Then the date was to be "mid-June." Rollout occurred on May 25, 1978, with first flight set for June or July. Then the first flight date moved to August 25th. In early September, it was to be by "month's end." Finally, on November 8, 1978 — still only two years since Canadair exercised its option to produce the plane — the first CL-600 flight took place. The original 6,500 lb st ALF 502 engine was used in that flight because of continuing problems with the newer and larger 502L.

The prototype CL-600 was flown to a site in the Mojave Desert for a 43-day, 25-flight test program. During 1978, the number of orders was variously placed at 111, 121, 166, 127, 102, and 108. Federal Express ordered 25 stretched versions weighing 43,000 pounds and using a more powerful engine for its freight services. An experienced observer opined early in 1978 that the CL-600 could be the "hottest selling large corporate aircraft on the market." [54]

Canadair continued to warrant that the CL-600 would have a range of 5,117 miles (minus a 10% tolerance) and maintain a high-speed, level-flight cruise speed of 580 mph (about Mach 0.86) at 36,000 ft. Deposits amounting to $4.375-$6.5 million were to be returned if these (and other) standards were not met. Canadair boasted that the CL-600 would be both the fastest and the most economical large corporate jet available. Some of the political figures who opposed the government's policy of using the Challenger as a vehicle for stimulating the Canadian aerospace industry questioned whether the warranted performance levels could be attained and, in particular, whether the objectives of high-speed and low operating costs were compatible with one another. [55]

Events of 1979 showed that the Challenger program did, indeed, have some problems. While plans went ahead for the stretched Challenger E version, tests on the first and second prototypes of the CL-600 showed that the weight would have to be reduced if the plane was to perform at the warranted levels. The horizontal tail had to be shortened a bit. Excessive vibration was said to exist in the fan gear in the new 502L engines. Fuel consumption was higher than expected, bringing the range down to 3,800 miles. Rather than delaying deliveries, Canadair promised to have the engines changed and to provide modification kits to buyers of the first batch of planes. By November 1979, worried customers were beginning to turn to the "proven" G-III. [56]

Serious problems with the 502L engine persisted. Avro Lycoming proved unable to deliver acceptable engines on schedule. While the range of the CL-600 was said to be 3,800 miles in February 1980, this figure had dropped to only 3,300 miles by September 1980. The 3,300 mile range could be achieved, it was reported, only at the relatively slow cruise speed of Mach 0.70. Even the officially-announced long-range cruise speed was then only Mach 0.76 (501 mph). Canadair assured customers that the addition of 1,700 pounds of fuel capacity and further modifications to reduce drag would increase the range to 3,680 miles. Gross takeoff weight, rather than being reduced, rose to 40,200 pounds, however. The first prototype crashed in April 1980 when a parachute used in stall tests failed to detach. The fourth plane was damaged in taxiing due to a brake failure. The program went ahead, nonetheless.

Canadian certification was granted in August 1980. That certification was subject to weight limitations because of wing, wheel and brake design considerations. There were also restrictions on all-weather operations because of the stress that icing might impose on the wings. FAA certification was given on November 7, 1980, conditional on modifications to an improperly functioning stick-shaker stall warning system. Only nine passengers — not the 19 for which the plane was designed — could be accommodated with the restrictions. Canadair was at the time doing extensive studies of the design of the wing root, wing leading edges, engine nacelles, the exhaust system, the tailplane, and the addition of winglets, to clean up drag problems and bring the plane up to something nearer to the original design goals. Canadair still had orders for 170 CL-600s and the standard green price was $7.0 million.[57]

Most of the restrictions on the CL-600 were removed by both the Canadian authorities and the FAA in early 1981. Additional testing on new thrust reversers, the 1,700-pound fuselage fuel tank and for all-weather operations was required, however. Full certification at the 40,200-pound gross weight was expected before the end of the year. Engine shipments from Avro Lycoming were still late, but 15 CL-600s had been sent to completion centers by midyear and deliveries to customers had begun. About five were in operation by August. Canadair had let it be known in March that customers would shortly be able to buy CL-600s with the 8,650 lb st GE CF34-1A rather than the 7,500 lb st Avro Lycomings, with an extra $900,000 tacked onto the green price. It was the earlier version of this engine that Canadair had rejected years before because of its price.

The GE-powered CL-600 was referred to as the CL-601 by August and first flight was scheduled for the spring of 1982. A serious re-evaluation of the Challenger E program was also begun shortly after midyear. Its gross weight, required field lengths and costs had edged up while its range, cruise speeds and climb rates had gone down.[58]

The market for Canadair Challengers was "confused" in early 1982. Numerous modifications were being made to aircraft on the assembly line. Delivery schedules were slipping. Winglets had been added to the CL-601 and retrofits for the CL-600s were under consideration. While 40 CL-600s had been shipped from the factory, only 12 were in service. First flight of the 601 occurred on April 10, 1982, and the first production version flew on September 17th of that year. The need for the higher-powered 601 was all the more obvious when the FAA approved the fuselage tank for the 600 and simultaneously limited the craft to but five passengers.[59]

Canadair had delivered a total of about 59 CL-600s to final customers by the end of 1982. With the green price averaging perhaps US$8.0 million on these sales, Canadair may have had total revenue of US$472 million. Its development and production costs approached US$1.5 billion, however, leaving it with a loss in excess of US$1 billion on the program, not including the costs of the now abandoned Challenger E. The FAA certified the CL-601 on March 11, 1983. As certified, the 601 incorporated four-foot winglets and a fuel tank in the fuselage to supplement the wing tanks, and had a gross weight of 42,250 pounds and a range of 4,100 miles at a long-range cruise speed of Mach 0.74. There were accommodations for up to 19 passengers. With a green price of $10.2 million, the plane was a far cry from that envisioned in 1976.

Parliament granted Canadair an emergency loan of CA$200 million in 1982. The company sustained an operating loss of CA$361 million during that year. An additional emergency loan of CA$240 million was given in 1983. Then there was a proposal to write-off over CA$1.0 billion in development costs. The government undertook an extensive review of production methods, costs, engineering, marketing, and finance, and then appointed a new executive committee. Four vice presidents retired and a new CEO was appointed. Work began in mid-1983 on a new composite wing for the 601, with R&D for this project alone budgeted at CA$1.2 million. Avro sued Canadair for CA$100 million for breach of contract and Canadair counter sued for CA$109.6 million for the delays and lost sales caused by the 502L engines. These suits were eventually settled out of court.

After these events — particularly after the huge write-off of past costs — the view emerged that what had occurred was a "painful experience," but that "from here on the Challenger is a money-maker." Despite all of the problems, most of the users of the 600s and 601s liked the planes. Canadair looked ahead to a 25-30% share of a total market of perhaps 3,550 medium and heavy business jets over the following ten years.[60]

Canadair sold only six Challengers in 1983 and, on a fully allocated cost basis, lost another CA$334.2 million. The 1983 operating loss was put at only CA$83.8 million. Following the general outlines of the earlier proposal to write-off development costs, a massive restructuring of the company was arranged in 1984, with one new company, Canadair Financial, assuming the debt and Canadair, Ltd., the manufacturing company, continuing in a debt-free mode. Four CL-600s and 16 CL-601s were produced in 1984. The Canadian Department of National Defense bought eight CL-600s from the remaining inventory in 1985. No CL-600s were delivered new after that sale. A profit of CA$6.0 million on total sales of CA$376 million (with products other than the Challengers included) was realized in 1984.

The newly elected conservative government decided to privatize Canadair and, in 1984, solicited proposals from more than 100 private companies. Profits of about CA$20 million were realized in 1985, when only nine CL-601s were produced and 13 were delivered to completion centers and final customers.[61]

One of the requirements set by the government for firms bidding to buy Canadair was that the production and further development of the existing line of airplanes be continued. Bombardier, Ltd. and the Canadian Development Investment Corporation signed an agreement privatizing Canadair on August 18, 1986. Among the planes then under development was a new version of the CL-601, the 601-3A. The 601-3A was the CL-601 fitted with 9,140 lb st GE CF34-3A engines and state-of-the-art digital avionics. First

flight of the 3A was on September 28, 1986. Both Canadian and FAA certification were given in April 1987.

The gross takeoff weight of the 3A at certification was 43,100
pounds. The supercritical wing was loaded at a high 95.8 lb/sq ft. The added
power of the new engines brought increased fuel efficiency, but the general
operating characteristics — cruise speeds, range, and runway requirements —
were much like those of the 601. Six 601s (labeled 601-1As with GE
CF34-1A engines) and ten 601-3As were produced in 1986. Corresponding
numbers for 1987 were two and nineteen. No 601-1As were made after 1987.
Production of the 601-3As reached 26, 21, and 18 in 1989, 1990 and 1991,
respectively.[62]

A Canadair commuter version of the CL-601-3A nominated the Challenger RJ was announced in 1989. It was based on a 225-inch stretch of the
basic 601 fuselage, with the engines of the 3A. Then an extended range 3A,
the 601-3A/ER was announced. The 3A/ER had a gross takeoff weight of
44,600 pounds, 1,500 pounds above the basic 3A. The extra weight was accounted for entirely by added fuel capacity that increased the range to 4,140
miles. There was also a 601-3A/GW model, with the weights of the ER but
without the added fuel capacity. A 601-3A/S version was offered as well. It
was a less expensive, transcontinental model without the avionics necessary
for transoceanic navigation. In 1990, Canadair put the operating costs of the
601-3A at $4.36 per mile, based of 600 hours of operation per year and an av-
erage speed of 465 mph. With accommodations for 14 passengers, this comes
to about $0.31 per seat mile; with nine seats, the costs come to about $0.48
per seat mile. A 1990 evaluation by *Business and Commercial Aviation* concluded that, "[t]he Challenger Division has its corporate act together at long
last, and — more important — it has a calm confidence that it will remain a
major factor in the transcontinental/intercontinental business jet market."[63]

The Challenger RJ regional jet went into commercial service in 1992.
A Corporate Jetliner 601RJ version of this plane was also developed. It can
accommodate 18 to 30 passengers, has a maximum takeoff weight of 51,000
pounds, a maximum cruise speed of 528 mph (Mach 0.79 at 37,000 ft) and a
long-range cruise speed of 488 mph (Mach 0.74 at 41,000 ft). With full fuel
(but not full payload) the 601RJ has a range of over 3,300 miles.

130

Canadair provided provisional specifications for yet another heavy business jet, the Global Express, in 1993. The Global Express is to have a gross takeoff weight of nearly 91,000 pounds. For comparison, the 601-3A has a gross takeoff weight of 41,300 pounds, and the Gulfstream G-IV/SP has a gross takeoff weight of 74,600 pounds. With full fuel but only eight passengers, the Global Express is to have a range of 7,450 miles at Mach 0.80. The range with the same loadings will fall to less than 5,750 miles at Mach 0.88. A version of the BMW Rolls Royce BR 710 will be used if it is decided to put the plane into production.[64]

Observations on Rivalry in the "Heavy Iron" End of the Market for Business Jets

Table 5-5 provides some comparative data on the Gulfstream, Dassault and Canadair "heavy iron" business jets. While these data are limited to the G-IV, the Falcon 900 and the Canadair 601-3A as of 1985, they are fairly indicative of the relationships among the offerings of large business jets by the three manufacturers during the 1980s and into the 1990s. The Gulfstreams were the most expensive to buy, whether looked at in terms of price per plane, price per seat, or price per pound. Further, based on prices, weights, and fuel consumption per aircraft mile and per payload pound mile, the Gulfstreams also were the most expensive to operate. It is true, nonetheless, that Gulfstream sold considerably more "heavy iron" business jets than did the other two manufacturers. In the twelve-year period 1980 through 1991, Gulfstream delivered 248 G-III and G-IV aircraft to U.S. customers. Dassault had the Falcon 50s and Falcon 900s available during the same period, and delivered 171 of them to U.S. customers. Canadair was unable to deliver its Challenger 600 until 1981. It put a total of 160 Challenger 600s, 601s and 601-3As into customers' hands in the 1981-1991 period.

Gulfstream was undoubtedly favored by having had the successful G-I and G-II aircraft in the market well ahead of competitive offerings by Dassault or Canadair. How strong this benefit was, however, must in no small measure be the result of Gulfstream's own good management of technological and market opportunities. That is, had the G-I and G-II not been very good aircraft with excellent post-sales support, the fact of their existence

Table 5-5 Comparative Data on Gulfstream, Dassault and Canadair "Heavy Iron" Business Jets, 1985			
Item	G-IV	Falcon 900	Canadair 601-3A
Equipped Price (millions)	$15.0	$13.5	$13.1
Passengers	14-19	12-19	9-19
Gross Takeoff Wt.	69,700 lb	45,500 lb	43,100 lb
Wing Load (lbs/sq ft)	73.3	86.3	95.8
Long-Range Cruise Speed	511 mph	495 mph	481 mph
VFR Range:			
Seats Full	5,180 mi	4,736 mi	4,170 mi
Tanks Full	5,600 mi	5,037 mi	4,448 mi
Aircraft Miles per Pound of Fuel (Seats Full - Long Range Cruise)	0.15	0.2	0.20
Payload:			
Maximum	4,700 lb	4,000 lb	6,415 lb
Full Fuel	1,600 lb	3,100 lb	2,000 lb
Payload Pound-Miles per Pound of Fuel:			
Maximum Payload	705 lb-mi	800 lb-mi	1,283lb-mi
Full Fuel	240 lb-mi	620 lb-mi	400lb-mi

Source: *Business and Commercial Aviation,* May 1985, p. 46.

prior to the 1980s could have had an adverse effect on Gulfstream. Gulf-stream in fact invested heavily in reputation — reputation for safe, high-performance, high-reliability aircraft — and received its return on this invest-ment through a stable and growing base of customers who could not be easily persuaded to buy from another manufacturer.

These comments hardly mean that Gulfstream's participation in this market was without substantial risk. Gulfstream's initial entry, like that of Dassault and Canadair, involved large sunk costs. These costs were necessary for undertaking exploratory R&D on general design concepts, for searching into the various technology bases to assess whether it was feasible to pursue particular facets of a design, for evaluating the probable performance attrib-utes of a "paper airplane" that had never been flown, for estimating the size of the market for that airplane and for assessing alternative production methods and production costs with runs of various sizes.

Most of these pre-sales costs are truly sunk; only a small fraction of the resources used for these purposes would be transferable to other projects should the one in question not result in revenues adequate for their recovery. Even worse, the failure of the project for which the resources are committed could make it more, not less, difficult to succeed with other projects. There can be little question, for example, that the continued delays and failures in the early phases of the Challenger 600 program made it more difficult for Ca-nadair to sell the eventually excellent Challenger 601-3A. Moreover, had there not been a massive writing-off (at the expense of the Canadian taxpayer) of the approximately $1.0 billion in development costs, the Challenger 601-3A program could never have gone ahead. That is, save for the public bailout, Canadair would have gone out of existence in the mid-1980s. It re-mains highly questionable whether a positive return on the real value of the total resources devoted to the Challenger program has yet been realized.

There are other risks associated with the sunk costs aspects of enter-ing and remaining in the market for a high technology product. First, neither the amount of pre-sales sunk costs nor the time over which they will be in-curred can be easily forecast. For reasons not entirely obvious, the forecasts that are made tend to be overly optimistic. We have covered the massive cost and time overruns experienced by Canadair in developing the Challenger

CL-600/601. While Gulfstream never had problems of similar magnitude, the initial version of the Gulfstream III required far more R&D and extended over a far longer period than had originally been foreseen. That project was eventually aborted as it became clear that additional R&D expenditures could not be recovered from sales revenues. Dassault ran into analogous cost and time overruns with the Falcon 50. It turned out that the Falcon 50 reached the market so late that Dassault had to introduce the improved Falcon 900 fairly quickly.

Dassault's decision to bring out the Falcon 900 as a follow-on to the Falcon 50 illustrates a second feature of the sunk-cost risks in a market characterized by continuing technological opportunities. The need to devote resources to the development of new products does not stop after successful innovation. The learning that occurs in the first element of the process leads to ideas about improving the product. This is augmented by developments in science and technology that occur outside of the firm in question. Great pressure exists to use that knowledge in creating yet another airplane, partly because of the urges characteristic of the Schumpeterian entrepreneur.

William P. Lear epitomizes these urges, but it would be a mistake to think that they are absent from Allen Paulson, of Gulfstream, or from the many other designers, developers, and executives in the industry. A consequence of this is that the failure of a firm to obsolete its own products will almost certainly result in another firm's doing so. This applies with as much force to Gulfstream as to the other manufacturers we see here. The loyalty of Gulfstream customers arose in large measure precisely because Gulfstream did obsolete its own offerings — not only by introducing new basic models but also by providing product-enhancing retrofits for its earlier models. Had Gulfstream not done these things, it would have been easier for competitors to sway customers from purchasing the Gulfstream aircraft. The G-I had to go to the G-II, the G-II to the G-III, and so on, if Gulfstream was to retain its market position. Similarly, the Falcon 50 had to go to the Falcon 900 and the Challenger 600 had to go to the 601 and the 601-3A if Dassault and Canadair were to stay in the market. Competing against the new variants of airplanes by reducing the price of an old one is not an effective option. Sunk costs are involved in each of the model-to-model iterations, however. Substantial pre-sales commitments of time and resources are a continuing phenomenon with substantial risks that these investments will not be recoverable.

In conventional economic analysis, entry is encouraged when existing firms are making supracompetitive profits. Absent such profits, entry is discouraged and exits are likely. In markets that are competitive in the Schumpeterian sense, the fact that existing firms are failing to make profits is not necessarily a deterrent to entry. The Schumpeterian entrepreneur may attribute the losses experienced by the existing firms to their failure to utilize technologies in an effective way. That is, the firm or individual considering entry will see — correctly or incorrectly — that its new product will incorporate superior attributes that will make it successful despite the records of the others who have tried. The failures of the others may in fact be a stimulus for the potential entrant. To the entrant, the failures show that buyers are not strongly attracted to the existing array of goods. Entry based on beliefs of this sort may underlie chronic tendencies towards "overbidding." In any case, it is clear that existing firms cannot ignore the possibility of competitive entry even when the market from their point of view is extraordinarily weak.

We find no evidence from the experience in the "heavy iron" end of the market to suggest that being first — or perhaps better, being more experienced — insulates a firm from these risks or helps appreciably in managing the risks. There is great difficulty, however, in defining what is meant by being more experienced. Gulfstream was ahead of Dassault and Canadair in building and marketing heavy business aircraft. Dassault, on the other hand, had earlier and more extensive experience than Gulfstream in building and marketing business jet aircraft. Both had antecedent experience in developing high-performance military aircraft, but it is not obvious that this translated into an advantage for either. One could even speculate that Gulfstream's decision to contract with the military side of Grumman in the development of the supercritical wing for the first G-III project contributed to its difficulties.

In summary, there are many, many ways any firm can make serious errors in its attempts to enter and hold market positions in a market such as the one we see here. Looked at in detail, one can ascertain to some extent the particular events that lead to the success of one firm and the failure of another. In microcosm, the resulting market structure appears to be the result of these events. Looked at in less detail, the resulting market structure may seem to be the result of a stochastic process. Richard Nelson once observed in conversation that "[s]een from the moon, the market structures emerging from Schumpeterian competition look like the results of random processes." His work with Sidney Winter exemplifies that view. We see less of the randomness but the same ultimate result: market structures in Schumpeterian competition are endogenous to that competitive process. It is far more true that the ways largely exogenously-created technological opportunities are seized determine the structure of the market than that the structure of the market determines the ways technological opportunities are either created or seized.

Notes

1. Historical information on Grumman is from *Jane's Encyclopaedia of Aviation*, 1989. See also F. J. Knight, *Gulfstream: A Tribute to the Ultimate Biz-Jet, 1958-1991*, Hanley Swan, U.K.: Self-Publishing Association, Ltd., 1992.

2. K. Munson, *Private Aircraft: Business and General Purpose Since 1946*, London: Blandford Press, 1967, p. 158.

3. *B&CA*, Planning and Purchasing Issue, 1960.

4. E. J. Bulban, "Gulfstream I Turbofan Version Studied," *AWST*, September 9, 1974, pp. 53-54.

5. *B&CA*, June 1965, p. 18; *AWST*, May 10, 1965, p. 43; D. A. Brown, "Grumman Gulfstream II Aimed at Ease of Maintenance," *AWST*, November 29, 1965, p. 82ff.

6. *AWST*, March 7, 1966, p. 271; September 26, 1966, p. 29; October 10, 1966, p. 33; May 22, 1967, p. 87.

7. *AWST*, October 21, 1967, p. 114; March 18, 1968, p. 306; D. A. Brown, "Corporate Experience Aids Gulfstream 2," *AWST*, October 9, 1967, p. 56; R. G. O'Love, "Attack Angle System Set for Gulfstream 2," *AWST*, October 9, 1967, p. 89.

8. *AWST*, March 10, 1969, p. 236-237.

9. *AWST*, November 16, 1970, p. 89; *AWST*, Inventory Issues, 1974, 1975, 1976.

10. *FI*, November 20, 1975, p. 756; *B&CA*, October 1975, pp. 74, 106, 145; R. N. Aarons, "A Closer Look at Gulfstream," *B&CA*, May 1981, p. 53.

11. *B&CA*, June 1972, p. 44.

12. *B&CA*, November 1974, p. 84.

13. *AWST*, March 8, 1971, p. 159.

14. *AWST*, September 9, 1974, p. 55; *B&CA*, October 1974, p. 28.

15. *AWST*, May 24, 1976, p. 11; *FI*, November 20, 1976, p. 1476; *B&CA*, August 1976, p. 18; September 1976, p. 31.

16. See H. C. Smith, *The Illustrated Guide to Aerodynamics*, 2nd ed., Blue Ridge Summit, PA: 1992, especially pp. 35-36, 193-200.

17. E. J. Bulban, "General Aviation Backlog Strong," *AWST*, March 21, 1977, p. 183.

18. *AWST*, March 21, 1977, p. 119; *B&CA*, January 1977, p. 84;   February 1977, p. 19; April 1977, p. 74.

19. *AWST*, May 30, 1977, p. 17.

20. D. A. Brown, "Business Jet Competition Intensifies," *AWST*, June 29, 1977, p. 57; "Tip Tanks Boost Gulfstream 2 Range," *AWST*, June 19, 1978, p. 85; *B&CA*, July 1980, p. 87.

21. *B&CA*, March 1978, p. 25; September 1978, p. 57; *FI*, April 15, 1978, p. 1037; *AWST*, April 10, 1978, p. 17.

22. *AWST*, September 11, 1978, p. 76.

23. *AWST*, May 21, 1979, p. 20; September 24, 1979, p. 55; December 10, 1979, p. 17.

24. R. N. Aarons, "Certification is Near for the Challenger and the G-III," *B&CA*, September 1980, p. 53.

25.   *AWST*, March 10, 1980, p. 21; March 24, 1980. p. 7; September 8, 1980, p. 13; September 29, 1980, p. 20.

26. *AWST*, March 29, 1981, p. 59; D. W. Almy, R. N. Aarons and J. W. Olcott, "B/CA Analysis: Gulfstream III," *B&CA*, January 1983, p. 77.

27. Aarons, "A Closer Look . . . ," *loc. cit.*

28. *Jane's All the World's Aircraft*, 1987-88, p. 432.

29. *B&CA*, August 1982, p. 23; September 1982, p. 162; *FI*, August 27, 1982, p. 562.

30. *FI*, March 12, 1983, p. 645; *AWST*, March 28, 1983, p. 59; May 2, 1983, p. 15.

31. D. W. Almy and J. W. Olcott, "601 + 900 + IV = Heavy Competition," *B&CA*, February 1984, p. 55; G. Warwick, "G-IV Gulfstream Goes Further," *FI*, September 14, 1985, p. 28; *AWST*, January 30, 1984, p. 13; *FI*, September 1, 1984, p. 325; *B&CA*, October 1985, p. 114.

32. *AWST*, March 25, 1985, pp. 25, 36; June 24, 1985, p. 26; September 16, 1985, p. 26; September 23, 1985, p. 26; *Jane's All the World's Aircraft*, 1987-88, p. 432.

33. D. M. North, "Advanced Cockpit Display, New Engines, Mark Gulfstream 4," *AWST*, November 10, 1986, p. 46; R. N. Aarons, "Status Report: Gulfstream IV," *B&CA*, May 1986, p. 47; J. W. Olcott, "Inflight Report: Gulfstream IV," *B&CA*, January 1987, p. 30; *FI*, February 22, 1986, p. 14; November 1, 1986, p. 20; *AWST*, February 9, 1987, p. 30; February 23, 1987, p. 29; April 6, 1987, p. 31; April 27, 1987, p. 45.

34. *B&CA*, April Issues, 1987-1991.

35. *B&CA*, April 1991, p. 48; *AWST*, November 4, 1991, p. 20.

36. *AWST*, April 20, 1992, p. 67; M. Mechan, "Gulfstream V Launch Includes BR 710 Engine," *AWST*, September 14, 1992, p. 92; M. A. Dornheim, "Stable Growth Ahead for Business Aviation," *AWST*, March 15, 1993, p. 97.

37. *FI*, October 28 - November 3, 1992, p. 22; F. George, "The Newest Gulfstream." *B&CA*, October 1992, p. 52.

38. *AWST*, November 4, 1991, p. 20.

39. *AWST*, January 18, 1971, p. 55; May 31, 1971, p. 224; November 1, 1971, p. 17.

40. C. E. Schneider, "Pan Am Seeks Falcon Use Contracts," *AWST*, January 4, 1971, p. 52; D. E. Fink, "Falcon 20T Aimed at New Market," *AWST*, April 19, 1971, p. 49; *AWST*, May 31, 1971, p. 224; April 10, 1972, p. 66; May 1, 1972, p. 60; September 4, 1972, p. 74; August 6, 1973, p. 48; *B&CA*, August 1973, p. 31; *FI*, March 8, 1973, p. 333; May 3, 1973, p. 670.

41. *B&CA*, June 1974, p. 17; November 1974, p. 30; December 1974, p. 39; *AWST*, May 20, 1974, p. 18; May 27, 1974, p. 60; October 7, 1974, p. 52; November 4, 1974, p. 57; *FI*, June 13, 1974, p. 767.

42. *FI*, September 25, 1976, p. 963; January 29, 1977, p. 233; *B&CA*, June 1975, p. 108; December 1975, p. 116; September 1976, p. 129.

43. *B&CA*, February 1977, p. 86; FI, January 29, 1977, p. 233; June 24, 1978, p. 1911; J. W. Olcott, "Inflight Report: Dassault Falcon 50," *B&CA*, September 1978, p. 59.

44. *B&CA*, April 1980, p. 88; September 1980, p. 57; *FI*, August 29, 1981, p. 633; November 14, 1981, p. 1500; January 1, 1983, p. 12; R. Parrish, "Falcon 50 Operator Survey," *B&CA*, March 1983, p. 38.

45. *AWST*, June 6, 1983, p. 26; D. W. Almy and J. W. Olcott, "601 + 900 + IV = Heavy Competition," *loc. cit.*

46. D. M. North, "Increased Cabin Size, Long-Range Capabilities, Mark Falcon 900," *AWST*, March 4, 1985, p. 52; J. W. Olcott, "Inflight Report: Dassault Falcon 900" *B&CA*, May 1985, p. 44; "B/CA Update: Falcon 900," *B&CA*, June 1987, p. 40; "Dassault Falcon 900B," *B&CA*, October 1991, p. 64; R. L. Parrish, "Dassault's Falcon 900," *B&CA*, August 1988, p. 56; "Falcon 900 in Intercontinental Operations," *B&CA*, November 1990, p. 52; *AWST*, September 23, 1985, p. 107; January 20, 1986, p. 100; *FI*, September 1, 1984, p. 325.

47. *B&CA*, August 1992, p. 20.

48. These paragraphs depend in part on R. Rashke, *Stormy Genius: The Life of Aviation Maverick Bill Lear*, Boston: Houghton Mifflin, 1985, pp. 329-336.

49. *AWST*, September 30, 1974, p. 31; E. J. Bulban, "New Lear Business Jet Being Planned," *AWST*, December 9, 1974, p. 57.

50. *AWST*, December 15, 1975, p. 62; Rashke, *op. cit.*, p. 530ff.

51. W. H. Gregory, "Canadair Acquiring LearStar 600 Rights," *AWST*, April 12, 1976, p. 17; *FI*, April 24, 1976, p. 1064; *B&CA*, August 1976, p. 19.

52. Rashke, *op. cit.*; W. C. Wetmore, "Canadair Sees Big LearStar 600 Market," *AWST*, July 26, 1976, p. 59; *B&CA*, September 1976, p. 129.

53. *AWST*, March 7, 1977, p. 25; July 18, 1977, p. 24; September 26, 1977, p. 69; C. Covault, "FAA Relaxation on Challenger Sought," *AWST*, April 4, 1977, p. 67; *FI*, March 19, 1977, p. 693; *B&CA*, September 1977, p. 132.

54. *AWST*, February 13, 1978, p. 63; March 13, 1978, p. 189; May 8, 1978, p. 23; May 29, 1978, p. 19; June 12, 1978, p. 66; August 14, 1978, p. 23; September 11, 1978, p. 47; November 13, 1978, p. 23; December 4, 1978, p. 52; D. M. North, "Wind Tunnel Backs Challenger Design," *AWST*, April 10, 1978, p. 56; "Challenger Rolls Out With 102 Orders," *AWST*, June 5, 1978, p. 19.

55. *FI*, August 12, 1978, p. 471; *B&CA*, September 1978, p. 54.

56. *AWST*, July 9, 1979, p. 22; July 30, 1979, p. 46; August 13, 1979, p. 11; September 10, 1979, p. 13; October 1, 1979, p. 16; November 5, 1979, p. 24; D. M. North, "Corporate Orders Set Records," *AWST*, September 24, 1979, p. 36; J. W. Olcott, "Update: Canadair Challenger," *B&CA*, February 1979, p. 49; J. MacMcClelland, "Industry's First All-AC Business Jet," *B&CA*, October 1979, p. 96; *FI*, April 7, 1979, p. 1047.

57. *AWST*, January 28, 1980, p. 75; February 25, 1980, p. 53; March 24, 1980, p. 14; March 31, 1980, pp. 15, 91; April 7, 1980, p. 231; April 28, 1980, p. 21; June 9, 1980, p. 13; June 23, 1980, p. 27; D. M. North, "Further Industry Growth Forecast," *AWST*, March 3, 1980, p. 213; "Challenger Gets Canadian Certification," *AWST*, August 18, 1990, p. 28; "Challenger Handling Qualities Assessed," *AWST*, September 22, 1980, p. 54; R. N. Aarons, "Certification is Near for Challenger . . . ," *B&CA*, September 1980, p. 53.

58. H. Field, "Canadair Challenger in the Air," *FI*, August 1, 1981, p. 318; J. W. Olcott and R. N. Aarons, "B/CA Analysis: Canadair Challenger," *B&CA*, September 1981, p. 66; *AWST*, February 16, 1981, p. 13; April 13, 1981, p. 25; June 22, 1981, p. 92; June 29, 1981, p. 13; D. M. North, "Sales Recovery Forecast for Turbofans," *AWST*, August 10, 1981, p. 77; "Canadair Delays Stretched Challenger E," *AWST*, August 31, 1981, p. 22.

59. D. M. North, "Used Aircraft Sales Parallel New Ones," *AWST*, January 4, 1982, p. 58; *AWST*, February 15, 1982, p. 13; April 18, 1982, p. 22; May 17, 1982, p. 22; July 26, 1982, p. 13.

60. D. M. North, "GAMA Forecasts Slight Delivery Gains," *AWST*, January 31, 1983, p. 67; "CF34 Upgrades Challenger Capabilities," *AWST*, May 16, 1983, p. 63; "Canadair Outlines Future Challenger," *AWST*, September 26, 1983, p.121; A. K. Marsh, "Parliament Studying Canadair Problems," *AWST*, June 20, 1983, p. 24; R. Parrish, "Canadair Challenger 600 Operator Survey," *B&CA*, September 1983,   p. 37; D. W. Almy and J. W. Olcott, "601 + 900 + IV = Heavy Competition," *loc. cit.*; *AWST*, March 28, 1983, p. 59; June 13, 1983, pp. 26, 93; September 12, 1983, p. 24; October 3, 1983, p. 44.

61. J. W. Olcott and R. N. Aarons, "New Engines Have Given the Challenger Competitive Performance . . . ," *B&CA*, May 1984, p. 49; *FI*, September 1, 1984, p. 325; *AWST*, April 14, 1986, p. 26.

62. *AWST*, October 13, 1986, p. 118; J. MacMcClelland, "Long Legs," *Flying*, July 1988, p. 52; R. A. Searles (ed.), "Observer: Challenger 601-3A Status Report," *B&CA*, June 1986, p. 89; J. R. Cannon, "B/CA Analysis: Canadair Challenger

601-3A," *B&CA*, October 1987, p. 40; F. George, "Avionics Analysis: Challenger 601-3A," *B&CA*, October 1988, p. 102; *B&CA*, May 1989. p. 100.

63. R. N. Aarons, "Canadair Challenger: A New Maturity," *B&CA*, March 1990, p. 50.

64. *B&CA*, April 1992, p. 45; G. Warwick, "Canadair Gives Global Express Longer Legs," *FI*, March 24-30, 1993, p. 6; R. Lopez, "Global Express Go Ahead Expected This Year," *FI*, April 14-20, 1993, p. 11; D. Hughes, "BMW Rolls Royce Wins Global Express Conpetition," *AWST*, March 22, 1993, p. 58

Chapter Six

The Market for Mid-Sized Business Jets After 1970

The Fate of the Early Entrants

JetStar   The Lockheed Aircraft Corporation faced "crisis years" after 1965.[1]   Although Lockheed had won the 1965 C-5 competition, it experienced massive costs overruns on the total package (fixed price) contract.   The AH-56A Cheyenne program ran into similar cost overruns and was threatened with termination in 1969.   In the same year, procurement of the C-5 was cut back from 115 to 81 aircraft.   The company had similar problems with its missile programs.   In response to a 1956 FAA request, Lockheed invested heavily in an SST design.   The FAA selected the Boeing version in December 1966 despite Lockheed's claim that the airlines preferred its concept. Lockheed then decided to use its C-5A design to re-enter the commercial transport market, a project that evolved into the widebody L-1011 TriStar. The L-1011 was ordered in quantity by several airlines, but always faced intense competition with the McDonnell Douglas DC-10.

Lockheed had a deficit of $32.6 million in 1969 and anticipated another large deficit in 1970.   The company was running out of cash despite an order backlog (including government programs) of over $5 billion.   Banks were unwilling to extend anything like the cash required and Lockheed was nearly bankrupt.   In August 1971, after heated debate, Congress passed Public Law 92-70, the Emergency Loan Guarantee Act, to protect lenders against losses on loans to Lockheed.   Lockheed became profitable again by 1974, only to run into a Senate inquiry and an SEC investigation of its practices in military sales in the U.S. and abroad.   The top management of Lockheed was replaced in early 1976.

In these circumstances it is small wonder that the JetStar was not upgraded and modernized more than it was.   As we noted in Chapter Three, the

JetStar 6 was modified to the JetStar 8 with the 97th production aircraft in 1967. The change amounted to no more than the use of the more powerful JT12A-8, 3,000 lb st engines. Table 6-1 gives data on U.S. deliveries of JetStars after 1970. A total of 66 JetStar 8s had been delivered worldwide when production of the type was suspended in 1973.

During the 1972-1974 period, AiResearch Aviation Company developed a retrofit program for the JetStar 6 and 8 using Garrett TFE731-1 turbofan engines. The retrofit program included not only the new engines, but also redesigned nacelles, pylons, firewalls, engine mounts, thrust reversers and slipper fuel tanks. The 1972 price for these upgrades (not including the aircraft) was set at $1.35 million per plane. Lockheed, recognizing that owners of the craft disliked the noise, range and short-field performance of the 6 and 8, cooperated with AiResearch in this program. Lockheed was not in a position to pursue the alternative of spending four to five years (and up to $100 million) to develop a new plane.

The AiResearch conversions were designated JetStar 731s. First flight of a JetStar 731, a model converted from a JetStar 6, was in July 1974. The first production model JetStar 731 was delivered in the spring of 1976. The range and cruise speed of the original JetStar were greatly increased by the modifications. In early 1977, a JetStar 731 flew from the 2,456-mile trip from San Francisco to Honolulu at an average speed of 445 mph. Demand for the 731 was brisk. A total of 55 JetStar 6s and 8s — nearly a third of those produced — were retrofitted to the 731 version.

The development of Lockheed's own JetStar II began in 1972. By 1973, Lockheed was telling business customers that the new plane would soon be ready. Lockheed's financial problems prevented it from committing to produce a new version of the JetStar at that time. Instead, Lockheed cooperated in the AiResearch 731 project. By 1975, Lockheed's overall financial picture looked brighter. But by then Dassault had begun intensive efforts to sell the Falcon 50 in the U.S. Lockheed realized that it needed to convince potential buyers that it was indeed going to produce a great new JetStar so as to forestall orders for the rival Falcon 50. The new JetStar II could be in customers' fleets two years ahead of the Falcon 50 if Lockheed could begin deliveries in 1976.

Unlike the AiResearch 731 versions, Lockheed's JetStar IIs were newly constructed airframes. The craft was powered by larger, quieter Garrett TFE731-3 3,700 lb st turbofan engines. There were, in addition, some changes in the wings to accommodate larger slipper fuel tanks with reduced drag, plus new electronic avionics systems, new corrosion-resistant materials in the wing planks and landing gear, an improved flight deck, tinted windows, and better air conditioning and pressurization. The JetStar II consumed about half as much fuel per pound of airplane per minute on the takeoff run as did the JetStar 8. The length of runway required for takeoff was reduced by 22% even though the II had a gross takeoff weight that was 6% higher. Fuel consumption at cruise speeds was also much less. *Business and Commercial Aviation* estimated that a typically equipped JetStar 8 sold for about $1,750,000 in 1973; a fully-equipped JetStar II was priced much higher — approximately $4,550,000 in 1975 and $5,035,000 in 1976. These prices are only slightly less than the $5.1 million and $5.5 million prices for the Gulfstream II in the same years. By 1979, the JetStar II was priced at $5.9 million and the Gulfstream II/TT at $7.1 million. The Falcon 50 had yet to be delivered, but orders were being taken for 1980 and 1981 deliveries of that plane at about $8.5 million.

Allied Stores took delivery of the first production JetStar II in September 1976, fifteen years after the first JetStar 6 was delivered to the Superior Oil Company. Lockheed believed that the JetStar II would be a serious contender for several years. As can be seen from Table 6-1, this proved not to be the case. Only 40 JetStar IIs were made before production was halted in 1979. The last JetStar II was delivered to the Iraqi government in 1980. Lockheed was out of the market for business jets. Buyers looking for aircraft in the price/performance ranges in which the JetStar II was attempting to compete were more attracted by the less expensive AiResearch 731 conversion or the far more modern Gulfstreams, Falcon 50 and the promised Canadair Challenger.[2]

Sabreliner We have seen that a nearly continuous stream of improvements is essential for a firm to maintain or improve its position in the market for business jets. North American Rockwell's Sabreliner had already lost its strong position as the 1970s opened. Through that decade and into the next, many new models of the Sabreliner were tried. None succeeded in restoring to the firm anything close to its earlier share of the market. The underlying problem, we suspect, is that none of the new Sabreliners went far enough to bring that plane up to the standards of competitors then on the market.

Table 6-1 U.S. Deliveries of JetStars, 1971-1979		
	Model	
Year	JetStar 8	JetStar II
1971	6	—
1972	10	—
1973	4	—
1974	—	—
1975	—	—
1976	—	3
1977	—	16
1978	—	7
1979	—	4

Source: AvData, Inc.

The Sabreliner 60, of 1967, was a derivative of the Model 40. The 60 was 38 inches longer than 40 and could accommodate two extra passengers. The wingspan of the 60 was 3 inches longer than that of the 40. The Model 40 was dropped from production when the 60 was introduced. Total deliveries of Sabreliners reached 27 in 1968, and then dropped to 23 in 1969, and to nine in 1970.[3]

Two new versions were being contemplated by the end of 1970. One was a "larger, faster" plane, first referred to as the Model 70 and then as the

Model 75.   The second new model was to be a "smaller, medium-priced" model dubbed the Sabre Commander.   Both were to be ready for delivery before the end of 1971.   The vertical dimension of the fuselage of the Model 75 was 9 inches greater than that of the Model 60 to provide more headroom. Larger, rectangular windows were substituted for the triangular ones on the Model 60.   Otherwise the airframes were essentially the same.   Five different interiors were available on the 75.

The Sabre Commander, or Model 40A, was basically the old Model 40 with the avionics and interior refinements of the Model 75.   It was priced initially at $995,000 to compete with the Cessna Citation and, as it then appeared, the Corvette.   The Sabre Commander 40A was really a high-performance aircraft, however, boasting a 560 mph high-speed cruise and a range (with 30 minutes of reserve fuel) of nearly 2,200 miles.[4]

The Model 75 was equipped with the same P&W JT12A-8 engines that were on Models 40 and 60.   Plans called for a change to the Garrett AiResearch ATF-3 as soon as that engine became available.   Development of the new engine was delayed and North American Rockwell decided in late 1971 to modify the Model 75 to use GE CF700-4 engines.   Simultaneously, major changes were made in the top management of the Sabreliner Division. Flight testing of prototypes of the new model, the 75A, began in November 1972.

The changes made in the Model 40 to reach the 40A were hardly startling.   A third window was added to each side of the cabin.   Thrust reversers were installed, but the P&W JT12-8 engines were retained.   The windshield de-icing system was improved.   The interiors were far more attractive, with four individual chairs and two smaller rear seats.   The commode was reviewed as a spot that would "probably find more use as a resting place for baggage than as . . . a toilet."   Other changes were made solely to reduce costs.   Full pressurization was eliminated from the nose compartment.   The avionics package was changed from the Arinc type to a "much less costly general aviation type."   The instrument panel "seem[ed] to cry for a redesign to bring together an integrated whole."   The 40A, like the 40, was "rugged, trustworthy and proven."   Also like the Model 40, the 40A had relatively high operating costs.   Based on a purchase price of $995,000, contemporary fuel prices and 500 hours of annual use, *Business and Commercial Aviation* estimated cost per passenger seat mile for the 40A at $0.25 in 1972. The operating cost of the Cessna Citation was about two-thirds of that — $0.15 or $0.16 per seat mile. Further, in October of 1972 Sabreliner announced that the price of the 40A would be raised to $1,145,000 or, with higher quality avionics, to $1,300,000.[5]

Production of the Model 60 continued while the 40A and 75/75A were being refined and put into production. Nine of the 40As, four 75s and three 60s (all with the P&W engines) were delivered in 1972. In 1973, deliveries totaled 23 40As, two 60s and 1 Model 75.

The Sabreliner Model 75A was displayed for the first time at the September 1973 NBAA meetings. In addition to the higher-powered GE engines, improvements over the Model 75 included Aeronca thrust reversers, a new nose-gear steering system, new anti-skid brakes, an improved self-storing entry door, and better air conditioning. The Model 75A was then priced at about $1.8 million. National Lead took delivery of the first production version in early 1974.[6]

The Model 40A did not sell well. Only seven were shipped in 1974, with the last delivered in September. North American Rockwell, as the company was known immediately after the 1973 merger, considered but ultimately rejected a proposal by its Sabreliner Division to develop a small business jet, the Commander 750, to compete directly with the Cessna Citation. The Model 75A was in production for only five years. Eleven 75As were delivered in 1974, 19 in 1975, two in 1976, 12 in 1977, and 13 in 1978. These shipments include 15 75As sold to the FAA to replace its fleet of DC-3s.

Table 6-2 provides U.S. shipment data for Sabreliners for years after 1970. The Model 60 — the 1967 improvement on the original Model 40 — sold about as well as the newer models up to 1979. Its price, fully equipped, was $1,435,000, a bit higher than that of the Learjet 35 and a bit lower than that of the Learjet 36. The Learjet 35 and 36 incorporated newer technologies, however, as we will see in the next section. The price of the Model 60 was bracketed between those of the Falcon 10 and the HS-125-600. These planes will be covered in later sections of this chapter also. The Falcon

10, a smaller version of the Falcon 20, was a fairly popular airplane in these years. The HS-125-600 did not sell particularly well, but HS-125 series was constantly updated in ways that surpassed the changes made in the Sabre-liners. The HS-125-700 was under development by 1976.

   ·   The Model 75A Sabre was priced between the HS-125-600 and the Falcon 20F. On every front there were comparably priced and excellent alternatives to Sabreliners. This clustering of relatively high-performance planes in the same general category created far more competition then the Sabres could stand.[8]

Table 6-2 U.S. Deliveries of Sabreliners, 1971-1981				
	Model			
Year	40A	60	75/75A	65
1971	—	7	—	—
1972	8	3	5	—
1973	16	1	1	—
1974	5	12	9	—
1975	—	—	17	—
1976	—	11	9	—
1977	—	12	9	—
1978	—	9	5	—
1979	—	4	3	4
1980	—	—	—	38
1981	—	—	—	27

Source: AvData, Inc.

The Sabreliner Division of Rockwell International was not unaware of the basic nature of its problems. Successive models had gotten heavier without coordinate improvements in the original aerodynamics. The use of higher-powered engines could not compensate for the decline in performance that accompanied this development trend. Neither could higher-powered engines — even more efficient, new engines — radically reduce the high operating costs of the Sabreliners. The Sabreliner's esteemed reputation, by itself, could only ensure the loyalty of old customers and attract new ones for a limited time.

Work on a new product line began in late 1975.[9] In mid-1976, Sabreliner proclaimed an "extensive development program." Significantly, it announced a contract with the Raisbeck Group for incorporating "aerodynamic technology into a new wing design for all future Sabreliners."[10] The new wings, based on the NASA supercritical design, would make possible the addition of 1,000 gallons of fuel capacity as well as aerodynamic improvements.

Two new production models were planned: the 65A, with 3,700 lb st Garrett TFE731-3 engines and the 80A, with the GE CF700-2 3,500 lb st turbofan engines. In addition, a comprehensive retrofit program was defined. The 40A, with the retrofitted aerodynamic improvements, would become the Model 40B. Similarly, the Model 60 would be retrofitted to the 60A, and the 75 to the Model 80A. Certification for these retrofits was scheduled for dates ranging from the fourth quarter of 1977 to the second quarter of 1978. A Model 45, which was the 40B with Garrett TFE731-3 engines, and a Model 65, the 60A with TFE731-3 engines, were also being developed. Sabreliner seemed intent on regaining its previous market position.

Rockwell International did not immediately assent to these plans. Approval was given in January 1977 for the modification of a Model 60 to the 65A. The modifications were to incorporate the new wings, with work done by Raisbeck in Northridge, California, and TFE731-3 engines and new nacelles, with the work done by Grumman at its Long Island plant. The Sabreliner Division produced the rest of the airframes and assembled the planes in Los Angeles. The installation of interiors and other avionics and finishing work took place in Perrysville, Missouri, near St. Louis.

Flight testing of the prototype 65A began in July 1977 at the Los Angeles International Airport. The new NASA-type wing was six feet longer than that on the Model 60. It was expected that the new wing, new engines and extra fuel capacity would result in a range 1,000 miles greater than that of the 60. A price in the neighborhood of $3.2 million was contemplated, but orders were not being solicited. The second pre-production model was not scheduled to fly until June, 1978. Sabreliner said that it would offer full modification of Model 60s to the 65A standards once the latter was certified. Raisbeck offered to retrofit the Model 60s to Model 60As, retaining the P&W engines. Raisbeck had the same retrofits available for the old 40s and 75As.

A major re-organization of the Sabreliner Division occurred in the fall of 1977. The various major components were henceforth to be shipped to Perryville, for assembly and finishing. Headquarters of the division was moved to St. Louis. The marketing of the Model 65A was started at a firm price of $3.1 million. Development of the Model 80A was also announced. The 80A was described as a modern version of the 75A, with three to four feet added to the fuselage for two additional passengers, supercritical wings and more powerful Garrett TFE731-3R 3,700 lb st engines. Deliveries as early as December 1979 were foreseen.[11]

Rockwell committed to production of the Model 65A, or Model 65 as it had by then been called, in early 1978. The performance data used in sales promotions were guaranteed by Rockwell. Deliveries were sold out through September 1979. Raisbeck reported bookings of $8 million, including $3 million for its kits for the Model 65 and $5 million for retrofits of other Sabreliners. The Model 85, a stretched 75A, was in design while Raisbeck was at work on the Model 80A, the retrofitted 75A. Rockwell rejected the idea of building a plane to fit between the Models 65 and 85.

In 1979, troubles appeared on the Model 65. After 16 had been produced, it was discovered that the anti-skid brakes locked on aborted takeoffs. Deficiencies were also found in the leading-edge flap system. Raisbeck's work on retrofits and in producing wings for new Sabreliners ran into technical and cash-flow problems. Raisbeck entered a contractual agreement with Midcoast Aviation to join forces on the upgrades, but this venture proved unsatisfactory. Raisbeck's repair certificate was revoked and, consequently, 23 modified Sabreliners were grounded. Raisbeck filed for Chapter 11 bank-ruptcy. Rockwell decided to use its own repair certificate to complete the eight Sabreliners then being modified and to find ways to get the other 23 into the air.[12]

The Model 65's problems were corrected and it was certified in No-vember 1979. Six were delivered before the end of the year. The Model 65 was then the only new Sabreliner in production. Rockwell had received 46 wing kits from Raisbeck prior to the bankruptcy and was making arrange-ments either to produce the kits itself or to obtain them from other vendors. The equipped price of the Model 65 was about $4,880,000 and customer interest, especially by companies already operating a Sabreliner, was said to be strong. Rockwell was setting up its production line to produce at a rate of three per month. Rockwell succeeded in delivering 41 Model 65s in 1980, 38 of them to U.S. customers.

Work on a stretched Model 75A continued. A Model 85 was de-signed, but this plane was delayed because the engines that had been selected were not available. The British government had withheld support for the Rolls-Royce jet engine program and the RB.401-07 engine was a casualty of this decision. A different stretch of the 75A, the 8OC, was designed. The 80C was described as a 10-passenger craft with a range of about 3,000 miles. It incorporated an 18-24 inch plug in the fuselage of the 75A, the Raisbeck supercritical wings and 4,000 lb st Garrett TFE731-5 engines.[13]

By mid-1980, the future of the Model 65 program had become uncer-tain. A slackening in demand became apparent even as the planes under con-struction were delayed by parts shortages. The Sabreliner Division was suffering large losses. The El Segundo plant where the wing and fuselage were built was to be occupied by Northrop by January 1982. The equipped price of the plane had been increased to $5,100,000. To add to the problems, it turned out that the Model 65 failed to meet its performance guarantees. Rockwell was forced to find ways to squeeze better performance from the engines. In addition, the de-icing system had to be changed. Under the cir-cumstances, Rockwell decided to stop production of the Model 65 after the 75th plane was completed. Rockwell had no other new planes ready to put into production and no facilities ready to produce even the older models.

Rockwell was, nonetheless, active in servicing the Sabreliners then in use. It also had a program for modifying Model 40s and was working on a similar program for the Model 60s.[14]

The final Model 65 was finished in May 1981. But the Sabreliner did not die a quiet death at this point. The Sabreliner Division presented an extensive modification/retrofit program to Rockwell International in 1981. A new production line would be required, with the concomitant start-up costs, of course. It would take something in the order of 30 months before the first delivery would be possible. The plan was to modify 65s to 65As (with new vertical tail, windows and entry door), to stretch the 65A fuselage and add TFE731-5 engines to create the 80C, and to go ahead with the postponed Model 85 with either ALF502L or GE CF34 turbofan engines. The Model 85 was to be six feet longer and seven inches wider than the 80C, but otherwise had much in common with the 65A. The Sabreliner Division saw its proposal to restart production as one that would create "a whole new ballgame."

Rockwell International elected not to support the proposed "new ballgame." Instead, it sold the Sabreliner Division to Wolsey & Co., an investment banking firm, in 1983. Support for the 600-odd Sabreliners in service was to be continued, but there would be no new production. Wolsey reorganized the former Rockwell division as the Sabreliner Corporation and announced that it would welcome joint venturers — joint venturers with money — so that it could proceed with the plans for the 65A, the 80C and the 85. An Italian helicopter manufacturer, Costruzioni Aeronautiche G. Agusta, was negotiating with Sabreliner in 1984-1985 for rights to build the Model 85 in Italy, with the finishing to be done in the U.S. For a time it seemed that McDonnell Douglas might have an interest in joint venturing on the Sabreliner. In 1986, the Sabreliner Corporation itself considered a new program to re-engine the Model 60. In 1989, the company sought "financial partners" to re-open the Model 65 production line. Nothing came of any of these plans; the last new Sabreliner was a Model 65 that came off the line in May 1981.[15]

Gates Learjet In sharp contrast with both the JetStar and the Sabreliner, William Lear announced the Model 24 in 1965, a year after the 23 hit the market. After Gates acquired Lear in 1966, the Lear Jet designation was changed to Gates Learjet. Gates Learjet continued the strategy of introducing new models. By 1970, Models 24C, 24D, 25D and 25C had been introduced. All used the same wing and the same GE CJ610-6 5,900 lb st engine. The fuselages were also basically the same, but those in the Model 25 category were 4.3 feet longer. The 24C was the least expensive, selling green for $698,000 in 1970. The 25C was the most expensive, with a green price of $950,000. In the same year, the Sabreliner 40 sold green for $1.1 million.

The Model 24C was intended to compete with the Cessna Citation. It did not succeed in this mission and was dropped from production in 1971, at almost the same time as the first Citations were being delivered. Gates, like others in the industry, was experiencing the effects of a marketwide recession at the time. There was concern, too, about the safety of the Learjets. Walter Reuther, the head of the United Automobile Workers, was killed in the crash of a Model 23A in May of 1970. While this accident was attributed to a malfunctioning altimeter, others seemed to involve problems with the Learjet's flight characteristics in level, high-speed flight.[16]

The newly-issued FAR (Federal Air Regulation) Part 36 noise standards also posed problems for Gates. The sound levels of the Learjets far exceeded the standards that the FAA was going to enforce beginning in 1974. Work was undertaken in 1971 on a Model 26, a Model 25 with quieter Garrett TFE731-2 turbofan engines, but this engine proved to be too heavy and too large for the small Learjets. Gates and GE joined forces to develop a sound suppresser for the GE CJ610-6 but, even if that proved an acceptable solution, it would not have been ready by the required 1974 date. No other acceptable turbofan engine was available. Gates, of course, petitioned the FAA for an extension of the deadlines for compliance with the requirement.

Work on the Learjet 35, a transcontinental model, and on the Learjet 36, an intercontinental model, began in 1972. These planes did use the TFE731-2 engines. William Lear — no longer associated with the Learjet program — was working on the design of a supercritical wing to retrofit on all of the existing models.[17]

Orders for Learjets rose markedly in 1972-73. Gates had to choose between adding to capacity or allowing a large accumulations of backorders. The company was cautious because the 1969-1970 period had been marked by overproduction, a repetition of which would have been costly. On the other hand, long delays between orders and deliveries might well cause some customers to turn to other manufacturers. Further, a large queue of back-orders tended to be somewhat spongy; duplicate orders and cancellations could cause that queue to shorten precipitously before the corresponding deliveries were made. Gates opted not to increase capacity even while it attempted to get all of the production possible out of the lines then in operation. In 1971, 22 Learjets were delivered, 14 of which were 24Ds. In 1972, a total of 37 were shipped, with 16 of them being 24Ds and 15, 25Bs. In 1973, out of 54 Learjet deliveries 26 were 25Bs and 17 were 24Ds. Profits of $9.2 million on sales of $172.4 million were recorded in the 1973 fiscal year.[18]

Gates attempted to stretch the Model 25 into a Model 26, with the Garrett TFE731-2 engines, but found that the modification posed many problems. It was eventually abandoned. Gates announced Models 35 and 36 at the July 1973 Paris Air Show. The Model 35 was shown at the September NBAA meeting. Models 35 and 36 were identical save for the extra 1,260 pounds of fuel and the two fewer passengers carried by the 36. Gates, in fact, referred to them as Model 35/36. The TFE731-2 3,500 lb st engines met the FAR 36 noise requirements and had 18.6% more thrust (at sea level) than the GE CJ610s on the earlier Learjets. The new engines also consumed 39.6% less fuel at takeoff thrust. The airframe, while retaining the distinctive Lear appearance, was new. The fuselage of the 35/36 was 13.25 inches longer, and the wingspan 3.9 feet longer than the comparable dimensions of the 25s.

The 35s and 36s were still a relatively small airplanes, with gross takeoff weight of only 17,000 pounds. They were so small, in fact, that the realistic number of passengers is "really seven and four for practical purposes," not the eight and six that were listed. For comparison, the Sabre 75A had a gross takeoff weight of 22,000 pounds, the HS-125-600, 22,000 pounds, the Falcon 20F, 27,320 pounds and the Gulfstream II, 58,500 pounds. The full fuel (but not full load) range of the 35 was 3,027 miles and that of the 36 was 3,621 miles. These ranges exceeded those of all other business jets then available except for the Gulfstream II. The Model 35 had an initial price of $1,395,000 and the Model 36, $1,445,000.[19]

The Model 35/36 was certified in July 1974, after a largely trouble-free development. The first 35 was delivered in late December of that year. In 1975, 34 Model 35s and 14 Model 36s were shipped. *Business and Commercial Aviation* reported that operators accustomed to the 24s and 25s liked the 35s and 36s almost without reserve. Those migrating from larger transcontinental or intercontinental aircraft felt "a bit squeezed." Still, *Business and Commercial Aviation* estimated the total operating cost of the 35/36, based on six passengers, at only $0.115 per seat-mile, far below that of any other long-range business jet then available.[20]

Gates, like the other manufacturers of business jets, began investigating the NASA supercritical wing in 1974. The Raisbeck Group acted as consultants in this research. Raisbeck subsequently exercised rights to retrofit existing Learjets with the new design, with manufacturing done by a third firm, Dee Howard. The Howard/Raisbeck Mark II wing system was said to yield "improved stall characteristics . . . [r]eduction in stall speeds . . . [i]mprovement in low speed handling characteristics . . . [r]eduction in takeoff and landing distances . . . [i]mprovement to high density-altitude takeoff performance . . . [and r]eduction of high-speed drag."[21] Many operators of the 23, 24 and 25 series of Learjets converted their aircraft to the Mark II system. Nearly all reported both improved performance and substantial reductions in operating costs.

Gates, partially in response to the Howard/Raisbeck retrofit program, modified the wings of all Learjets produced after July 1976. This redesign was not nearly as radical as the Howard/Raisbeck version, but resulted nonetheless in better performance and lower operating costs. Models 35 and 36 became Models 35A and 36A. The Model 24E was added. The 24E effectively re-introduced the low-priced 24C that had been dropped from production in 1971. In addition to the modified wing, the Model 24E featured less expensive avionics than other Learjets. It was intended to compete against the Citation and turboprops such as the King Air 200, the Mitsubishi MU-2 and the Merlin III. It was priced at $929,330 in 1976.[22]

Gates' sales of Learjets remained remarkably strong. Worldwide deliveries came to 18 24Ds, 14 25Bs, 34 35s, and 13 36s in 1975. The new wing improved the demand for new Learjets despite the availability of the

Howard/Raisbeck retrofits. Gates went ahead with plans for new models, nonetheless. The 24E, 24F, 25D and 25F were certified for altitudes up to 51,000 feet with a new GE CJ610-8A engine. The Model 54/55/56, announced in 1977, was to be a completely new, larger airplane, with walk-around headroom. The 54, 55 and 56 differed from one another only in fuel capacity, number of passengers and, hence, their gross weight, range, and field performance.

Model 28/29 represented fundamental improvements on the 25 series aircraft. The 28/29 and the 54/55/56 all had elements of the NASA super-critical wing and NASA winglets. Prototypes of the 28/29, with "Longhorn" winglets, flew in early 1978. First flight of the 54/55/56 "Longhorn" was in April 1979. The first six 28/29s were delivered in 1979, a year that marked the shipment of the 1,000th Learjet. The first 15 55s were shipped in 1981. While most of the industry was experiencing declining orders by the spring of 1980, Gates was increasing its production in anticipation of record sales.[23] The 28/29, which used GE CJ610-8A 2,950 lb st engines, was not particularly successful. Only nine 28/29s were built.

Learjets continued to be involved in an inordinate number of crashes. There were six fatal Learjet accidents worldwide in 1977 alone. Five more occurred in the United States in 1979 and 1980. The first two of these involved Lear 25s, one with the Howard/Raisbeck wing and the other with the new Lear wing. In both instances, there were small amounts of ice on the wings and the aircraft stalled prior to "stick shaker warning." There were three other accidents involving Lear Series 20 planes during approach or go-around. In two other cases, Lear 25Bs (with the original wings) were flying at high-altitude cruise levels and suddenly crashed to the ground in a near-vertical path without apparent warning. It was suspected that these planes had been exceeding maximum operating speeds. Investigation showed that one of them had been equipped with a switch to disconnect the klaxon speed warning system. Subsequent inspections found six other Learjets with similar cutoff switches. Part of the problem seemed to be that some pilots enjoyed "cow-boying" Learjets as though they were fighter planes.

An August 1980 FAA directive mandated new high- and low-speed procedures for all Series 20 and 30 Learjets. Later the same year, the FAA required that the pitch mode of Series 20 autopilots be disconnected. The maximum speed of the 20s was reduced from Mach 0.81 to Mach 0.76 pending the installation of a new pitch trim system in the autopilots. In 1981, the Series 20 Learjets were restricted to a maximum altitude of 45,000 feet until a new longitudinal trim system was installed. Still, in May of 1982, another Lear 23 crashed while descending from 41,000 to 39,000 feet. In one report, the NTSB discussed "the aircraft's marginal controllability characteristics when flown at and beyond the boundary of its high-altitude speed envelope."[24]

Gates' sales remained relatively strong through this period. One hundred and twenty Learjets were shipped in 1980; 29 25Ds, one 29, 88 35As, and two 36As. In 1981, 138 Learjets were delivered, including 93 35As and 15 55s. Sales of Learjets slowed after 1981. Ninety-nine were delivered in 1982, 45 in 1983, 33 in 1984 and 33 in 1985. The 35A was the largest selling model. While this plane was developed with a different fuselage, different wings, and different engines from those in the earlier Learjets, it was still very much the sort of plane William Lear had envisioned 30 years earlier. The 35A had a gross takeoff weight of only 17,000 pounds. It was small, fast and economical to operate.

Gates dropped the 54/55/56 designations in 1981. Instead, the Model 55 was offered as a straight 55, a 55ER, a 55LR and a 55 XLR. The 55ER (extended range) was certified in 1983. It had an extra fuel tank in the tailcone baggage compartment. The 55LR had yet an additional tank between the standard fuselage tank and the tailcone tank. Retrofits for previously produced 55s were available. In July 1983, Gates received certification for an improvement package for the 55s. The package included modifications to the leading edge of the wings and a system to increase the power of one engine automatically if the power from the other dropped by five percent or more. Another improvement package was certified in 1984. That package included improved wheel brakes, new wheels and axles, newly designed wheel compartment doors and increased use of epoxy materials. Again, retrofits were available. Gates introduced the Model 55B in 1986. It had an all-digital flight deck, aerodynamic refinements in the wing and changes in the interior.[25]

Gates delivered the last 25D in December 1983 and announced a temporary shutdown of the 35A/36A and 55 lines in September 1984. The

35A/36A line was reopened in March 1985; the 55 line, in May. The lines closed again in December 1984 and reopened for limited production in late February 1986. Reflecting in part an industry-wide slowdown, Gates Learjet sales declined by $158.6 million from fiscal year 1982 to fiscal year 1985. Net earnings fell from a record high of $22.4 million in fiscal 1982 to a loss of $10.6 million in fiscal 1985. Calendar 1985 saw Gates Learjet with a loss of $23 million.

A new CEO was named in April 1985. Gates worked on a number of upgrade programs for the 35A/36As and 55s in this period, but the financial stress under which Gates Learjet was operating caused the introduction of all of them to be deferred. In August of 1986, a group of outside investors pledged $100 million to Gates Learjet in return for a majority interest in the firm. The head of the group suggested that Learjet was suffering from self-inflicted wounds. The trouble with the company, he opined, stemmed from the fact "that it did no research and development for [the past] five years." To conserve its resources, Gates Learjet withdrew from a joint program with Piaggio to develop the futuristic Avanti turboprop. It sold its Jet Electronics and Technology subsidiary in December 1986. The outside investment group, acting under the name Integrated Acquisition, Inc., formally acquired a 64.8% interest in Gates Learjet in September 1987.[26]

The Learjet 31 was announced in October 1987. The 31 mated the fuselage and engines of the 35A/36A with the modified wings of the 55B. Delta-shaped fins were added on the lower rear fuselage for improved stability. *Business and Commercial Aviation* estimated the operating costs of this craft at $0.20 per passenger mile (eight passengers) in 1990. The 55C — the 55B with the delta fins and other modest changes — was also announced. Gates' CEO observed at the time that, under the new ownership, "[w]e are re-establishing our thrust; taking leading technology [and] converting it to performance."[27] A profit was expected for 1987.

The 55C was favorably reviewed, but was hardly a reason to expect Learjet's sales to increase. The 55s had never approached the 35s in sales. Learjet still failed to prosper. The CEO named in 1985 resigned in early 1988. A new CEO was selected from the Gates management team. The President of Integrated Resources, Inc. (formerly Integrated Acquisition) became the Chairman. The change in management did not cure the situation. Integrated Resources, Inc. filed for Chapter 11 bankruptcy in June 1990. At that point, Bombardier, Inc., the Canadian firm that had rescued Canadair's Challenger program, acquired Integrated Resources' share of Learjet. Bombardier provided Learjet with stable financial resources and promised to invest in new aircraft development. Learjet continued its U.S. operations as a subsidiary of Bombardier.

Plans were made in 1990 to lengthen the fuselage and upgrade the engines of the Model 31 and the 55s.[28] These plans were changed in 1991. The announcement of an upgraded Model 35A — soon to be called the Learjet 31A — and of a new Model 60 elicited renewed buyer interest in Learjets. Yet another CEO — an outsider with a strong background in the marketing of business jets — was selected in 1991. He sought to achieve "40-45% of the business jet market by the year 2000," a seemingly impossible goal.

Deliveries of the Learjet 31A began in September 1992. The plane uses Garrett TFE731-2 3,500 lb st engines. It is a small plane, with an empty weight of 9,914 pounds and a gross takeoff weight of 15,500 pounds. Thus, it has the power of the Learjet 35/36 but weighs only a bit more than the Learjet 25. Learjet claims a maximum cruise speed of 530 mph (Mach 0.82 at 45,000 feet) and a long-range cruise speed of 483 mph (Mach 0.77 at 49,000 feet) for the 31A. It has a full-fuel range of about 1,750 miles. The plane boasts state-of-the-art digital avionics. The price with standard equipment was $4,575,000 in 1992.

Rollout of the production model of the Learjet 60 occurred in May 1992. While a derivative of the Learjet 55, the 60 is considerably larger and more powerful than its ancestor airplane. The passenger cabin is 28 inches longer and another 15 inches was added to the fuselage near the engines. The P&W PW305A engines each produce 4,600 lb st in contrast with the 3,700 lb st of the engines on the Learjet 55. The gross takeoff weight of the 60 is 23,100 pounds; that of the 55 is 20,500. The equipped price of the Learjet 60 was set at $8,295,000 (1991 dollars).

The Learjet 60 was certified in January 1993 and deliveries began shortly thereafter. As the Learjet 31A and Learjet 60 were entering service, a new Learjet 45 was announced. The 45 will have an entirely new wing based on recent NASA developments. It is a mid-sized plane for up to eight passengers, with gross takeoff weight of 19,700 pounds. Preliminary plans call for use of Garrett TFE731-20 3,500 lb st engines that will yield a range of over 2,500 miles and a maximum cruise speed of Mach 0.81. First deliveries were scheduled for 1996 at a price of $5,395,000 (1992 dollars).

Despite an extreme slump in sales of business jets generally, Learjet recorded a ten-year high in deliveries in its fiscal year ending in March 1993. Orders were then increasing and Learjet forecast another ten percent increase in sales during the next fiscal year. The influence of Bombardier and the new management seems to have been strongly positive.[29]

Israeli Aircraft Industries   We noted in Chapter Three that the 1967 merger of North American Aviation and Rockwell-Standard Corporation required the divestiture of the latter's Jet Commander business. Jet Commander was sold to the government-owned Israeli Aircraft Industries (IAI). IAI contracted with Aero Commander to complete production of the Jet Commander 1121 through the 150th unit. Production was moved from Bethany, Oklahoma, to Lod International Airport, Tel Aviv, beginning in 1968, but no additional 1121s were built.

IAI had not to that point produced civilian aircraft. In fact, the only plane it had manufactured was the Fouga Magister, a twin-jet military trainer made under license from Henry Potez, the French firm responsible for the MS-760. IAI had considerable experience, nonetheless. It did all of the major repair and maintenance for the Israeli Air Force and, additionally, serviced and repaired about 300 planes per year for customers from many countries. After its acquisition of the Jet Commander — and concurrent with the 1968-1970 slump in the U.S. aerospace industry — IAI succeeded in attracting to Israel "about 200 aeronautical engineers from such companies as Grumman, Lockheed, Boeing, McDonnell Douglas, and North American."[30] These included people with experience in the design and manufacture of business jets.

Sales of the Jet Commander 1121 were weak at the time IAI acquired the line. There were few unfilled orders and there was an inventory of unfinished and partially finished planes. IAI renamed the Jet Commander the IAI Commodore Jet 1121. A privately-owned U.S. sales organization, Commodore Jet Sales, Inc., was franchised in Arlington, Virginia, by a U.S. subsidiary of IAI, Commodore Aviation, Inc. Many of the green 1121s in inventory in Oklahoma were changed to the Commodore Jet 1121B, with the original GE CJ610-1, 2,850 lb st engines replaced by GE CJ610-5, 2,950 lb st engines. An 1121C, the 1121B with a different interior, was also offered. At the same time, IAI was working in Israel on a Model 1123. The 1123, while incorporating major changes from the 1121, was a stretch of that design.

The first prototype of the Model 1123 crashed in 1970 because of a defective flap actuator. The first production model flew in April 1971. The second production version was shown at the Paris and Reading Air Shows in the following two months. The 1123 was certified by the FAA in December 1971, but sales efforts were purposely not pushed pending the workoff of the 1121 inventories. To speed this workoff, the 1121s were being offered by Commodore Jet Sales at discounts ranging from $123,000 to $143,000 .

IAI decided to discontinue Commodore Jet Sales as the U.S. sales representative in early 1972. Piper Aircraft was initially selected to conduct marketing in North America, but hurricane damage to its Pennsylvania facilities caused IAI to seek another sales agent. Atlantic Aviation Corporation was selected in September. Atlantic's distributorship of the HS-125-600 was transferred to Beech Aircraft and Atlantic stopped ongoing negotiations with Gates Learjet and Aerospatiale (for the Corvette) when it reached its agreement with IAI.

Atlantic Aviation ran a "name-the-jet" contest and a new name, 1123 Westwind, was chosen. An intensive sales effort began in the U.S. The 1123 Westwind had GE CJ610-9, 3,450 lb st engines. The fuselage was 22 inches longer than that of the 1121. It incorporated new avionics, a new electrical system, improved air conditioning, fully-modulated anti-skid brakes, an emergency landing gear extension mechanism and independent emergency brakes. The 1123 had capacity for an additional 1,535 pounds of fuel. A number of changes were made in the control surfaces — including the addition of drooped leading edges to improve slow-speed handling. The longer fuselage permitted the maximum number of passenger seats to increase from eight to ten. It also provided space for more baggage and an improved lavatory. Atlantic Aviation designed four different interiors as customer options. The 1973 price, fully equipped, was $1,050,000. Sixty percent of the parts, representing eighty percent of the materials costs, came from U.S. suppliers, including Rockwell.[31]

IAI was totally committed to defense work during the October War, 1973. Nonetheless, IAI was able to announce an 1124 Westwind by April of 1974. Only 36 1123s were to be produced, and the last two of these were used as prototypes for the 1124. The new plane was not fully defined when it was announced, but IAI indicated that the Garrett TFE731-3, 3,700 lb st turbofan engine (or a 4,000 lb st version) would be used. Changes in the wing design and fuselage were also under consideration. Atlantic Aviation said it would take $50,000 refundable deposits on the 1124. Retrofits of the engines for the 1123 were also promised. A thrust-reverser system for the 1123 was made available as a $50,000 option. Because of the low price paid to Rockwell for the Jet Commander program, IAI expected to reach a break-even point with sales of 45 planes. The 1123 was then selling for $1,155,000 in 1974 and it was expected that the 1124 would sell for $1,550,000 or more.[32]

IAI touted the 1124 Westwind as the "first of the Jet Commander/Commodore Jet series to have been fully developed in Israel."[33] The 1124 Westwind still had the external appearance of the Jet Commander, however. The wing was unswept and set slightly above the mid-fuselage level. The entire aircraft seemed "low-slung," with little ground clearance. Still, many important engineering changes were hidden by the family resemblance. The fuselage structure was strengthened so that the higher-powered TFE731-3 engines and a Grumman-designed thrust reverser could be used. The leading edges were redesigned and de-icing boots were added. Spoilers were installed on the upper wing surfaces. The landing gear was strengthened to accommodate the 23,000-pound gross weight. A new dorsal fin improved directional stability. Controls were improved, with hydraulic power for some of the systems, new fuel feed, new engine controls and improved fire detection and fire-fighting systems. New wheels, tires and brakes — designed and supplied by Goodyear — were incorporated. The cockpit was redesigned and made more spacious. Each of these may seem unimportant, but together they made the 1124 quite different from the 1123. IAI hardly gained clear superiority relative to its rivals with the 1124, however.

In comparisons of the 1124 with the Falcon 10, the Learjet 35, and the Sabre 60, planes against which the 1124 was designed to compete, *Business and Commercial Aviation* rated the 1124 well above average in passenger comfort and accommodations, above average in certification values (e.g., ratio of maximum useful load to empty weight) and range capabilities, but below average in general performance (e.g., climb rate, maximum cruise speed, economical cruise speed), and below average in efficiency (e.g., passenger seat miles per hour, miles per pound of fuel, passenger seat miles per pound of fuel).[34] The 1124 Westwind sold quite well, however. Twelve were delivered in the U.S. in 1976, 18 in 1977, and 16 in 1978. The equipped price of the plane was about $2,327,400 in 1978. Even though operators indicated general satisfaction with the plane — even seeing it as a bargain — IAI was aware that the 1124 would not be the airplane to see them through the next decade.

As the 1124 was being certified in various countries in early 1976, IAI was already working on follow-on designs, one of which was to have supercritical wings. The 1125 Westwind 1 was announced in mid-1978 and available for delivery in the U.S. by early 1979. There was no change in the engines, but the 1125 had seven inches more headroom, a removable 700-pound capacity fuel tank in the forward baggage compartment and a new interior. The first plane with the added headroom was Aircraft No. 240 in the Jet Commander/Commodore Jet/1123/1124/1125 series; Aircraft No. 242 was the first with the added fuel tank. The 1125 Westwind 1 was priced at $2,480,000 in 1979. Twenty-three were delivered in the U.S. in that year, 20 in 1980, 11 in 1981, seven in 1982 and six in 1983. By that date, there were only three non-Israelis among the 20,000 IAI employees.[35]

An improved Westwind 1 was being studied before the first one was delivered. This version, the Westwind 2, was introduced at the September 1979 NBAA meeting. Again, the engines were not changed. The Westwind 2 did have a redesigned wing, and winglets were mounted on the tip tanks.

Thrust reversers and new avionics were also included. The Westwind 2 still bore a marked resemblance to the original Jet Commander. The price of the Westwind 2 was $3,147,000 in 1980, about $500,000 more than the price of the Westwind 1 in that year.[36] Atlantic Aviation opined in March of that year that, "[t]he operators now have a broader acceptance of [the Westwind] on its merits, rather than any political or support-related considerations".[37]

IAI's worldwide sales of Westwind 1s and 2s reached 72 in 1980. Seven Westwind 2s were delivered in the U.S. in 1980, 20 in 1981, 16 in 1982 and 13 in 1983. Recall that these were years during which the industry was experiencing a sharp contraction and when Gates Learjet sales were declining precipitously. These years were also marked by complaints by the domestic manufacturers and labor leaders about the policies of foreign governments that were resulting in an increasing share of the U.S. market being occupied by planes manufactured abroad.[38]

After five years of research on advanced-technology wings, IAI moved from the old Jet Commander design when it announced the Astra at the September 1980 NBAA meetings. The Astra was presented only as a model at that time, but the presentation showed swept wings, thick at the roots, mounted low on the fuselage. One Astra was ordered during the meetings. Deliveries were scheduled to start in the third quarter of 1984. In October 1982, IAI said that rollout of the Astra was expected by October 1983, with first flight six months after that. Deliveries were then scheduled to begin in March 1986. Rollout occurred on schedule in September 1983. IAI considered advancing the timetable for certification and thought that deliveries might start as early as the summer of 1985.

Although the fuselage of the Astra looked somewhat like that of the earlier Westwinds, the only parts in common were the engine nacelles and the empennage. The fuselage was nearly eight feet longer and two inches wider, and had eight inches more headroom. The new wing, built in one piece, had a 34-degree sweep in the inboard section and a 24-degree sweep on out to the tip. The TFE731-3A engines were each to deliver 3,650 lbs st. Extensive use of composite materials kept the gross takeoff weight down to 23,650 pounds, the same as that of the Westwind 2. With a crew of two and four passengers, the craft was to have a full-fuel range of over 3,000 miles at a cruise speed of

Mach 0.80 and of over 3,800 miles at Mach 0.72. Shortly after rollout, IAI said that it was investing $100 million in R&D on the Astra and another $50 million in new tooling for the plane. A price of about $6.0 million was planned.[39]

First flight of the Astra occurred in March 1985. FAA certification was given in August 1985. First delivery to a U.S. customer was on June 30, 1986. As of 1986, compared to other business jets in the 20,000-30,000 pound weight class, the Astra had the longest range (slightly longer than the BAe 125-800), carried the second highest payload (the BAe 125-800, with 10% higher gross weight, carried 650 pounds more), and had the second highest cruise speed (the Gates Learjet 25G was about 7 mph faster).[40] A 1987 *Business and Commercial Aviation* analysis concluded that "IAI's considerable technical skills, honed through design of supersonic fighter aircraft, and a very competitive pricing policy make the . . . Astra a far-reaching and worthy consideration among medium-size business aircraft."[41]

IAI made a number of changes in the Astra beginning with the 30th unit in 1989. A new IAI-owned sales and support organization, Astra Jet Corporation, had by then been formed in Princeton, NJ, to work with Atlantic Aviation and other distributors throughout the world in promoting the IAI product. A new designation, Astra SP (for "special performance," "special pilot" refinements, "special passenger" comfort) was given at that point. The engines were changed from TFE731-3As to TFE731-3Bs, adding 50 lb st to each. The range was increased by about 60 miles, cruise speed was increased slightly, and the hot-day, high-altitude takeoff performance was improved. A new digital avionics package was installed. New seats and an improved galley were provided. The price was increased from $5,995,000 for the Astra to $6,550,000 for the Astra SP. There was a six- to eight-month order backlog, with production running at about 1.5 per month.[42]

IAI pursued a "one-plane product line" strategy (i.e., one business jet, along with military fighters) after its acquisition of Rockwell's Jet Commander. New models in the Commodore Jet/Westwind/Astra series largely replaced the existing models rather than adding to the product line. IAI achieved notable success with this strategy, at least through 1990. The post-1989 recession in the U.S. hurt IAI's sales. Only 12 Astras, not the 18 planned, were delivered in 1991. The Gulf War and the 10% luxury tax that became effective in the U.S. on January 1, 1991, added to the problems of IAI and the other manufacturers. Astra Jet hoped that 12-15 Astras would be sold in 1992.

IAI began exploring a new, heavier Astra IV business jet in 1992. The Astra IV would seat a many as 19 passengers. Partners to share the financial risks and production were being sought. *Business and Commercial Aviation* reported that the Yakolev Aircraft Corporation in Russia was one of the firms being considered.[43]

Hawker-Siddeley/British Aerospace   In December 1969, Beech Aircraft and Hawker-Siddeley entered into a contract under which Beech was to serve as the completion center and marketing agent for the HS-125 in North America and selected other areas. Atlantic Aviation and Garrett AiResearch Corporation had been performing these functions for Hawker. Beech set up the Beech Hawker Corporation in 1970. By the end of that year, Beech Hawker had sold four of the existing stock of completed HS-125-3ARs, re-designating them BH-125s. Beech Hawker set up facilities to complete interiors and exteriors and to install the avionics. The first BH-125-400 had been completed by May 1971.

The 125-400 featured a newly-designed flight deck, a larger baggage compartment, polarized and adjustable cabin-window shades, fluorescent cabin overhead lighting and options for a hot-food galley, foldout tables, a stereo sound system, cabin/cockpit interphones and a cabin instrument readout panel. The 1970 equipped price for the 125-400 was $1.2 million.[44]

Hawker-Siddeley was working on two other 125s in 1970. One was the 125-600, a stretch and improvement on the 125-400. A prototype of the 125-600 flew in January 1971. The 125-600 was scheduled to reach the U.S. market as the BH 125-600 in late 1971, but shipments of the green aircraft were delayed when Rolls Royce was unable to deliver the new Viper Mk. 601 3,750 lb st engines. Engines for the 125-400s were available and production of that plane continued. The other plane under development was the 125-200, a smaller aircraft that was still in the product definition stage. The 125-200, if introduced, was to compete against advanced turboprops and the new Citation.[45]

Beech Hawker introduced the BH-125-600 at the September 1972 NBAA meetings. Changes from the 125-400 included a two-foot extension of the fuselage forward of the wing, a six-inch extension of the nose radome, a new radar system, larger dorsal and ventral fins, elimination of a bulge in the fuselage at the cockpit, the new engines and engine pods, modified anti-skid brakes and new ailerons. With a gross takeoff weight of 25,000 pounds — 1,500 more than the 125-400 — the 125-600 was normally configured for eight passengers, but could accommodate as many as 14. The plane could cruise at 510 mph (Mach 0.76 at 31,000 feet) and had been tested to Mach 0.848 in Great Britain. *Business and Commerical Aviation* estimated the operating costs of the BH-125-600 (with eight seats) at $0.15 per seat mile in 1972.

Hawker-Siddeley sold the first two 125-600s to the British Ministry of Defense. Beech Hawker bought 50 125-400s and 600s that year with scheduled deliveries stretching over three years. The first green 600 reached Wichita in October 1972. In addition to itself, Beech Hawker used Atlantic Aviation and Page Airways as retail sales agents in the U.S.[46]

U.S. sales of the BH-125-600 did not go as well as expected. Beech delivered 16 125-400s to U.S. customers in 1971 and 1972. In 1973, only three 125-400s and five 125-600s were shipped. By September of 1973, Beech had an inventory of five unsold 600s. Beech expected to sell 15-20 600s in 1974 and succeeded in delivering 12 in the U.S. and five more in other countries. Only two were delivered in 1975.[47]

Beech and Hawker-Siddeley did not renew their agreement when it expired in September 1975. Hawker-Siddeley set up its own marketing and support organization, Hawker-Siddeley Aviation, Inc., in Washington, D.C. It was clear, however, that the 125-600 was not going to do well regardless of the sales efforts that might be put forth. The price of the 600 stood at $1,687,000 in 1974, compared to $1,267,000 for the 125-400 a year earlier. The higher price was not the primary problem, though. The main obstacle to selling the 125-600 was the Rolls Royce Mk. 601 turbojet engine. Fuel prices had risen since the 1973 oil crisis and that engine was a fuel guzzler compared to the turbofan engines then being installed on rival aircraft. Further, the Mk. 601 engine was very noisy — far too noisy to come close to meeting the new FAR Part 36 noise requirements.[48]

Hawker-Siddeley announced the HS-125-700 in May 1976. An appropriate Rolls Royce was not available so Hawker opted for the Garrett TFE731-3-1H, 3,700 lb st turbofan engine. These engines consumed 0.82 pounds of fuel per lb hour at 40,000 feet and Mach 0.75 cruise speed in contrast with the 1.10 pounds per lb hour consumed by the Mk. 601. This added fuel efficiency, aided by many aerodynamic refinements, gave the 700 a range that was 50% greater than that of the 600. That range could be achieved, however, only with a reduced payload and with longer takeoff distances. Still, for any stage length and payload the 600 was capable of, the 700 could achieve the same performance using less fuel. The TFE731 also met FAA noise standards. Deliveries began as scheduled for mid-1977, with 12 going to U.S. customers before the end of the year. Garrett also provided the TFE731 in retrofit packages for all of the earlier 125 series aircraft.[49]

The production model 125-700s had a much-improved flight control system and a redesigned flight deck. The 1977 price was $3,220,000, 50% higher than the $2,075,000 price of the 125-600 in 1976. Nineteen were delivered in the U.S. in 1978, 19 more in 1979, 20 in 1980, 21 in 1981, 18 in 1982, and 11 in 1983. By 1981, the price had risen to $5,845,000 and by 1983, to $5,995,000. Hawker-Siddeley had begun studying a new model, the 125-800, in 1977, but the incentive to introduce that plane was reduced by the continuing acceptance of the 700. There was a two-year backlog for deliveries of the latter model as late as June 1981. By the autumn of 1981, an airplane that represented the 500th of the 125 series and the 100th 125-700 was delivered to a U.S. customer.[50]

British Aerospace was formed in 1977 when the British Aircraft Corporation, Hawker-Siddeley and Scottish Aviation were nationalized. British Aerospace became a public limited company in 1981 when the government sold a portion of its holdings to the private sector. The remainder of the government's holdings were sold in 1985. Details of the BAe 125-800 — the plane Hawker-Siddeley had been developing since 1977 — had been kept secret until May 1983 when its first flight occurred. The 800 used TFE731-5 turbofan engines. These provided 4,300 lb st, 600 pounds more than the engines of the 125-700. The wingspan of the 800 was 4.5 feet longer than that of the 700, with the outer portions of the wings based on the supercritical design. A drooped leading edge was adopted to improve stall characteristics. BAe's work on the wings of the Airbus A300 and A310 contributed to the new airfoil for the 800.

The avionics package on the first 800s improved on that of the 700, but was still analog. After December 1984, the 800 had an all-digital cockpit. It was the first business jet so equipped. The new wrap-around windscreen on the 800 gave it a sleeker look and improved visibility. The 800 was five inches longer than the 700. With a reconfiguration of interior paneling, air conditioning and emergency oxygen, about five additional inches of cabin width was provided. The result was a "wide-bodied" look. The gross takeoff weight of the 800 was 27,400 pounds, 1,900 more than the 700. The range was increased by nearly 400 miles. The 125-800 was certified in March 1984. The 700s were to be phased from production, with the 800s gradually replacing them until a production rate of three per month was achieved. Sixteen BAe 125-800s were delivered in 1984, 27 in 1985, 26 in 1986, 34 in 1987, 31 in 1988 (including the 700th in the series), and 17 in 1989.[51]

BAe began working on a replacement for the 125-800 in early 1987. The BAe 1000 — the twelfth variant of the 125 — was announced in October 1989. The 1000 represented a major reworking of the 800. The TFE731 engines were replaced by the Pratt & Whitney PW305 engines, with 5,200 lb st. The digital avionics suite was improved to include fully automatic digital engine controls (FADEC) and a Honeywell Laseref III inertial reference system. The fuselage was made with new panels and was 33 inches longer than that of the 800. An extra cabin window was added to each side. The wing, while strengthened, was essentially that of the 800. Gross takeoff weight was increased by 2,600 pounds. The performance envelope of the BAe 1000 was quite different, too. There was a 49% improvement in range at Mach 0.77 and a 27% improvement in range at Mach 0.70. The added power reduced required takeoff distance by 9%. The 1990 price of the 1000 was set at $10,950,000. In early 1990, first flight was expected by mid-year; certification was scheduled for late summer 1991.[52]

In late 1991 — prior to first delivery of the BAe 1000 — there were 486 Model 125s based in the United States, 185 in Europe, 33 in South America, 33 in Africa, 30 in the Middle East, and 28 in Pacific Rim countries. The 1000 was certified in Great Britain in October 1991 and in the U.S. in December 1991.[53] An *AWST* evaluation six months later concluded that, "the 1000 will be hard to beat. Passengers will find the cabin well suited to long trips, and flight crews will appreciate the aircraft's more powerful engines, upgraded systems and sophisticated avionics suite."[54] Twelve BAe 1000s were delivered in 1991 and sales were strong through 1992.

Observers who have suggested that the 1000 will be the last iteration of the Model 125 may or may not prove to be correct. BAe announced in April 1992 that it would divest a major portion of its corporate jet division to get funds for future developments. The company said that it could not develop aircraft beyond the BAe 1000 without outside investments. It was estimated that developing a new plane would cost $500 million. It was recognized, however, that finding a buyer could be "a bit of a hard sell" since the 125-800 and the 1000 "represent a design stretched to the end of its rope." By the end of 1992, BAe announced that it would not sell the line. Negotiations with Raytheon had been broken off because BAe would not agree to Raytheon's plans for shifting major portions of the production to the U.S. The negotiations later resumed and the sale to Raytheon was announced in 1993. Raytheon owned Beech Aircraft at the time. It appeared that Raytheon, like Bombardier, was planning to offer two (or more) lines of business jets.[55] Whatever happens after the Raytheon acquisition, the 30 years of successful innovations represented in the 125 series is a truly impressive record.

Dassault and the Falcon Jets   Unlike IAI and BAe but like Gates Learjet, Avions Marcel Dassault (AMD) followed a "multiple business jet" strategy. At the same time that it was developing the sophisticated Mirage fighters, AMD was extending its line of business jets. By 1971, as noted in Chapter Three, the Fan Jet Falcon was available as the standard Falcon 20, the Falcon 20C, the Falcon 20D, the Falcon 20E and the Falcon 20F.

The Falcons were relatively large planes with high-speeds and good range. According to *Business and Commercial Aviation* estimates, the operating cost of a company-owned and -operated Falcon 20 configured with ten seats was around $0.18 per passenger seat mile. Thirty-seven were delivered in 1968 and 50 in 1969. Only 22 were shipped in 1970, as the sales of business aircraft generally suffered a sharp decline.[56]

The Falcon 20T, which evolved indirectly to the Falcon 50, was under development in 1971. We covered this aspect of AMD's product developments in Chapter Five. The smaller Falcon 10 was also being readied for sale.

A Falcon 10 prototype made its first flight in December 1970. This test model was powered by GE CJ610 2,850 lb st turbojets. The production version was to use Garrett TFE731-2 3,230 lb st turbofans. Designed to carry four passengers with a commode and service bar or up to eight passengers without those facilities, the 10 was described as a 0.7 scale model of the 20. In reality, the Falcon 10 was a new airplane. With a gross takeoff weight of 18,247 lb st, it was only two-thirds as heavy as the Falcon 20s, about 3,000 pounds heavier than the Learjet 25, and about 2,000 pounds lighter than the Sabre Model 60.

The wing of the Falcon 10 was adopted by AMD from the wing of a Mirage fighter. The combination of the new engine and this complex wing gave the 10 a high-speed cruise of Mach 0.85 and a normal cruise speed of 525 mph (Mach 0.81 at 40,000 feet). It was priced green at $1,150,000 in 1971. Pan Am ordered 40 of them for distribution in the U.S. While some regarded Dassault's move toward a smaller plane as a response to the Citation, the 10 was not a "minijet" in the same sense as was the Citation. The latter weighed only 10,350 pounds, had 2,200 lb st engines, cruised at 400 mph, and was priced fully-equipped at $695,000. The Falcon 10 and the Citation were not close substitutes.[57]

Certification of the Falcon 10 was expected in December 1972, but the first of the prototypes crashed in France during a test flight in October. Investigators concluded that an intentional, sudden change from full right to left rudder at high-speed had overstressed the fuselage, causing it to break into two pieces in mid-air. The pilot and flight test engineer were killed.

Structural changes were made and the two remaining prototypes of the 10 were flying again by June 1973. One of them flew from Paris to Corsica at an average speed of 568.5 mph, a record for planes of its type. The first production model, a demonstrator, arrived in the U.S. in early September on an itinerary that included several U.S. cities and a tour through South America. The plane was back in Dallas for the NBAA meetings on September 24. One Falcon 10 was delivered to a U.S. customer in 1973, 16 in 1974, 21 in 1975, 14 in 1976, 14 in 1977, 19 in 1978, 16 in 1979, 16 in 1980, nine in 1981, two in 1982, five in 1983 and one in 1984. U.S. sales represented about 60% of total sales. The plane stayed the same through this period while the price, fully equipped, went from $1,475,000 in 1974 to $4,058,790 in 1983.[58]

Falcon operators praised the performance of the Falcon 10 even as they criticized the service they received from Pan Am's Falcon Jet Corporation, AMD's agent for Western Hemisphere sales and service. As sales began to weaken in 1979-80, AMD decided to make some improvements in the Falcon 10 and, as we will see, the Falcon 20. The improved Falcon 10 was renamed the Falcon 100. A fourth window was added on the right side of the fuselage opposite the door. State-of-the-art avionics were included in the standard package. The interior was done over, and the luggage compartment was enlarged. Experiments with composite materials for wing panels were abandoned after structural failures occurred during testing. The Falcon 100 was announced in late 1981 at the same price as the 10. Two Falcon 100s were delivered in the U.S. in 1983, four in 1984, two in 1985, three in 1986, three in 1987, five in 1988 and one in 1989. The Falcon 100 was dropped from the *Aviation Week and Space Technology* Inventory Issue after 1991.[59]

AMD did not press developments of its 20 series aircraft during the 1970s even though the basic design of these planes was by then well over a decade old. Dassault was, of course, occupied in the early 1970s with the Falcon 10 and, after 1974, with the "heavy iron" Falcon 50 and derivatives of the 50. By 1972, only the 20D and 20F were being sold in the U.S., with the latter having GE CF700-2D2, 4,315 lb st engines and the former, CF700-2D, 4,250 lb st engines. Eight Fs (and Es) and ten Ds (and Cs) were delivered in the U.S. in that year. Eleven Fs and and 18 Ds were delivered in 1973. No Falcon Ds were delivered in the U.S. after that. U.S. deliveries of the Falcon

F never exceeded ten per year after 1974. Two were delivered in 1974, the last year it was shipped.

AMD announced a retrofit program for the 20 series Falcons in May 1976. Beginning three years later, the GE engines could be pulled and Garrett ATF3-6, 5,050 lb st engines installed in their place. The retrofit would extend the range of the aircraft and reduce fuel consumption and runway requirements. At the same time, Dassault announced the Falcon 20G, a 20F with the same Garrett AiResearch engines. Pan Am's Falcon Jet Corporation was bidding in a competition for a U.S. Coast Guard contract for a medium-range surveillance plane, using the 20G as its entry. The Coast Guard, over the protests of U.S business jet manufacturers, awarded Falcon Jet a contract for 41 Falcon 20Gs in January 1977, with deliveries to begin in July 1979. Something in the order of 68% of the value of the parts came from U.S. suppliers, satisfying the requirements of the "Buy American Act." The Coast Guard procurement made it seem quite certain that a civilian version of the 20G would also be produced.[60]

Avions Marcel Dassault had merged with Breguet Aviation in 1971. In 1979, 20% of the stock was taken over by the French government; the government's holdings were increased to 46% in late 1981, giving it effective control of the company.

The Coast Guard Falcon was designated the HU-25A Guardian. In the course of developing it, the concept of the 20G changed significantly. The 1979 delivery date for the HU-25A slipped more than two and a half years as AMD and Garrett attempted to modify the plane and the engine to meet contract specifications. The Coast Guard was still refusing to accept the HU-25A as late as January 1982.

Garrett found ways to increase the thrust of the engine from 5,050 lb st to 5,440 lb st and AMD defined a Falcon 20H — a civilian version of the HU-25A, with the more powerful engines. At the same time that the Falcon 10 was renamed the Falcon 100, the Falcon 20H became the Falcon 200. The 200 was expected to be ready for delivery in June 1983.[61]

The Falcon 200 ended up as a six-to-eight passenger version of the Falcon 20, with Garrett ATF3-6A, 5,200 lb st turbofan engines. It had new avionics, new cockpit display arrangements, new nacelles, modifications in the mid-span wing fences, improved air conditioning and a redesigned interior. The first 200 was delivered in the U.S. in December 1983. Three more were delivered in 1984, eight in 1985, one in 1986 and three in 1987. There were no U.S. deliveries of the plane after that. The last delivery of a Falcon 200 worldwide occurred in April 1988.[62]

Dassault proposed a widebody Falcon 20/200 to the French Ministry of Transport in 1983. This plane was to accommodate 12-15 passengers and have a range of 4,000 miles. In the same year, Century Aircraft and Falcon Jet Corporation offered engine retrofits for Falcon 20Ds and 20Fs that would make them faster, give them greater range, and decrease operating costs. The 1983 proposal to the Ministry went ahead as the Falcon X program. By 1987, Dassault described the Falcon X as a eight to nineteen passenger, twin-engined craft, with a fuselage cross-section that was smaller than that of the Falcon 900, but larger than that of the Falcon 20/200. The wings were to incorporate new-generation, laminar-flow technology and canards were to be mounted on the forward fuselage.

Dassault launched production of the Falcon X in June 1989. The plane's cross-section had been increased from the earlier plans and was now the same as that of the Falcon 900. The fuselage was about two-thirds as long as that of the 900. The typical configurations would be for eight to ten passengers. The Pratt & Whitney PW305 and the GE/Garrett CFE738 engines, both rated at 5,600 lb st, were competing for Dassault's selection.

The Falcon X was christened the Falcon 2000 in October 1989. The new plane was described as a replacement for the 20/200 series Falcons, but it is not clear whether it is intended as a small "heavy iron" business jet or a large mid-sized offering. Like the 20/200s, it is to have two, not three engines. Like the 50/900, it boasts a stand-up cabin and a walk-in luggage compartment. Dassault began searching for a partner to produce the plane. The plans were for the other company — a non-French company — to produce the aft fuselage and engines nacelles while Dassault produced the rest of the plane. The French government, which as controlling stockholder had approved of the plans to develop the 2000, was asked to provide financial support. First flight was scheduled for 1992; first deliveries, 1994.[63]

An Italian firm, Alenia, joined Dassault in the Falcon 2000 venture. Some parts of the wings and fuselage are to be manufactured in Turino. The 2000 has a VIP cabin layout for 8-12 passengers, but up to 19 could be seated. The gross takeoff weight is planned at 35,000 pounds, compared to 45,500 pounds for the Falcon 900. The GE/Garrett CFE738-1-18, 5,725 lb st engine is used. Maximum cruise speed is Mach 0.85 and normal cruise is Mach 0.80. These speeds match those of the Astra SP and, among the mid-sized jets, are exceeded only by those of the new Citation 10. The range (with a 1,000-pound payload) is predicted to be 3,520 miles. The Citation 7, the Sabreliner 60, the BAe 1000, and the proposed Learjet 60 all have ranges equal to or greater than the Falcon 2000.[64]

The Falcon 2000 began flight tests in March 1993. Certification was expected by the end of 1994. A price of $15,340,000 was announced. The production model will be the first business jet with full, all-weather avionics and "heads-up" cockpit display (HUD) panels. Dassault claimed that it had 50 options by February 1993 and predicted that 300 would be sold over the following 12 years.[65]

In 1993, Dassault had two business jets in production, the Falcon 50 and the Falcon 900B. The Falcon 2000 was being flight tested and the Falcon 9000 was in the early stages of development. Even as Dassault was launching the 2000, another firm was offering a competitive retrofit program for the old Falcon 20s. The retrofit involves replacing the original GE engines with Garrett TFE731-5 engines and other modernizations. The retrofitted 731 Falcon 20s sell for between a third and a half of a new Falcon 2000.[66] Dassault was striving to stay in the market, but its future was far from clear.

New Participants in the Mid-Sized Segment of the Market

Cessna Even as Cessna was enjoying the initial success of the Citation in the low end of the market in the 1972-1975 period, it was studying ways to introduce higher-performance aircraft. Many business customers graduated to the Citation from planes like the Beech King Air turboprop, with consequent sales losses to Beech and other turboprop manufacturers. In the same way, Cessna saw that, without its having more advanced offerings, customers would turn to Learjets, Falcons and other mid-sized or large jets when they wanted to upgrade from the Citation. "Cessna did not go into the high-volume Citation program to develop a new market for competitors when owners of its 400-mph turbofan wanted to add or move up to a higher-performance airplane."[67] The Citation I and II, scheduled for deliveries in 1976 and 1978, respectively, were expected to help in retaining customers, but Cessna needed a considerably more sophisticated plane.

Cessna announced the Citation III (and the Citation I and II) at the September 1976 NBAA meetings. The Citation III was described as a competitor of the Falcon 50 and LearStar 600. The Falcon 50 and the LearStar (later Canadair) 600 were being readied at that time for the heavy end of the market. Cessna said the the III would incorporate NASA supercritical wings and be capable of cruising at 540 mph with 9-13 passengers. Power was to be from Garrett AiResearch TFE731-3, 3,700 lb st turbofan engines. Transcontinental and intercontinental versions were planned, with a price estimated at $2.3-$2.4 million in 1976 dollars. Buyers were invited to put down deposits to assure themselves of positions. Deliveries were scheduled to begin in 1980.[68]

The Citation III, while considerably heavier than the Citation, Citation I and Citation II, was not in fact designed for the "heavy-iron" part of the market. In 1978, preliminary specifications called for a gross takeoff weight of 17,150 pounds. The range for the standard version was to be 2,500 miles; for the extended-range version (with gross takeoff weight of 19,100 pounds), 3,000 miles. Drawings showed a horizontal stabilizer mounted in the lower mid-section of the vertical tail, but a T-tail was adopted before the end of 1978. In early September 1978, the standard Citation III was priced at $2,995,000 and the extended-range version at $3,195,000 (1979 dollars), with deliveries of the first block of 25 aircraft scheduled to begin in 1981. It was announced a bit later that month that the first block and most of the second block were sold. Prices were increased to $3,295,000 and $3,495,000 for the second block. Orders were being accepted for 1983 deliveries only.

A number of changes beyond the redesigned tail were made in 1978. The headroom in the cabin and the storage space were increased. Dual wheels were now on the undercarriage. Winglets had been tried and abandoned. Composites were used in some of the control surfaces. There was to be extensive use of bonding (epoxy gluing) of the joints between metal panels. The maximum operating altitude was increased to 51,000 feet. The economic cruise speed of the Citation III was cited as Mach 0.73. First flight of the first prototype occurred in May 1979.[69]

Cessna reported in early 1980 that the Citation III would be certified in October of the following year. No delivery positions were available until the fourth block in 1984. The prices for that block were set at $3,795,000 for the standard version and $3,995,000 for the extended-range model. Then it was announced that there would be a six-month slippage in the schedule due to hard-to-get tooling and an expanded test program. Shortly after mid-year, Cessna indicated that there would be changes in the design — the trailing edges of the wings, ailerons, elevator, hydraulic system, nose wheel and door were all to be modified. There were rumors that Cessna was facing severe cash flow problems and was likely to be acquired.[70]

Cessna elected in 1981 to drop the extended-range Citation III. Type certification of the standard Citation III was given in April 1982. Approval to operate at 51,000 feet into known icing conditions was granted in July 1982. The first production version, a demonstrator, was provided to Cessna Marketing in December. Deliveries to customers began in March 1983 and a total of 18 were delivered before the end of the year. As certified, the Citation III had a gross takeoff weight of 21,000 pounds, nearly 4,000 pounds more than that called for in the original design. The TFE731-3B-100S engines were each rated at 3,650 lb st. The normal configuration had eight passenger seats. Maximum cruise speed was Mach 0.85. Normal short-range cruise speed was 509 mph and long-range cruise speed, 404 mph. The range of the Citation III was 2,500 miles. The 1984 price, fully equipped, was $6,120,000. Fifty Citation IIIs were delivered in 1984, far outstripping the deliveries of the rival Falcon 20F, BAe 125-700, Learjet 55, and Westwind business jets.[71]

A 1983 *Business and Commercial Aviation* comparison showed that, relative to these other aircraft, the Citation III had pronounced strengths in cabin pressurization (with a 9.7 pound differential), required field lengths, climb rate, maximum certified altitude and several measures of fuel efficiency. Its worst grades were in areas measuring maximum payload and climb rate with one engine. The Citation III was a bit below average in cabin size, as well. Overall, the III was above average in 20 of the 28 parameters evaluated. The equipped price of the Falcon 20F was $6,188,790; of the BAe 125-700, $5,995,000; of the Learjet 55, $5,216,015. Thus, while its fuel efficiency would lead to relatively low operating costs, the Citation III was, if anything, priced higher than its principal rivals.[72]

There were 140 Citation IIIs in operation by July 1987. While Citation III was still selling relatively well in that year, Cessna had announced the SII Citation in October 1986 and, in so doing, it created a good deal of competition for the III. A prototype of the Citation V, a stretched Citation II, was flying by early 1988, putting further pressure on the Citation III. Improvements were being made in the BAe, Learjet and Falcon offerings. There were some grumblings from owners about the III, too. Only two FAA Airworthiness Directives had been issued, but over 100 service bulletins had been sent out by Cessna. Some of the first models spent considerable amounts of time in the shop. There were other shortcomings, as well. The III lacked true transcontinental range. Some of its systems were installed in ways that made service difficult. Repair and maintenance work at Cessna's service centers was not consistently good. Parts under warranty were often short-lived and not always available when needed.[73]

General Dynamics acquired Cessna in September 1985, pledging that it would support continued development of the Citation series. Several new Citations were being studied at that time, among them possible successors to the Citation III. By 1988, a Citation IV, a stretched III with significantly greater range, was being discussed in the press. Cessna formally announced the IV (and the CitationJet) at the September 1989 NBAA meetings. The IV, which was not scheduled for deliveries until 1993, was to weigh 2,000 pounds more than the III, use higher-powered Garrett TFE engines, include digital avionics, and have a range of over 3,100 miles. In the interim before the IV was ready, an improved Citation III was planned. Effective with completion of the 179th Citation III in January 1990, an entirely new, digital avionics package and other changes in the avionics suite were included as standard equipment. The interior was redesigned. Engine nacelles were fabricated of metal rather than composites. A number of other changes in the airframe introduced with serial numbers 169 through 178 were continued. The base price, with standard equipment, was set at $6,775,000.[74]

Cessna officials met regularly with the Cessna Advisory Council, a group of 15 business jet operators. In 1990, the Council expressed interest in derivatives of the Citation III, one "a lower-priced version" and the other a plane with "greater payload, range and larger engines."[75] After studying these proposals, Cessna dropped its development of the Citation IV, concentrating instead on two new planes, the Citation VI, the lower-priced derivative, and the Citation VII, the larger, more powerful derivative.

The Citation VI and Citation VII use the same airframe. The VI is numbered the CE-650/VI; the VII is the CE-650/VII. They are 52.2 feet long and have a wingspan of 53.3 feet. Each accommodates seven to nine passengers. The Citation VI uses the Garrett TFE731-3B-100 3,650 lb st engine and the VII uses the Garrett TFE731-4R-2S 4,100 lb st engine. The gross takeoff weight of the VI is 22,000 pounds; that of the VII, 22,450 pounds. The high cruise speed of the VI is 532 mph (at 39,000 feet). Its long-range cruise speed is 465 mph (at 41,000 feet). Its full-fuel range is about 2,130 miles. The Citation VII has a high cruise speed of 541 mph (at 39,000 feet), a long-range cruise speed of 480 mph (at 43,000 feet) and a full-fuel range of about 2,037 miles. The initial price of the Citation VI was $6.8 million while the first Citation VIIs were sold for $8.6 million. The Citation III was priced at $8.1 million in 1990.

The first Citation VI was delivered in June 1991. The first Citation VII was delivered in May 1992. By 1993, the Citation VII seemed to be the "flagship" of the Cessna fleet. A typically-equipped VII then cost $9,403,000. A typically-equipped Citation VI cost $7,889,000.[76]

Five months after announcing the Citation VI and VII, Cessna announced its Citation X. The X is not a direct derivative of the Citation III. It is to be Cessna's "top-of-the-line aircraft," a plane of "truly preemptive performance."

The Citation X, while still considerably smaller than the Gulfstream IV, Falcon 900B and Canadair 601-3A, is much larger than the Citation VI and VII. It will be 72.2 feet long and have a wingspan of 63.9 feet. The planned gross takeoff weight is 31,000 pounds. Powered by Allison GMA-3007C, 6,000 lb st engines, the Citation X is to have a maximum cruise speed of Mach 0.90 (600 mph at 40,000 ft), a normal cruise speed of Mach 0.86 (570 mph at 40,000 ft) and a long-range cruise speed of Mach 0.82 (540 mph at 40,000 ft). A full-fuel range of 3,800 miles is estimated. The 1993 equipped price was announced as $15.5 million.[77]

Textron Corporation acquired Cessna from General Dynamics in January 1992 for $600 million in cash. Dassault had bid $300 million. General Dynamics had paid $663.7 million for Cessna in 1985. Cessna generated profits of $100 million in 1991 and profits of $200 million per year were forecast by the mid-1990s. Cessna was far and away the world's largest seller of business jets. The 2000th Citation was completed in June 1993.[78] The overall market for these aircraft was continuing to decline, however.

Mitsubishi The crowded field of producers of mid-sized business jets did not prevent others from attempting to enter. One of these entrants was Mitsubishi Heavy Industries, Inc., of Japan.

Mitsubishi had vast experience in the aircraft industry. It began production of aircraft in 1921 and by 1945 had manufactured about 18,000 planes and 52,000 aircraft engines. The Zero fighter was one of its products. After World War II, Mitsubishi became a principal supplier to the Japan Air Self Defense Force (JASDF). Mitsubishi was the prime contractor in the T-2 supersonic jet trainer program and the follow-on F-1 supersonic fighter. Mitsubishi has also been co-producer of a number of U.S. aircraft, including the McDonnell Douglas F-4EJ, Lockheed P-3C Orions, and Sikorski S-61 helicopters. Mitsubishi had sales of $6.3 billion in 1980, ranking as the 28th largest industrial corporation outside of the U.S.[79]

Mitsubishi was involved in the U.S. business aircraft industry as early as 1964. Mooney Aircraft Corporation, under license from Mitsubishi, assembled Japan-manufactured parts of the MU-2 turboprop beginning in about 1965. Mitsubishi organized its own U.S. subsidiary, Mitsubishi International, and did its own assembly in Texas after 1970. The MU-2s were equipped with AiResearch TPE engines and U.S.-made instruments and sold successfully through the early 1980s. The last versions of the MU-2s were called the Solitaire and the Marquise.

Mitsubishi announced its MU-300 business jet in 1978. Details were sketchy, but it was indicated that flight tests would begin shortly in Japan and that the plane would thereafter be brought to the U.S. for FAA testing and certification. When the plane was rolled out in 1979 ceremonies at Mitsubishi's San Angelo plant, it was called the Diamond 1. The name derived directly from the English translation of Mitsubishi. The Diamond 1 was about the same size as a Citation II and used the same JT15D-4 engine. The Mitsubishi offering had very different performance specifications, however. It had swept wings and a T-tail. The maximum cruise speed was Mach 0.78. The range (with reserve fuel) was over 1,400 miles. The gross takeoff weight was listed at about 14,000 pounds and the cabin could be configured for five to nine passengers. The initial price was $1,880,000 with deliveries set to start in 1981. Mitsubishi declared that it had sold 54 positions and expected to have sold 100 by the date of first delivery. Production was to exceed three per month. While the major airframe components were to be made in Japan, 70 percent of the value of a completed unit (including labor) was U.S. content.[80]

The Diamond 1 prototype was flying in Japan in 1978. FAA testing was underway in mid-1980. Mitsubishi reported that it had 80 orders at that time. The Diamond 1 program then began to slip. Certification was first delayed by two months, then by six more months, and then to a total of 18 months. Part of this delay was attributable to more stringent FAA certification standards put in place after the crash of a DC-10 at Chicago's O'Hare Airport in 1979. Certification was finally given in July 1982 and deliveries began in the next month. Reviewers accorded the Diamond I favorable evaluations. Still, by the time Mitsubishi was ready to ship the planes, the recession and the fact that 15-20% of the orders were from speculators and brokers combined to reduce the order backlog significantly. Nonetheless 23 Diamond 1s were delivered in 1982, nine of them in December.[81]

Mitsubishi announced in 1983 that it would introduce an improved Diamond 2 in the mid-1980s. A larger Diamond 3 was promised for 1987-88. In the interim, the Diamond 1 was fitted with P&W JT15D-4D engines to improve performance at higher temperatures. The new model was designated the Diamond 1A. Retrofits were made available for the Diamond 1s. Even with the new engine, a *Business and Commercial Aviation* analysis rated the plane well below average in maximum payload, useful load, climb rate, tanks-full range and seats-full range. It ranked somewhat above average in measures of fuel efficiency. There were no attributes with respect to which the 1A had compelling advantages. Twenty-three Diamond 1s and five 1As were delivered in the U.S in 1983. One Diamond 1 and nine 1As were delivered in the U.S. in 1984. The final 11 Diamond 1As were shipped in 1985.[82]

The Diamond 2 appeared on schedule. While retaining the same dimensions as the Diamond 1 and 1A, the Diamond 2 was new in important respects. P&W JT15D-5, 2,900 lb st engines were used. This engine did not improve the range since the Diamond 2 had no additional fuel capacity. It did allow a greater payload and, of course, a higher gross weight. Improved electronic fuel controllers added to the plane's efficiency. With these changes, a new *Business and Commercial Aviation* analysis showed the Diamond 2 to have much the same shortcomings as did the 1 and 1A.[83]

Beech Aircraft, as we have noted in several places, was searching for ways to offer a business jet throughout the 1970s and into the 1980s. In December 1985, Beech — then a subsidiary of Raytheon — acquired the Diamond program, redesignating the Diamond 2 the Beechjet 400. It was reported that Beech paid less than $10 million for the deal. The assembly facilities were moved from Texas to Beech's plant in Wichita. The components that came from Japan were to be continued under the initial arrangements. Beech announced a green price of $3.05 million and, with avionics, a $3.5 million price for the Beechjet. Beechjets, assembled from unfinished Diamond 2s, were to be ready for delivery by June 1986. While it was finishing these planes, Beech began investigating a larger version of that plane.[84]

The first Beechjet 400 was delivered in June 1986. Nine were delivered in the U.S. that year. The 400 had the same P&W JT15D-5 engines, but an extra 100-gallon fuel tank was added. The interior was redesigned to conform generally with that of Beech's KingAir turboprop. Maximum takeoff weight was increased to 15,780 pounds. The range was increased a bit from the Diamond 2, up to 1,930 miles VFR with four passengers and to 1,530 miles IFR with four passengers. Beech continued its research into an all-composite, Burt Rutan-designed twin-engined business jet and on its super-modern Starship design as it began delivering the Beechjet 400. Observers wondered whether the Beechjet 400 and one or both of these other proposed aircraft would not undo one another. Beech claimed that they were comple-ments, not substitutes.[85]

Beech delivered only six Beechjets in the U.S. in 1987. Twelve were delivered in the U.S. in 1988 and eight in 1989. An improved Beechjet 400A, to be produced entirely in Wichita, was announced at the 1988 NBAA show. The 400A had new digital avionics and, through re-location of fuel tanks, a slightly larger interior. Interior soundproofing was improved. Other struc-tural changes were minor. A June 1991 *Business and Commercial Aviation* analysis compared the 400A with the Citation II, Citation V, Learjet 31A/ER and Learjet 35A. The Beech offering was still distinctly below average in payload, runway requirements and range with full payload.

The U.S. Air Force selected a 400T (T-1A) version for its tanker/ transport trainer in 1990. A total of 211 were to be procured. Orders for the civilian 400A spurted thereafter, leaving Beech with orders for 60 for delivery in 1992 and 13 for 1993. International orders were particularly strong. Beech was thus expanding its production while many others in the industry were contracting. Beech's marketing strengths, including attention to getting owners of King Airs to migrate to the 400A rather than competitive aircraft, were recognized as being very important in the success of the 400A. The plane was proving to be a strong rival of Cessna's Citation V.[86] It was pre-sumably the same marketing strengths and a desire to compete against the Citation VI, Citation VII and other larger planes that motivated Raytheon to acquire the BAe-125 line in 1993.

Summary Observations on the Mid-Sized Segment of the Market

After 1970, the first two manufacturers of business jets were gradual-ly forced from the market. The Sabreliner and the JetStar, lacking fundamen-tal improvements, were displaced by newer airplanes. Learjet, strong for a time, began to experience difficult times after it cut back on R&D in the early 1980s and failed to bring out distinctive new models. After it was acquired by Bombardier in 1990, Learjet has strengthened its product line and experienced a revitalization.

BAe continued to invest in improvements in the 125 series. In the process, it held and improved its market share. Now that the BAe series is part of the Raytheon/Beech family, it may do even better. Israeli Aircraft Industries, after taking over the relatively unpopular Jet Commander series, upgraded that aircraft and then replaced it with the Astra series. IAI has improved its market position, but continues to have a fairly small share. The recession in sales of business aircraft and the lack of a basically new airplane seem to have hurt IAI. Dassault, with its Falcons, did less well in the mid-sized category after 1970 than in the "heavy iron" end of the market. Its Falcon 2000 may, of course, become a market success.

Cessna, a late entrant into the mid-sized field with its Citation III, has done remarkably well. Cessna's accomplishments have been made despite changes in ownership and without reliance on any significant military contracts. Through the 1980s, Cessna was working on many new models — jets, turboprops, propeller aircraft — and did so through periods of poor sales as well as in periods when sales were strong.

Beech took over the Diamond line at a time when Mitsubishi was apparently failing with it. Surprisingly, Beech has increased the sales of the Beechjet 400 without making really fundamental changes in the aircraft it acquired from Mitsubishi. Success in shifting owners of the turboprop KingAirs to the Beechjets has been an important part of this story. Whether Beech can continue in this vein remains to be seen, but the acquisition of the BAe line by Raytheon may give a boost to Beech/BAe overall sales efforts.

Notes

1. These paragraphs rely on R. J. Francillon, *Lockheed Aircraft Since 1913*, Annapolis, MD: Naval Institute Press, 1988, pp. 37-45.

2. *Ibid.* pp. 394-398; *AWST*, September 20, 1971, p. 56; October 2, 1972, p. 16; February 26, 1973, p. 71; March 5, 1973, p. 9; April 23, 1973, p. 68; April 30, 1973, p. 25; June 18, 1973, p. 11; April 15, 1974, p. 74; June 10, 1974, p. 53;

July 8, 1974, p. 56; July 15, 1974, p. 299; August 19, 1974, p. 71; September 30, 1974, p. 32; February 10, 1975, p. 31; March 8, 1976, p. 54; March 15, 1976, p. 189; April 12, 1976, p. 56; May 3, 1976, p. 103; July 12, 1976, p. 24; August 23, 1976, p. 20; February 7, 1977, p. 63; February 5, 1979, p. 9; February 12, 1979, p. 25; September 29, 1979, p. 70: C. E. Schneider, "JetStar May Be Re-Engined," *AWST*, July 3, 1972, p. 39; W. C. Wetmore, "Reengined JetStar Investment Kept Low," *AWST*, August 11, 1975, p. 56; E. J. Bulban, "General Aviation Backlog Strong," *AWST*, March 21, 1977, p. 188; D. M. North, "New Engines Improve JetStar Handling," *AWST*, May 15, 1978, p. 4; *B&CA*, June 1972, p. 30; April 1972, p. 26; July 1974, p. 92; November 1974, p. 39; June 1975, p. 108; September 1976, p. 30; March 1977, p. 43; R. N. Aarons, "The Ultimate Mod," *B&CA*, September 1972, p. 88; H. Field, "JetStar II," *FI*, July 2, 1977, p. 25; *FI*, March 8, 1973, p. 373; November 1, 1973, p. 49; June 13, 1974, p. 767; May 1, 1975, p. 698; November 20, 1975, p. 756; January 1, 1977, p. 104; February 24, 1979, p. 526.

3.   *B&CA*, April 1971, p. 51.

4.   *AWST*, March 8, 1971, p. 59; July 5, 1971, p. 48; July 12, 1971, p. 48; September 27, 1971, pp.18-19; C. E. Schneider, "Sabre 75 Retains Handling Qualities," *AWST*, November 8, 1971, p. 58; *B&CA*, April 1971, p. 50.

5.   *AWST*, April 17, 1972, p. 20; May 1, 1972, p. 11; May 15, 1972, p. 23; October 2, 1972, p. 23; November 20, 1972, p. 73; *B&CA*, February 1972, p. 34; October 1972, p. 23.

6.   *AWST*, March 19, 1973, p. 86; June 4, 1973, p. 20; June 25, 1973, p. 66; September 24, 1973, p. 51; March 11, 1974, p. 95; *B&CA*, January 1973, p. 44; February 1973, p. 14; April 1973, p. 59; September 1973, p. 67; *FI* , January 10, 1974, p. 30; May 22, 1975, p. 823.

7.   *AWST*, March 17, 1975, p. 183; June 16, 1975, p. 71; March 15, 1976, p. 191; February 7, 1977, p. 67; March 13, 1978, p. 197; February 12, 1979, p. 63; *FI*, October 2, 1976, p. 1013; January 15, 1977, p. 104.

8.   *B&CA*, April 1974, pp. 58-61.

9.   *AWST*, November 3, 1975, p.14.

10.   E. J. Bulban, "NBAA Show Stresses New Technology," *AWST*, September 20, 1976, p. 29.

11.   *AWST*, January 3, 1977, p. 11; July 11, 1977, p. 25; D. A. Brown, "Business Jet Competition Intensifies," *AWST*, June 27, 1977, p. 57; J. M. Lenorowitz, "New Sabreliner Uses Supercritical Wing," *AWST*, July 18, 1977, p. 66; E. J. Bulban, "Sabreliner Reorganization Underway," *AWST*, September 12, 1977, p. 68.

12.   *B&CA*, September 1978, p. 58; J. W. Olcott, "The Raisbeck Group . . . ," *B&CA*, December 1979, p. 53; E. J. Bulban, "New Programs Highlight Show," *AWST*,

September 18, 1978, p. 14; B. A. Smith, "Problems Delay Sabreliner Certification," *AWST*, September 3, 1979, p.65; *AWST*, May 14, 1979, p. 11; B. M. Elson, "Firms Join Forces on Sabreliner Work," *AWST*, January 21, 1980, p. 19; *AWST*, February 11, 1980, p. 20; February 18, 1980, p. 92.

13. *AWST*, March 31, 1980, p. 89; D. M. North, "New Wing, Engine Mark Sabreliner 65," *AWST*, April 7, 1980, p. 72.

14. D. M. North, "Rockwell Weighs Future of Sabreliner 65 Program," *AWST*, July 28, 1980, p. 16; "Convention Reflects Belt Tightening," *AWST*, October 13, 1980, p. 46.

15. D. M. North, "Sabreliner Proposes 3 New Versions," *AWST*, June 29, 1981, p. 23; "Sabreliner Plans to Start New Aircraft," *AWST*, January 9, 1984, p. 22; "Sabreliner, Agusta Negotiate Pact," *AWST*, October 1, 1984, p. 18; *AWST*, July 11, 1983, p. 14; July 2, 1984, p. 13; November 5, 1984, p. 11; June 9, 1986, p. 13; March 27, 1989, p. 27.

16. *AWST*, January 4, 1971, p. 53; February 22, 1971, p. 24; March 29, 1971, p. 54; June 4, 1973, p. 27.

17. *AWST*, April 17, 1972, p. 9; July 3, 1972, p. 42; *B&CA*, December 1972, p. 28.

18. *AWST*, February 19, 1973, p. 14; September 24, 1973, p. 64; *B&CA*, July 1973, p. 28.

19. *B&CA*, October 1973, p.46; *AWST*, October 8, 1973, p. 69; *FI*, September 12, 1974, p. 317.

20. *AWST*, July 15, 1974, p. 299; January 6, 1975, p. 56; *B&CA*, August 1975, p. 50.

21. *B&CA*, November 1976, p. 110; E. J. Bulban, "Modification Firms Boosting Efficiency, Reducing Costs," *AWST*, October 15, 1979, p. 56.

22. *B&CA*, June 1976, p. 51.

23. E. J. Bulban, "Record Sales Bring Hefty Backlog into 1980," *AWST*, September 26, 1977, p. 48; "NBAA Focuses on New Models," *AWST*, October 3, 1977, p. 16; *FI*, May 7, 1977, p. 1244; *AWST*, November 10, 1978, p. 58; October 9, 1978, p. 59; December 4, 1978, p. 63; February 19, 1979, p. 21; May 7, 1979, p. 16; June 4, 1979, p. 5; D. M. North, "Further Industry Growth Forecast," *AWST*, March 3, 1980, p. 215; "Gates Presses Series 50 Certification," *AWST*, April 14, 1980, p. 60.

24. *AWST*, April 2, 1979, p. 49; August 11, 1980, p. 29; November 3, 1980, p. 38; November 10, 1980, p. 62; May 11, 1981, p. 15; August 24, 1981, p. 23; May 17, 1982, p. 22; D. M. North, "Similarity of Learjet Crashes Causes NTSB to Weigh Study," *AWST*, June 9, 1980, p. 22; *FI*, January 21, 1978, p. 165; June 20, 1980, p. 1450; August 30, 1980, p. 747; J. W. Olcott, "Pilot, Know Thy Aircraft,"

B&CA, January 1982, p. 152; "Learjet Safety: Facts and Fiction," *B&CA*, July 1987, p. 40.

25. D. M. North, "Gates Series 50 Certification," *AWST*, April 14, 1980, p. 60; "Learjet Series 50 Deliveries to Start," *AWST*, April 27, 1981, p. 161; "Gates Learjet Model 55 Offers Economy, Size Increase," *AWST*, September 7, 1981, p. 42; *AWST*, September 22, 1980, p. 11; March 9, 1981, p. 231; March 23, 1981, p. 28; *FI*, August 28, 1979, p. 509; R. N. Aarons, "Status Report: The New Jets," *B&CA*, September 1978, p. 53; R. Parrish, "Report from the Learjet Fan Club," *B&CA*, September 1980, p. 72; "B/CA Analysis: Gates Learjet 55," *B&CA*, October 1981, p. 68; J. W. Olcott and R. N. Aarons, "Extended Range GE-Powered Learjets," *B&CA*, January 1982, p. 46; F. George, "The Digital Learjet 55," *B&CA*, May 1987, p. 51; *FI*, September 25, 1982, p. 942; *Jane's All the World's Aircraft*, 1987-88, pp. 418-421.

26. *AWST*, September 24, 1984, p. 26; March 4, 1985, p. 21; May 20, 1985, p. 24; March 3, 1986, p. 24; June 8, 1987, p. 13; *Jane's All the World's Aircraft*, 1987-88, p. 418; R. L. Parrish, "B/CA Operator Survey: The Learjet 55," *B&CA*, December 1983, p. 46; "Gates Learjet Gears for the Future," *B&CA*, September 1986, p. 49; *FI*, March 24, 1984, p. 746; November 10, 1984, p. 1233; November 8, 1986, p. 29.

27. *AWST*, October 5, 1987, p. 26; F. George, "Learjet 55C," *B&CA*, October 1988, p. 88; R. N. Aarons, "The Learjet 31/31A," *B&CA*, October 1990, p. 70.

28. E. H. Phillips, "Delta Fins, Simplified Systems Increase Learjet 55C Reliability," *AWST*, October 31, 1988, p. 74; J. MacMcClelland, "The Twenty-Five Years of Lear," *Flying*, September 1989, p. 58; *AWST*, July 2, 1990, p. 30; R. N. Aarons, "The New Learjet 31," *B&CA*, March 1988, p. 40; *FI*, December 10, 1988, p. 31.

29. *AWST*, July 29, 1991, p. 59; R. N. Aarons, "New Life for Learjet," *B&CA*, July 1990, p. 41; *AWST* September 21, 1992, p. 13; J. MacMcClelland, "Report Card Day for Learjet 31: It Gets an 'A,'" *Flying*, October 1992, p. 74; J. W. Olcott, "Learjet 31A," *B&CA*, April 1992, p. 48; F. George, "Learjet's Model 60," *B&CA*, September 1992, p. 66; *B&CA*, October 1992, p. 22; *B&CA*, November 1992, p. 26; *B&CA*, December 1992, p. 34; *FI*, February 17-23, 1993, p. 18; *FI*, April 28-May 4, 1993, p. 20; *Flying*, April 1993, p. 26; M. A. Dornheim, "Stable Growth Ahead for Business Aircraft," *AWST*, March 15, 1993, p. 95.

30. J. Holahan, "Those Airplanes from Israel," *B&CA*, June 1971, p. 41.

31. *Ibid.*; *AWST*, January 18, 1971, p.55; June 7, 1971, p. 50; October 4, 1971, p. 52; December 27, 1971, p.17; September 11, 1972, p. 76; April 30, 1973, p. 100; C. E. Schneider, "1123 Reflects Israel's Market Drive," *AWST*, April 30, 1973, p. 94; *B&CA*, May 1973, p. 49.

32. *FI*, April 11, 1974, p. 452; *AWST*, September 30, 1974, p. 31.

33. D. A. Brown, "Westwind Designed to Competitive Goals," *AWST*, March 1, 1976, p. 62.

34. *Ibid.*; D. A. Brown, "Westwind Shows Higher Performance," *AWST*, September 20, 1976, p. 54; *B&CA*, March 1976, p. 41; November 1976, p. 43.

35. R. N. Aarons, "Operator Survey: 1124 Westwind," *B&CA*, July 1978, p. 58; *AWST*, March 1, 1976, p. 63; July 11, 1977, p. 9; June 5, 1978, p. 107; *FI*, August 12, 1978, p. 464.

36. *AWST*, September 18, 1978, p. 14; October 1, 1979, p. 16; January 21, 1980, p. 13; October 13, 1980, p. 9.

37. As quoted by D. M. North, "Further Industry Growth Forecast," *AWST*, March 3, 1980, p. 215; See also D. M. North, "Westwind 2 Offers Increase in Range," *AWST*, January 25, 1982, p. 74; *FI*, July 26, 1980, p. 235.

38. *FI*, October 26, 1985, p. 13.

39. D. M. North, "Convention Reflects Belt Tightening," *AWST*, October 13, 1980, p. 40; "IAI Introduces Astra, Westwind Sales Rise," *AWST*, April 20, 1981, p. 55; D. A. Brown, "Israel May Advance Astra Certification," *AWST*, September 19, 1983, p. 63; *AWST*, October 25, 1982, p. 13; February 28, 1983, p. 65; September 5, 1983, p. 28; September 12, 1983, p. 33; *B&CA*, April 1982, p. 110; April 1983, p. 78; G. A. Gilbert, "Status Report: IAI Astra," *B&CA*, October 1983, p. 114; Ian Goold, "IAI Rolls Out the Astra," *FI*, September 3, 1983, p. 641.

40. *AWST*, March 26, 1984, p. 27; December 2, 1985, p. 50; *Jane's All the World's Aircraft*, 1987-88, p. 150; J. W. Olcott, "Inflight Report: The IAI Astra," *B&CA*, September 1985, p. 68.

41. J. W. Olcott, "B/CA Analysis: IAI's Astra," *B&CA* August 1987, p. 40; J. Marsden, "Israel's Astra," *FI*, January 5, 1985, p. 22; H. Hopkins, "Star in the Making," *FI*, September 7, 1985, p. 23.

42. *B&CA*, November 1989, p. 62; *AWST*, October 16, 1989, p. 42; E. H. Phillips, "Astra Jet Corp. to Implement Total Support Program Next Year," *AWST*, October 15, 1990, p. 101.

43. E. H. Phillips, "Business Aviation Industry Poised for New Era of Growth," *AWST*, October 28, 1991, p. 36; *B&CA*, May 1993, p. 119.

44. *B&CA*, January 1971, p. 36; *AWST*, December 15, 1969, p. 26; May 3, 1971, p.61; E. J. Bulban, "HS-125 Paves Way for Beech Expansion," *AWST*, January 5, 1970, p. 21.

45. *AWST*, May 31, 1971, p. 215.

46. J. Holstreet, "What Has Beech Done to the DH 125?," *B&CA*, March 1972, p. 40; J. Fricker, "At Long Last the Dash 600," *B&CA*, September 1972, p. 46;

AWST, June 19, 1972, p. 9; September 4, 1972, p. 16; October 23, 1972, p. 22; H. J. Coleman, "New Version of HS-125 Offers Improved Handling Qualities," *AWST*, August 14, 1972, p. 50; H. Field, "Extended Executive," *FI*, August 24, 1972, p. 273.

47. *AWST*, September 24, 1973, pp. 36, 37, 64; *B&CA*, August 1973, p. 42.

48. *AWST*, July 14, 1975, p. 22; *FI*, November 20, 1975, p. 755.

49. *FI*, May 22, 1976, p. 1346; June 26, 1976, p. 1695; *B&CA*, September 1976, p. 131; *AWST*, May 17, 1976, p. 23; September 13, 1976, p. 53.

50. *FI*, May 14, 1977, p. 1314; November 14, 1981, p. 1482; *B&CA*, May 1977, p. 45; *AWST*, June 13, 1977, p. 11; July 24, 1978, p. 67; August 28, 1978, p. 9; November 5, 1979, p. 13; June 22, 1981, p. 91; D. M. North, "TFE731 Boosts HS.125 Performance," *AWST*, January 27, 1978, p. 61; R. N. Aarons and J. W. Olcott, "B/CA Analysis: British Aerospace HS 125-700," *B&CA*, October 1980, p. 51.

51. *Jane's All the World's Aircraft*, 1987-88, p. 294; D. Velupillai, "125-800: Coast-to-Coast Flier," *FI*, June 4, 1983, p. 1680; *AWST*, May 30, 1983, p. 56; D. A. Brown, "HS 125-800 Enters Flight Test Phase," *AWST*, June 6, 1983, p. 91; G. C. Larson, "British Aerospace 800: Heavy Competition," *B&CA*, July 1983, p. 72; "The First All-Digital Business Jet," *B&CA*, February 1985, p. 47; R. L. Parrish, "Operator Survey: BAe 125-800," *B&CA*, December 1985, p. 52; J. W. Olcott, "BAe 800," *B&CA*, December 1988, p. 63; *FI*, January 25, 1986, p. 12; July 23, 1988, p. 4; J. MacMcClelland, "Best Seller: BAe 800," Flying, November 1988, p. 28.

52. A. Winn, "BAe 1000; Business Airliner," *FI*, October 7, 1989, p. 32; J. Fricker, "BAe 1000; The Ultimate 125," *B&CA*, October 1989, p. 96; *B&CA*, May 1990, p. 112; Flying, July 16, 1990, p. 25; *AWST*, October 1, 1990, p. 41.

53. R. N. Aarons, "BAe 1000," *B&CA*, October 1991, p. 104; *AWST*, October 8, 1990, p. 83; E. H. Phillips, "BAe 125-1000 Nears End of Flight Tests; Certification, Deliveries Planned for Fall," *AWST*, September 9, 1991, p. 79.

54. E. H. Phillips, "Range, Cabin put BAe 1000 in Intercontinental Class," *AWST*, June 15, 1992.

55. *AWST*, April 20, 1992, p. 66; *B&CA*, April 1992, p. 47; *B&CA*, June 1992, p. 22; *B&CA*, November 1992, p. 26; *Flying*, April 1992, p. 30; D. M. North and C. A. Shifrin, "Raytheon Acquires BAE Corporate Jets," *AWST*, June 7, 1993, p. 46.

56. *AWST*, January 18, 1971, p. 55; March 8, 1971, p. 146; April 19, 1971, p. 49; May 31, 1971, p. 224; November 1, 1971, p. 17; H. D. Kysor, "Six Roads to Business Aviation," *B&CA*, January 1971, p. 44; H. Field, "Masterly Mystere," *FI*, February 24, 1972, p. 298.

57. *B&CA*, January 1972, p. 29; G. Eremea, "Dassault Falcon 10," *B&CA*, September 1971, p. 56; May 31, 1971, p. 228; June 14, 1971, p. 73; November 1, 1971, p. 17.

58. *AWST*, October 16, 1972, p. 23; November 6, 1972, pp. 23, 36; April 2, 1973, p. 71; June 25, 1973, p. 62; September 10, 1973, p. 23.

59. J. Salerno and R. N. Aarons, "Operator Survey: Falcon 10 and 20," *B&CA*, June 1981, p. 59; R. N. Aarons, "Status Report: On the Drawing Boards and in the Flight Test Hanger," *B&CA*, September 1981, p. 74; *FI*, November 14, 1981, p. 1482.

60. *AWST*, May 31, 1976, p. 56; January 17, 1977, pp. 11, 26; *B&CA*, October 1976, p. 22; February 1977, p. 19; *FI*, January 15, 1977, p. 104; January 29, 1977, editorial page.

61. *Jane's All the World's Aircraft*, 1987-88; D. M. North, "Sales recovery Forecast for Turbofans," *AWST*, August 10, 1981, p. 75; *AWST*, January 11, 1982, p. 26.

62. *AWST*, January 31, 1983, p. 22; H. Hopkins, "F200 Sets High Standard," *FI*, September 24, 1983, p. 820.

63. *AWST*, March 16, 1987, p. 28; September 14, 1987, p. 17; October 9, 1989, p. 37; October 30, 1989, p. 30.

64. *AWST*, June 8, 1992, p. 38; *B&CA*, May 1991, p. 109.

65. G. Sedbon, "Dassault Prepares for Falcon 2000 Debut," *FI*, December 23, 1992 - January 5, 1993, p. 17; *Flying*, October 1992, p. 32; *B&CA*, September 1992, p. 71; G. Sedbon, "Falcon 2000 to Fly in March," *FI*, February 17-23, 1993, p. 18; M. A. Dornheim, "Dassault's Falcon 2000: New Big Cabin Twinjet," *AWST*, March 29, 1993, p. 42; *FI*, March 10-16, 1993, p. 5; *B&CA*, April 1993, pp. 22, 36; J. MacMcClelland, "Falcon 2000 Rolls Out on Schedule," *Flying*, May 1993, p. 82.

66. R. L. Parrish, "731 Falcon 20," *B&CA*, August 1992, p. 42.

67. *AWST*, March 19, 1973, p. 87.

68. E. J. Bulban, "NBAA Show Stresses New Technology," *AWST*, September 20, 1976, p. 28; *B&CA*, November 1976, p. 120.

69. *B&CA*, September 1978, p. 55; April 1979, p. 88; *AWST*, September 11, 1978, p. 47; March 26, 1979, p. 60; D. M. North, "General Aviation Deliveries Hit Peak," *AWST*, September 18, 1978, p. 17; "General Aviation Sales to Grow," *AWST*, March 12, 1979, p.188; "Corporate Orders Set Records," *AWST*, September 24, 1979, p. 42; *FI*, October 13, 1979, p. 1219; *Jane's All the World's Aircraft*, 1987-88, p. 404.

70. *AWST*, July 7, 1980, p. 24; D. M. North, "Cessna Modifying Design of Citation 3," *AWST*, July 14, 1980, p. 105; "Cessna Predicts Sales Increase,"

AWST, November 10, 1980, p. 61; J. W. Olcott and J. MacMcClelland, "Status Report: Cessna Citation III," *B&CA*, January 1980, p. 39.

71. *AWST*, June 29, 1981, p. 23; July 12, 1982, p. 15; September 20, 1982, p. 24; October 4, 1982, p.23; January 31, 1983, p. 26; September 23, 1985, p. 59; D. M. North, "Citation 3 Marks New Design Approach," *AWST*, June 13, 1983, p. 91; G. C. Larson, "Reflections," *B&CA*, September 1982, p. 50.

72. J. W. Olcott, "B/CA Analysis: Cessna Citation III" *B&CA*, July 1983, p.40; *FI*, April 23, 1983, p. 1105.

73. R. N. Aarons, "Cessna's Citation II and S/II and III in Head-to-Head Competition," *B&CA*, October 1986, p.50; *AWST*, September 23, 1985, p. 59; R. L. Parrish, "B/CA Operator Survey: Cessna Citation III," *B&CA*, November 1987, p. 40.

74. *FI*, June 18, 1988, p. 11; June 24, 1989, p 45; A. Postlewaite, "Citation's New Page," *FI*, October 8, 1988, p. 21; R. N. Aarons, "Cessna's New Citation V," *B&CA*, May 1988, p. 52; "Cessna's Citation V," *B&CA*, July 1989, p. 49; "Cessna's Enhanced Citation III, *B&CA*, January 1990, p.42; E. H. Phillips, "New Derivative Aircraft Enhance Upbeat Atmosphere at Exhibition," *AWST*, October 90, 1989, p. 36.

75. Roy H. Norris, Senior Vice President, Cessna Aircraft, as quoted by *AWST*, May 7, 1990, p. 31.

76. E. H. Phillips, "Optimism, Jet Debuts Dominate Annual Convention of NBAA," *AWST*, October 8, 1990, p. 78; *B&CA*, April 1992, p. 30; R. N. Aarons, "Cessna Citation VII," *B&CA*, July 1992, p. 48; *B&CA*, May 1993, p. 83.

77. *Flying*, May 1991, p. 16; N. Moll, "Citation X is a 10," Flying, June 1991, p. 106; E. H. Phillips, 'Business Aviation Industry Poised for New Era of Growth," *AWST*, October 28, 1991, p. 38; E. H. Phillips, "CitationJet Nears Certification: Prototype Citation 10 to Fly Next Year," *AWST*, September 21, 1992, p. 45; *B&CA*, June 1992, p. 20; *B&CA*, July 1992, p. 36; *AWST*, March 29, 1993, p. 43.

78. "Cessna Officials Expect No Changes After Acquisition by Textron Corp.," *AWST*, January 27, 1992, p. 36; *B&CA*, March 1992, p. 19; *B&CA*, June 1993, p. 36.

79. *Jane's All the World's Aircraft*, 1987-88, p. 181; J. W. Olcott, R. Parrish and R. N. Aarons, "B/CA Analysis: Mitsubishi's Diamond I," *B&CA*, September 1982, p. 54.

80. *AWST*, August 7, 1978, p. 18; March 10, 1979, p. 65; *FI*, August 12, 1978, 464; *B&CA*, October 1979, p. 21; W. Goodman, "Diamond I Debut," *FI*, September 8, 1979, p. 764; D. M. North, "General Aviation Imports Grow in the U.S."*AWST*, June 11, 1979, p.164.

81. *AWST*, February 5, 1979, p. 5; June 2, 1980, p. 22; August 25, 1980, p. 11; May 25, 1981, p. 25; June 1, 1981, p. 25; August 3, 1981, p.78; August 10, 1981, p. 77; May 24, 1982, p. 24; D. M. North, "Diamond I Performance Matches Goals," *AWST*, September 6, 1982, p. 222; "GAMA Forecasts Slight Delivery Gain," *AWST*, January 31, 1983, p. 67; J. W. Olcott, R. Parrish and R. N. Aarons, "B/CA Analysis: Mitsubishi Diamond I," *B&CA*, September 1982, p. 54; *FI*, August 11, 1980, p. 1787; R. Whitaker, "Diamond I: Mitsubishi's First Business Jet," *FI*, July 18, 1981, p. 163; H. Hopkins, "Diamond I Flight Test," *FI*, November 13, 1982, p. 1441.

82. D. M. North, "Business Flying Outlook Turns Upward," *AWST*, March 14, 1983, p. 243; *AWST*, October 24, 1983, p. 62; *B&CA*, April 1984, p. 83; J. W. Olcott and R. N. Aarons, "B/CA Analysis: Mitsubishi Diamond IA," *B&CA*, July 1984, p. 82.

83. *AWST*, May 14, 1984, p. 58; May 27, 1985, p. 109; J. W. Olcott and R. N. Aarons, "B/CA Analysis: Mitsubishi Diamond II," *B&CA*, January 1985, p. 48.

84. *FI*, December 4, 1985, p. 14; *AWST*, December 9, 1985, p. 26; February 3, 1986, p. 61; April 14, 1986, p. 13; May 12, 1986, p. 26; P. Proctor, "Beech Prepares to Transfer Mitsubishi's Diamond Assembly to Wichita Facility," *AWST*, December 16, 1985, p. 22.

85. D. M. North, "Higher Thrust Turbofans, New Interior Mark Beechjet Executive Aircraft," *AWST*, August 11, 1986, p. 48; *AWST*, August 11, 1986, p. 51; J. W. Olcott, "Inflight Report: Beechjet 400," *B&CA*, August 1986, p. 44; R. Blech, "Beechjet 400 — The Diamond's New Setting," *FI*, May 30, 1987, p. 21.

86. F. George, "Beechjet 400," *B&CA*, March 1989, p. 44; J. W. Olcott, "B/CA Analysis: Beechjet 400A," *B&CA*, June 1991, p. 50; *AWST*, April 2, 1990, p. 48; E. H. Phillips, "Economic Concerns Threaten Growth of Corporate Aviation," *AWST*, October 1, 1990, p. 40; J. MacMcClelland, "The Beechjet 400A at Home in America," *Flying*, July 1991, p. 62; E. H. Phillips, "400A Offers Sophistication of Larger, Costlier Aircraft," *AWST*, August 10, 1992, p. 50.

Chapter Seven

Schumpeterian Rivalry and the Market for Business Jets

Introduction

We have been looking in some detail at the development of the market for business jet aircraft. Throughout, the emphasis has been on the nature of the rivalry among the suppliers of those aircraft — on "competition from the new [airplane], the new technology, the new [entrant], the new type of organization."[1] Virtually no attention has been given to the standard "structure-conduct-performance" paradigm of industrial organization economics. In market circumstances such as those portrayed in the past chapters, we find little sense in exploring how market structure may have influenced the conduct and performance of the firms in the industry. Where progressing sciences offer continuing opportunities for changes in valuable product characteristics, the predominant influences run in the opposite direction. The conduct of firms — conduct with respect to R&D, product and process innovations and marketing — largely determines their relative achievements. The structure of the market and changes in that structure reflect hardly more than the consequences of the varying patterns of achievements as first one and then another in a series of new products are offered.[2]

Table 7-1 shows how the United States and worldwide fleet of business jets has grown since the first Lockheed JetStar was delivered in 1961. By the end of 1992, there were 7,128 business jets licensed for use in the world, with 4,545 (63.8%) of them licensed in the United States. Cessna Citations, which entered service in 1971, accounted for over 27% of the worldwide total and about 26% of the U.S. total. Learjets are the second most frequently owned planes, constituting over 20% of the world fleet and 20% of the U.S. fleet. The Dassault Falcon and the BAe/Hawker-Siddeley series follow. In addition to the bizjets shown in Table 7-1, there were 207 jet airliners in use by businesses around the world, including 10 Boeing 747s, 21 Boeing 707s, 60 Boeing 727s, and 27 Boeing 737s.

193

Table 7-1
United States and World Fleet of Business Jet Aircraft,
December 1992

Type	United States	Rest of World	Total
BAe/HS-125 Series			
125-1/3	58	49	107
125-400	54	36	90
125-600	26	37	63
125-700	139	66	205
125-800	144	82	226
1000	12	12	24
BAe/HS Totals	433	282	715
Beechjet/Diamond Series			
I, IA	72	18	90
II	4	0	4
400, 400A	70	40	110
Beechjet/Diamond Totals	146	58	204
Challenger Series			
600	52	18	70
601, 601-3A	124	51	175
Challenger Totals	176	69	245

Source: AvData,Inc., as reported in *Flight International*, April 7-13,1993, p. 34

Table 7-1 (continued) United States and World Fleet of Business Jet Aircraft, December 1992			
Type	United States	Rest of World	Total
Citation Series			
Citation, Citation I	166	207	373
Citation I/SP	208	85	293
Citation II, S/II	441	288	729
Citation II/SP	52	39	91
Citation V	137	73	210
Citation III, VI, VII	175	67	242
CitationJet	5	0	5
Citation Totals	1184	759	1943
Falcon Series			
Falcon 10, 100	105	105	210
Falcon 20, 200	178	208	386
Falcon 50	132	94	226
Falcon 900, 900B	54	67	121
Falcon Totals	469	474	943
Gulfstream Series			
G-II, IIB	199	47	246
G-III	127	52	179
G-IV	138	59	197
Gulfstream Totals	464	158	622

Table 7-1 (continued) United States and World Fleet of Business Jet Aircraft, December 1992			
Type	United States	Rest of World	Total
Jet Commander/IAI Series			
1123,1123B	77	13	90
Westwind 1123	20	6	26
Westwind 1124, II	201	53	254
Astra, Astra SP	46	10	56
Jet Commander/IAI Totals	344	82	426
Learjet Series			
23, 24, 25	413	188	601
28, 29	3	6	9
31	29	30	59
35,36	391	232	623
55	98	46	144
60	1	0	1
Learjet Totals	935	502	1437
Lockheed JetStar Series			
6, 8	21	19	40
II	25	12	37
TFE731	40	15	55
Lockheed JetStar Totals	86	46	132

Table 7-1 (continued) United States and World Fleet of Business Jet Aircraft, December 1992			
Type	United States	Rest of World	Total
Sabreliner Series			
40, 40A	77	28	105
50	1	0	1
60	80	48	128
65	68	8	76
75,75A	43	21	64
80A	7	1	8
Sabreliner Totals	276	106	382
Other			
Corvette 600/601	1	32	33
HFB-320	10	11	21
MS-760	17	3	20
PD.808	0	1	1
SJ-30	1	0	1
North American T-39	3	0	3
Other Totals	32	47	79
Overall Total	4545	2583	7128

Technological Opportunities, Innovations and Market Structure

Table 7-2 summarizes the changes that have occurred in the market shares of the firms selling business jets in the U. S. market from 1961 through 1991. The shares are measured in terms of both the number and the value of business jets delivered in particular years. Deliveries of bizjet aircraft to the U.S. government as well as to private buyers are included in Table 7-2. Sales of planes designed primarily for airline use are not included.

The table lists all of the companies that have delivered business jets in the U.S. market, grouped by the families of aircraft associated with their names. For example, the third listed supplier is shown as "Lear Jet/Gates Learjet." The delivery data pertain to all Lear Jets/Learjets. The next manufacturer is "Aero Commander/Rockwell/Israel Aircraft Industries," with the data covering Jet Commanders, Commodore Jets, Westwinds and Astras. The ordering of the firms is based on the date of first delivery, beginning with the 1960 deliveries of Sabreliners (T-39s) by North American to the U.S. government and the 1961 entry of Lockheed. The data are aggregated into successive three-year periods thereafter. The three-year periods are used to smooth out abrupt year-to-year changes as well as to abbreviate the presentation. In addition to the percentage shares, Herfindahl Indexes for each of these distributions and the total number and value of the deliveries are given.

A Herfindahl Index (HI) is the sum of the squares of each of the percentages in a distribution adding to 100 percent. It is a measure of market concentration that reflects both the number and the size distribution of the firms. If only one firm supplies an entire market, the HI = 100 x 100 = 10,000. As the number of supplying firms increases and as the percentage of sales of each falls, the HI falls, approaching zero as a limit. Thus, the HI with 10 firms each of which supplies 10 percent of the total is (10 x 10) x 10 = 1,000; with 100 equal-sized firms, the HI = (1 x 1) x 100 = 100; with 1,000 equal-sized firms, the HI = (0.1 x 0.1) x 1,000 = 10.

The greater the variance in sizes, the larger is the HI. Thus, if there were 10 supplying firms, with one producing 55 percent of the total and the other nine accounting for 5 percent each, the HI = (55 x 55) + (5 x 5)(9) = 3,250. That is, when one (or a small number) of the firms produces the bulk

Table 7-2

Percentage Distribution of the Number and Value of Business Jets Delivered in the United States, 1961-1991 with Herfindahl Indexes

Manufacturer	1960		1961		1962-1964		1965-1967	
	% of Aircraft	% of Value	% of Aircraft	% of Value	% of Aircraft	% of Value	% of Aircraft	% of Value
North American/ Rockwell/Sabreliner	100.0	100.0	71.7	62.0	82.1	77.8	14.8	14.9
Lockheed	—	—	28.3	38.0	14.6	20.3	10.8	19.0
Lear Jet/Gates Learjet	—	—	—	—	1.4	0.7	25.6	18.6
Aero Commander/Rockwell/ Israel Aircraft Industries	—	—	—	—	0.5	0.3	20.3	14.4
Hawker-Siddeley/ British Aerospace	—	—	—	—	1.4	1.0	11.8	10.4
Dassault/Dassault-Breguet	—	—	—	—	—	—	16.3	21.6
Grumman/Gulfstream American/Gulfstream Aerospace	—	—	—	—	—	—	0.3	1.0
Hamburger Flugzeugbau	—	—	—	—	—	—	—	—
Cessna	—	—	—	—	—	—	—	—
Canadair	—	—	—	—	—	—	—	—
Mitsubishi/Beech Aircraft	—	—	—	—	—	—	—	—
TOTAL*	100.0	100.0	100.0	100.0	100.0	100.0	100.0	100.0
Herfindahl Indexes	10000.0	10000.0	5941.8	5288.0	6957.7	6466.5	1808.2	1712.1
Total Number of Business Jets Delivered in U. S.	15		46		212		508	
Total Value of Business Jets Delivered in U.S. (millions)	$4.5		$47.9		$226.7		$489.7	

* Totals in some columns are rounded to reach 100 percent

Source: AvData, Inc.; *Business and Commercial Aviation; Aviation Week and Space Technology.*

Table 7-2 (continued)

Percentage Distribution of the Number and Value of Business Jets
Delivered in the United States, 1961-1991 with Herfindahl Indexes

Manufacturer	1968-1970		1971-1973		1974-1976		1977-1979	
	% of Aircraft	% of Value	% of Aircraft	% of Value	% of Aircraft	% of Value	% of Aircraft	% of Value
North American/ Rockwell/Sabreliner	12.0	10.0	11.6	10.7	13.9	16.4	6.4	6.5
Lockheed	6.1	7.7	5.6	7.3	0.6	1.7	3.8	8.1
Lear Jet/Gates Learjet	29.0	15.9	20.6	14.2	27.2	21.2	30.8	23.2
Aero Commander/Rockwell/ Israel Aircraft Industries	5.0	2.5	5.1	3.5	4.2	3.8	8.2	7.5
Hawker-Siddeley/ British Aerospace	12.7	8.4	6.5	6.2	4.2	4.7	7.1	10.0
Dassault/Dassault-Breguet	12.0	13.3	13.8	15.5	15.0	17.6	10.3	11.6
Grumman/Gulfstream American/Gulfstream Aerospace	21.0	41.1	10.5	28.8	6.9	20.9	5.8	15.6
Hamburger Flugzeugbau	2.1	1.2	1.1	0.8	—	—	—	—
Cessna	—	—	25.1	13.2	27.9	13.6	27.6	17.5
Canadair	—	—	—	—	—	—	—	—
Mitsubishi/Beech Aircraft	—	—	—	—	—	—	—	—
TOTAL	100.0	100.0	100.0	100.0	100.0	100.0	100.0	100.0
Herfindahl Indexes	1797.9	2356.5	1590.4	1664.7	2019.7	1689.4	2023.2	1486.5
Total Number of Business Jets Delivered in U. S.	424		354		519		720	
Total Value of Business Jets Delivered in U.S. (millions)	$621.4		$482.1		$869.5		$1,779.1	

Table 7-2 (continued)

Percentage Distribution of the Number and Value of Business Jets Delivered in the United States, 1961-1991 with Herfindahl Indexes

Manufacturer	1980-1982		1983-1985		1986-1988		1989-1991	
	% of Aircraft	% of Value	% of Aircraft	% of Value	% of Aircraft	% of Value	% of Aircraft	% of Value
North American/ Rockwell/Sabreliner	6.4	7.4	—	—	—	—	—	—
Lockheed	—	—	—	—	—	—	—	—
Lear Jet/Gates Learjet	23.8	18.3	15.5	11.1	4.6	2.2	6.4	2.9
Aero Commander/Rockwell/ Israel Aircraft Industries	8.0	6.6	7.8	5.1	6.2	3.4	5.5	3.7
Hawker-Siddeley/ British Aerospace	5.8	7.3	7.4	7.5	12.7	10.7	8.3	7.5
Dassault/Dassault-Breguet	10.4	16.7	10.2	13.5	15.7	22.7	7.5	12.4
Grumman/Gulfstream American/Gulfstream Aerospace	5.1	13.6	9.4	24.5	16.8	32.6	15.0	34.2
Hamburger Flugzeugbau	—	—	—	—	—	—	—	—
Cessna	33.8	18.1	33.1	20.8	29.7	15.1	40.7	19.7
Canadair	4.5	10.8	7.7	13.6	6.9	10.2	10.8	17.0
Mitsubishi/Beech Aircraft	2.2	1.1	8.8	3.8	7.3	3.1	5.8	2.7
TOTAL	100.0	100.0	100.0	100.0	100.0	100.0	100.0	100.0
Herfindahl Indexes	2,006.7	1,395.8	1,780.6	1,620.0	1,732.6	2,050.6	2,228.1	2,086.1
Total Number of Business Jets Delivered in U.S.	1,013		625		434		361	
Total Value of Business Jets Delivered in U.S. (millions)	$4,380.3		$3,066.5		$3,750.8		$3,596.3	

of the total, the HI will be relatively high even though there is a large number of firms overall.[3]

Table 7-2 shows the HI for both the number and value of U.S. deliveries at 10,000 in 1960 when North American was the only supplier. All five of North American's deliveries that year were to the U.S. Air Force. In 1961, North American continued to supply only the military. Lockheed shipped all but two of its planes to private purchasers. During the triennium 1962-1964, Lear Jet, Hawker-Siddeley and Aero Commander began deliveries of Lear Jets, HS-125s and Jet Commanders. U.S deliveries reached 212, an average of 70.7 per year. Of the 212, only 44 were to private buyers. North American, based in large part on its continuing shipments to the Air Force, had 82.1% of the number and 77.8% of the value of deliveries in those years. About half of Lockheed's U.S. deliveries were to private customers. While Lockheed was the second largest shipper, it accounted for only 14.6% of the number and 20.3% of the value of total U.S. deliveries. Lear Jet, Aero Commander and Hawker-Siddeley began deliveries in 1964 and necessarily realized small shares for the full 1962-1964 triennium.

When it elected to sell Sabreliners to business customers in 1963, North American, it will be recalled, forecast "a commercial market of about 300 aircraft during the next 8-10 years . . . and that for the next two years the Sabreliner and Lockheed's JetStar [would] have the field to themselves."[4] That estimate of the size of the market proved very conservative. A total of 508 business jets were delivered in 1965-1967 alone. North American's view of the exclusive positions of the Sabreliner and the JetStar was also wrong, however. Lear Jet, Aero Commander and Hawker-Siddeley quickly eroded the North American-Lockheed duopoly. Lear alone had 25.6% of the number and 18.6% of the value of deliveries in 1965-1967. The Lear name — due perhaps as much to the personality of William Lear as to the plane itself — quickly became an almost generic designation for a business jet. Aero Commander, in what proved to be but a surge covering its initial order backlog, sold more business jets than did either Lockheed or North American in these three years.

Dassault began U.S deliveries in 1965 and it, too, outsold North American and Lockheed in the 1965-1967 years. Grumman entered with the

Gulfstream II, although that plane reached the market only at the very end of the period. Lockheed's total deliveries did not decrease absolutely, but its share fell to 10.8% of the number and 19.0% of the value of U.S. deliveries in 1965-1967. It delivered a smaller number of business jets in that triennium than did any other firm save the late-entering Grumman. North American (Rockwell International by 1968) was fourth in number of planes delivered, with only 14.8%. Unlike Lockheed and North American, Lear Jet and Dassault were openly exploring new and improved airplanes even as their first models were being delivered.

Table 7-2 shows that Lockheed and Rockwell International/ Sabreliner experienced generally decreasing shares after the mid-1960s. This was not a matter of simple arithmetic, where increasing numbers of sellers and an expanding market necessarily implied lower shares for incumbents. Lockheed and Rockwell International/Sabreliner were losing sales absolutely as well as relatively after 1968. Lockheed delivered no JetStars after the 1977-1979 period. Sabreliner dropped out after 1981. Gates Learjet had 29.0% of the number and 15.9% of the value of deliveries in the 1968-1970 years. After a slight decline in 1971-1973, these shares reached 30.8% and 23.2% in 1977-1979. But Gates Learjet did not sustain this commanding position. Its shares fell sharply after 1977-1979, accounting for only 2.2% and 2.9% of the value of U.S. deliveries in 1986-1988 and 1989-1991, respectively.

Dassault's shares remained relatively high and stable until the 1989-1991 years. Except for these later years, Dassault's share of the number of planes delivered ranged between 16.6% (1965-1967) and 10.2% (1983-1985). Its share of the value of U.S. deliveries reached 23.1% in 1965-1967 and was down to 11.6% in 1977-79. As late as 1986-1988, however, Dassault was clearly maintaining its market position. Dassault's subsequent decreases in shares in 1989-1991 were sharp, particularly when it is recognized that the total market contracted sharply during that period.

Grumman/Gulfstream American/Gulfstream Aerospace shipped 41.1% of the total value and 21.0% of the total number of U.S. deliveries in the 1968-1970 years. Except for 1974-1976, 1977-1979 and 1980-1982, Gulfstream has quite consistently represented 25% to 30% of the value of all U.S.

deliveries. Its share of the number of planes delivered has been much lower. The Gulfstream aircraft have commanded the highest prices of any business jet. The principal reason for the lower shares in the 1976-1980 period concerns the introduction of the G-III. Gulfstream, it will be recalled, ran into problems with the original version of the G-III, eventually abandoning it in favor of a less technologically advanced model.

Hamburger Flugzeugbau delivered a few HFB 320s in the 1968-1970 and 1971-1973 periods. Cessna entered in 1971 and achieved a 25.1% share of the number and a 13.2% share of the value of U.S. deliveries during its first three years. Unlike most of the other participants in the market, Cessna's shares have shown an almost steady increase since then. Its shares of the number of planes delivered have been much higher than its shares of the value of deliveries. The former came to 27.9%, 27.6%, 33.8%, 33.1%, 29.7% and 40.7% in the successive triennials from 1974-1976 onward. Cessna's shares of the value of deliveries ranged between 13% and 21% in these years. There is no indication as yet that Cessna is losing its market position.

Canadair's shares of both number and value of aircraft delivered have been gradually rising, reaching their highest levels in the 1989-1991 triennium. The new versions of the Challenger are likely to cause Canadair's share to increase further. The shares of Mitsubishi/Beech were at their highest in the 1983-1985 years.

Viewed in terms of the marketwide HIs, no pronounced trend towards either increasing or decreasing concentration is apparent from the data in Table 7-2 after the initial period when Lockheed, North American, Lear, Aero Commander and Hawker-Siddeley, as the first entrants, necessarily were the concentrated few. As others entered, the HI for the number of deliveries fell, reaching a low of 1,542.5 in 1965-67 and, for the years thereafter, a high of 2,228.1 in 1989-1991. The HI for the value of deliveries was at its low, 1,395.8, in 1980-1982. The peak of 2,356.5 in 1968-1970 is attributable to the introduction of the popular and high-priced Gulfstream II in that time frame. The HI for value of deliveries subsequently fell and then rose again to 2,086.1 in 1989-1991.

Even though no major changes have appeared in the HIs for business jets since the late 1960s, the changes in the fortunes of the individual companies weave an important story. While Nelson is correct in his observation that, viewed from the moon, the changes in shares appear to be the result of a stochastic process, our closer examination shows that the process is far from random. The clear lesson is that failure to continue an aggressive R&D program — both in good times and in bad — will result in the eventual loss of market position. Put more succinctly, a continuing R&D program will not ensure success, but the absence of one surely spells failure.

We have noted that Lockheed, after quickly developing the JetStar in Kelly Johnson's Skunk Works, relegated production of the plane to other facilities. Little attention was paid thereafter to further improvements and essentially no attention was paid to expanding the product line into basically new aircraft. Whether this was due to other more pressing problems faced by Lockheed or to poor development strategies, the results were the same. JetStar lost its popularity to subsequent entrants. Later efforts to revitalize the aircraft were of little avail. Lockheed's reputation as a technology leader in business aircraft was lost.

The North American/Sabreliner story differs from that of the JetStar only in degree. Product development was largely restricted to changes in the original Sabreliner. No R&D aimed at a fundamentally new aircraft or at developing a family of aircraft is apparent. Further, the first R&D aimed at significantly changing the Sabreliner started years after its introduction and seemed to lack focus even then. A number of projects were undertaken simultaneously and without mechanisms to sort out the good from the bad. Then, in the mid-1970s, when a major new technology, the NASA supercritical wing, was investigated, Sabreliner went to an external source, Raisbeck, for the work. Sabreliner appears to have retained much the same R&D strategy from 1978 through 1987 despite repeated failures of that strategy to improve the situation.

Lear Jet/Gates Learjet worked successfully during the 1960s and early 1970s on improving its initial aircraft and on expanding its line to somewhat different types of aircraft. It retained a sizable market share until the early 1980s. Gates, like Sabreliner, looked to an outside developer for the NASA supercritical wing technology in the mid-1970s. After 1981, the declining overall market and consequent financial stringencies may have provided good business reasons to slow the development of new versions, but doing so created even bigger problems for Learjet later on. A new model may have been particularly important in the light of the many crashes experienced with the earlier ones. But Gates did not have that new model. The result was a large drop in Gates' market share. Gates recognized this and, particularly after it was acquired by Bombardier in 1990, undertook strenuous efforts to regain its position. These efforts may or may not return Learjet to profitability.

The Jet Commander of Aero Commander/Rockwell reached the market later than had been planned and faced unanticipated and strong rivalry from Lear and Dassault. Post-introduction development efforts produced only modest improvements to the old airframe. A single-product development strategy was followed. Indeed, even Israeli Aircraft Industries worked on the same basic design for several years before a significantly new plane, the Astra, was introduced. IAI's share of the U.S. market has not been very large — considerably less than 10% of the value of shipments and possibly declining.

Hawker-Siddeley/BAe has made near-continuous improvements in the 125 series. We will discuss this further later in this chapter. Hawker-Siddeley/BAe also followed a single-product strategy, but achieved considerable success. Hawker-Siddeley/BAe has kept a 7%-10% share of the value of U.S. shipments since it took over the distribution from Beech. BAe's business jet division was reported to be profitable in 1991 despite the low level of industry sales.[14] Raytheon's 1993 acquisition of the BAe business jet division may result in some coordination between the R&D and marketing policies for the smaller Beechjet and the BAe lines of aircraft.

We have discussed the product strategies of Cessna and Gulfstream in Chapter Four, Five, and Six. The commitment of these companies to continuing development is obvious. Gulfstream has occasionally explored the addition of a mid-sized or small plane to its line, but has never done so. Gulfstream has been bent on supplying a state-of-the-art airplane for just those who want truly "heavy iron." Cessna's strategy has evolved to essentially one of supplying an airplane for every type of buyer save those who want truly "heavy iron."   Each has been inordinately successful in managing technology. Whether they can be profitable in the future remains to be seen.

Another point deserves attention. The change from propeller-driven to jet business aircraft entailed major shifts in technologies. We have seen that the success rate for those attempting to get into the market for business jets has not been high. The only subsequent change that appears to have posed considerable problems was the introduction of the NASA supercritical airfoil technology. Gulfstream encountered major problems with the wing design of the first G-III, however. Dassault had similar problems with the wing of the Falcon 50. Gates Learjet and Sabreliner (with Raisbeck) missed in getting a supercritical wing onto their planes in a timely way. IAI made minor changes in the wings of the Westwinds and introduced derivatives of the NASA wing technology only with the Astra. We have found no indications that Cessna had inordinate difficulties in developing the wing of the Citation III, although the story may simply be unreported.

We mention the development problems associated with the supercritical wing to emphasize again the strong influence on market structure that derives from the varying degrees of success firms experience in their attempts to seize technological opportunities. Even though the adoption of the NASA wing did not weed out old suppliers and create a whole set of new ones, it came near to having that effect. One can envision scenarios with only one of Gulfstream or Dassault in the heavy end of the market and with Canadair — for other reasons — out of it. Yet these scenarios did not transpire.

This pattern of relatively low concentration and changing shares for the individual companies contrasts sharply with that found by Phillips in the market for commercial aircraft between 1932 and 1965.[5] In the case of commercial aircraft, each major change in technology was accompanied by one or two of the participants gaining a dominant share through the life cycle of that technology. Douglas and Lockheed produced nearly all of the piston-engined, long-range aircraft added to the fleets of U.S. trunk carriers between 1934 and 1958. Boeing and Douglas produced nearly all of the long-range jet aircraft added to these fleets from 1959 through 1965. Concentration was always very high during each technological cycle, but there was no assurance that in the next cycle the same firms would continue their dominance.

Nelson and Winter have analyzed the market forces that tend to generate concentration, paying specific attention to Phillips' work.[6] Nelson and Winter suggest that, in a market such as that for commercial aircraft, firms make "draws" on technological opportunities for major changes — for example, from piston-engined to jet aircraft — only rarely. By the time of each such "draw," the latent gains from successful innovation are large. The R&D projects required to get a chance to realize the periodic large successes are very costly, however. Further (and adding a bit to the Nelson and Winter discussion), the firms that elect to enter the game need not do so simultaneously or even by adopting the same R&D strategies. When one of the firms becomes initially successful in one of these infrequent draws, entry by "imitators" producing "look-alike" products becomes unattractive if the followers have also to bear more or less the same high R&D costs as did the initial innovator. Even if that R&D were technologically successful, the followers find that, by the time they are ready to enter imitatively, the leader has already incorporated some less costly but important minor advances that make it more difficult to lure customers away from the first successful (not necessarily the chronological first) mover.

The Phillips and Nelson and Winter analyses are helpful in assessing why the same strong tendencies have not been apparent to date in the market for business jets. Note first, however, that some would regard the market for business jets as being quite concentrated. A market with five firms of equal size has an HI of 2,000, about that of the market for business jets. The Department of Justice (DoJ) and Federal Trade Commission (FTC) classify markets with HIs in excess of 1,800 as "highly concentrated."[7] Markets with HIs between 1,000 and 1,800 are "moderately concentrated," according the DoJ and FTC. Moreover, grouping all of the business jets into a single market for computing the HI surely tends to obfuscate important features of the market. The planes at the "heavy iron" end of the market are not substitutes for those at the low end. There is limited price-based substitutability among even the aircraft in the medium-size group. Buyers have differing performance requirements and, for the most part, restrict their choices to the small number of planes that meet those requirements. Different buyers consider different sets of alternatives, but each is presented with a small number of planes from which to choose. Viewed in this light, there may be less sub-stitutability in the market than the HI measure would suggest.

The tendency towards pronounced concentration in each generation of commercial aircraft was accentuated by factors not included in the earlier Phillips and Nelson and Winter studies. During the period covered, there was a relatively small number of trunk (long-distance) airlines. Four of them ac-counted for a vast preponderance of the acquisitions of new aircraft and they had roughly similar requirements for their heavy-volume trunk traffic. When one of them acquired a new plane that offered distinct performance and cost advantages (relative to planes then in the fleet and relative to other new planes), the other trunk carriers were likely to see much the same advantages from acquiring the same plane. There were, in addition, decreases in costs as-sociated with learning for both the manufacturer and the users as more of that model was produced and put into use. The technologically less pronounced but nonetheless important changes made in the aircraft after introduction were directed in large measure by that learning — and again, the similarity in the uses to which the several carriers put the plane meant that the same sort of changes would be useful to the group of them.

Niche markets for aircraft for carriers with different requirements ex-isted. During the years of the piston-engined planes, Martin and Convair in-troduced smaller, short-range planes with some success. Boeing and Douglas broadened their lines to capture most of the short- and intermediate-ranged jets, however. The tendency for one or two manufacturers to dominate the market was ever apparent.

The structure of buyers for business jets is very different from that for commercial airliners. There are a large number of business buyers, most of whom are likely to purchase only one or, at best, two or three planes of any vintage. In addition, as we have seen, the requirements of these buyers are highly disparate. Some want an airplane to get in and out of the small airports of towns and cities not far distant from one another. Cruise speed and range are of secondary importance. Others want a plane capable of carrying a few people longer distances, with travel time being very important. Yet others want a large plane with an intercontinental range. Some need to operate fre-quently from airports at high elevations and with heavy loads. An airplane that will impress customers with its luxury may be essential for some. For others, the avoidance of such a demonstration may be sought. The mixes of possible requirements are nearly limitless. It is clear that a plane that is nearly ideal for one may be utterly inappropriate for another. Thus, rather than all flocking to one or two aircraft as was the case in the commercial market, different buyers look to distinctly different aircraft to meet their needs. There is room — indeed, there is a <u>demand</u> — for a proliferation of types.

We noted in Chapter Two that, back in 1955-1956, the manufacturers of commercial and military planes saw the definition of a standard business jet as the *sine qua non* for getting such planes to the market. We see now the reason why standards for a common plane were not forthcoming. Buyers did not have common requirements and manufacturers who believed that they did suffered as a consequence. North American and Lockheed appear to have fallen into this category. They neither changed their first offerings nor broadened their lines to capture new buyers — buyers for whom the Sabreliner and JetStar were not attractive. By following this strategy, North American and Lockheed gave up whatever advantages they had gained in getting to the market first. The expansion of the market depended on inducing buyers with mixed preferences to buy new planes that were better in just the dimensions important to them. The market for commercial planes was not at all like this.

The Nelson and Winter simulations do not include the effects of entry on market concentration. In Phillips' empirical study of commercial aircraft, entry played an important role at the points when major new technologies were being introduced, but entry within the life cycles of those major technologies was rare and of little importance. Entry plays a different role in the case of business jets. Much as was the case for commercial planes, the radical innovation — the introduction of business jets — was accomplished by firms which had not previously been producing the earlier generation of business aircraft. In the commercial aircraft market, other firms followed, but then there were exits without offsetting entries. In the market for business jets, exits also followed the initial swarmings. Lockheed and Sabreliner left the market. It is possible that others may follow. New entrants have appeared and stayed, however. Grumman, Cessna, Canadair and Mitsubishi/ Beech came in, countering tendencies for the HIs to go up. Entry continues to be attractive. As of early 1993, Swearingen had developed the SJ30 to the point that entry seemed possible if sound financing and production facilities could be assembled. The Chichester-Miles Leopard and, possibly, a Honda business jet may join the SJ30 in competing against Cessna's new CitationJet at the low end of the market.

New models from existing manufacturers have entry-like effects, too. Bombardier appears to have revitalized Gates Learjet. The Model 31A, Model 45 and Model 60 Learjets may serve to recreate Gates' historic role in the mid-sized field. The Citation X, Cessna's new mid-sized model, is scheduled for first flight in 1993. Dassault's Falcon 2000 is also under development. At the high end, Dassault is developing the Falcon 9000 and Bombardier is committed to a $500 million-$1 billion outlay to bring out its Canadair Global Express replacement for the Canadair 601-3A.[8] In the interim, the 601-3A is being improved. Gulfstream's share at this end of the market is under attack, but it will have its G-V to ward off gains by Dassault and Bombardier. Given this potential for entry and for new models from existing companies, it would be premature to predict that the slight increase in the HIs since 1983-1985 portends a trend.

There is another aspect of market concentration that will deserve attention in the future. With Bombardier's having acquired both Gates Learjet and the Challenger and with Raytheon now owning both Beech and the BAe business jet business, it seems possible that a new ownership structure will emerge. That is, following the early example of Lear and Falcon, and later of Cessna, we may witness the further consolidation of what were previously independent manufacturers into multi-line firms. BAe may now go ahead with its proposed NBJ (new business jet) 45,000-55,000 pound model. The Swearingen SJ30 might go to either Raytheon or Bombardier, adding a low-end business jet to one or the other's offerings. Textron has Cessna and lacks only a heavy-iron business jet. Gulfstream American could conceivably be acquired to fill that void. Falcon already has an alliance with Alenia, but it also lacks a low-end plane. Whether IAI remains in the market will be largely a political decision, not one directed primarily by the market. Given the depressed condition of the overall market since the mid-1980s, further consolidations appear likely.

First-Mover Advantages

Our investigations into the market for business jets yield little to support the hypothesis that being first — whatever that means — confers an advantage. Evidence from the market for business jets is to the contrary. This was the case in the market for commercial aircraft, also. Boeing had the first all-metal, low-wing, monocoque construction, two-engined airliner in the B-247. Douglas' subsequent DC-2 and DC-3 stole the market. De Havilland's Comet was the first jet liner in commercial use, but Boeing later took the primary position in the market. In computers, too, Remington's Univac was first on the market, but the IBM 701, 650 and later models quickly dislodged the Univac. The market position of firms does not determine how technologies are used. Rather, the way technologies are used determines market positions. Market structure is endogenous to the process of Schumpeterian competition.

The first notorious attempt to commercialize a new set of radically different technologies undoubtedly encourages others to consider moves in the same general direction. The more evidence there is that evolving science affords opportunities for commercialization, the more likely it is that entrepreneurs will attempt to seize these opportunities. It is, of course, not inconceivable that the first mover could be so successful that none could or would seek to follow, but we find such a scenario implausible for products such as business jets. So long as the first mover does not preempt access to critical components of the technologies, the more plausible scenarios for products undergoing a series of innovative changes involve sequential learning. The followers learn from the experience of the first mover — learning both what the first mover did right and what the first mover did wrong. This is the swarming process that Schumpeter described in *The Theory of Economic Development.*

We are hardly contending that the first movers never have an advantage. In fact, it is not difficult to imagine cases in which the first mover is bound to win. Suppose, for example, that there is a clear dichotomy between an old process and a new one. That is, once some firm has succeeded in putting the new technology in place, no further improvements are possible. Suppose further that there is learning associated with use of the new process, with costs falling as the amount of usage increases. In these circumstances, the first mover will have clear advantages over subsequent users. Note the differences, however, between the conditions we assumed to guarantee that result and the conditions describing technological change in the market for business jets.

The Overbidding Question

The Schumpeterian entrepreneurs we have covered — corporate and individual — are driven by more than a motive for short-term profits. We see no way to quantify the extent of it, but there can hardly be doubt that the sum of the profits of the principal firms engaged in developing, producing and selling business jets has to this point been negative. The positive profits of Gulfstream, Cessna — and of Gates for a time, Dassault for a time, Lockheed for a time, BAe for a time, North American for a time — must be more than offset by the losses of the many who never succeeded in selling an airplane, by those whose entry was quickly followed by their exit, and by the once-successful participants who fell from the happy circumstance of being profitable.

In this sense, there has been "overbidding" in the market for business jets. Indeed, looking at only the averages, the unbiased, expected value of profits to a typical entrant has been and continues to be negative. The entrepreneurs do not see it that way, however. We have repeatedly seen them making sales projections that have no foundation in reality. Each sees itself as atypical, as being special, as being able to achieve what others cannot. Each feels it can beat the odds, almost as the habitual gambler does. And, while in time most habitual gamblers go broke, there seem to be others ready to take their place at the table. The process goes on.

We have no sense of how long Schumpeterian entrepreneurs will play in what is increasingly recognized to be a negative-sum game. In the case of business jets, the game has been going on for over thirty years and, despite abysmal market conditions and severe rivalry, the firms in the market are continuing to bring out new models, trying to improve sales and better their positions in the market. Attempts to enter continue to be reported. Analysis based on assumptions of rational, profit-maximizing behavior would suggest that some of the existing firms will sooner or later leave the market or be consolidated with other firms if for no reason other than the unavailability of capital.

The analysis would conclude, too, that entrants would be forestalled for the same reason. The structure of the market, one would think, will eventually stabilize, with fewer firms and higher concentration.

The Overall Demand for Business Jets

The size of the overall market has fluctuated enormously since the Sabreliner and JetStar made their appearances in 1960 and 1961. After rising rapidly to a total of 508 U.S. deliveries in 1965-1967, the number shrank to 354 in the 1971-1973 period. This decrease reflected the effects of the 1970-1971 recession and the fact that past order backlogs had been worked off. The market grew again through the 1970s as business conditions improved and new models appeared. U.S. deliveries reached 1,013 in 1980-1982, with 393 being shipped in 1981 alone. Recession hit again in 1982. In the years since then, sales of business jets have continued on a downward trend. The number of deliveries in the 1989-1991 period was about 36% of the number in 1980-1982. Sales remained flat in 1992. No strong revival was then in sight.

The persistent decrease in sales since 1981 has been attributed to a number of factors. Poor business conditions in 1982 and again since 1989 reduced the demand for business jets. The elimination of the investment tax credit in 1986 made aircraft more expensive to buyers and, as discussed below, reduced the incentives of aircraft manufacturers to invest in R&D. Product liability also had dampening effects. By 1985, Cessna reckoned that the cost of product liability insurance amounted to between 10% and 30% of the sales price, depending on the model. Noise-related restrictions were imposed on the operations of business jets at some airports. It has even been suggested that the low airfares charged by airlines have reduced the demand for business jets.[9]

Trajectories: Price and Performance Trends

Other factors were clearly involved in the slowing of demand. One was the fact that, while the new models introduced since 1980 continued to offer improvements in performance, the improvements were seen as modest. Some felt that a "technological plateau" had been reached.[10] In addition, the prices of business jets have increased rapidly. Note that the weighted average value per plane in Table 7-2 was $4.324 million in 1980-1982 and $9.962 million in 1989-1991, an increase of 130%. This 130% includes price increases associated with improvements in old models, higher prices for new and improved models and changes in the mix of aircraft. Care is needed properly to assess both the degree and the effects of these increases.

The *Business and Commercial Aviation* estimates of equipped prices for a Citation II were $2,518,475 in 1981 and $3,300,000 in 1990, an increase of 31%. A Citation III was priced at $4,298,400 in 1981 and at $7,900,000 in 1990, an increase of about 84%. The 1990 model had a new avionics suite and a wider selection of interiors. It was otherwise much the same as the earlier model. In 1981, a Learjet 55 was priced at $3,529,785. In 1990, an improved Learjet 55C had a price of $6,900,000, an increase of 95%. The price of the Falcon 50 was $8,750,000 in 1981 and $12,950,000 in 1990, an increase of 48%. A fully-equipped Gulfstream III cost $11.0 million in 1981. The improved Gulfstream IV of 1990 was priced at $23.5 million, 114% more than the 1981 model. For perspective, the Producer Price Index (PPI) for all commodities increased by 18.7% between 1981 and 1990. This index supposedly measures price change with quality held constant. The PPI for all durable manufactured goods rose by 25.2% between 1981 and 1990. The PPI for aircraft and aircraft equipment increased by 58.5%. There is no PPI for business jets alone. If the quality-constant prices of business jets rose at the same rate as did those for aircraft and aircraft equipment generally, business jet prices still went up by 23% more than did the prices of all durable manufactured goods.

It is impossible to estimate with any precision the extent to which these price increases affected the sales of business jets. Prices had been increasing in the previous decade, too. For example, the price of an equipped Cessna Citation was $695,000 in 1971. The improved Citation I sold for $1,696,000 in 1980, an increase of 144%. A Falcon 20F was priced at $1,650,000 in 1971 and at $4,825,000 in 1980, an increase of 192%. The price of an equipped BH-125-400 was $1,130,000 in 1971 while that of the improved HS-125-700 was $4,540,000 in 1980, and increase of more than 300%. An equipped Learjet 24D came to $798,735 in 1971 and an equipped

24F was $1,975,000 in 1980, 147% more. The PPI for all commodities rose by nearly 136% and that for all durable manufactured goods by 114% in the same period. The PPI for aircraft and aircraft equipment went up by a similar amount, 115%. It seems that the increases in the prices of business jets at least matched those for all aircraft and aircraft equipment.

Why have the prices of new business jets increased so rapidly? One reason is that the new airplanes both cost more to produce and were worth more to buyers than the antecedent models. Whatever the relevance of the price indexes described above may have for the groups of commodities they cover, the observed price increases for business jets may reflect nothing more than general inflation and the costs and value to buyers of the better airplanes.

At the same time that prices have been rising, there has been a pronounced technological trajectory with more than offsetting consequences. Table 7-3 summarizes some of the changes that have occurred in the HS-125 series between 1964 and 1992. Despite the strong outward resemblance of these successive models, it is apparent that the BAe 1000 of 1992 is a very different airplane from the HS-125-3A of 1965. The 1000 has a range nearly three times that of the 3A, cruises considerably faster, is quieter and is far more comfortable. The 1000 also has vastly improved avionics and control systems and, BAe hopes, will require less downtime for routine maintenance and unscheduled repairs. The 125 series is not at all unique: the Falcon, Learjet, Cessna, IAI and Gulfstream series all show much the same sort of improvements.

There is another very important aspect of the technological changes that helps to explain the observed price increases. The BAe 1000 does more than just fly further and faster and provide more comfort than did the earlier 125s. According to our estimates it provides these qualitative improvements at lower operating costs than did its predecessors. As shown in Table 7-4, the BAe 1000, in typical use, will cost about $0.21 per seat mile (1980 dollars). The HS-125-3A cost about $0.50 per seat mile (1980 dollars). Thus, at the same time performance was going up, operating costs were going down. These operating costs include the price paid for the airplane itself, principally in the form of depreciation and insurance charges.

Table 7-3

Changes in Characteristics of the HS-125, 1964 - 1992

Series	Year Introduced	Total Power (lb st)	Cabin Volume (cubic ft)	Maximum Gross Takeoff Weight (lb)	Maximum Range (mi)	Maximum Cruise Speed (mph)	Takeoff Runway Length (ft)	Time to Climb to 35,000 ft (min)
1A	1964	6,230	565	20,000	1,110	457	5,100	28
3A	1965	6,720	565	21,200	1,250	490	4,200	22
400	1968	6,720	565	23,300	1,510	499	4,970	24
600	1972	7,500	604	25,500	1,570	526	5,000	21
700	1977	7,400	604	25,500	2,660	501	5,800	26
800	1984	8,600	604	27,400	3,000	533	4,900	19
1000	1992	10,450	682	31,000	3,685	534	5,590	19

Source: G. C. Larson, "British Aerospace 800: Heavy Competition," *B&CA*, July 1983, p. 72; R. N. Aarons, "BAe 1000," *B&CA*, Otober 1991, p. 104; *AWST*, March 18, 1992, p. 113; *AWST*, Inventory Issues, various years.

Table 7-4 gives estimated operating cost per seat mile for several other business jets. We see that the 125 series is not at all unique. It appears that the CitationJet of 1992 will have operating costs more than 25% below those of the first Citation, even though the price of the CitationJet is several times that of the Citation. The Citation V has estimated operating costs that are about 20% below those of the Citation II. The estimated operating costs of the Falcon 200 are below those of the Falcon 20. The same is true of the Gulfstream IV compared to the Gulfstream II. The estimated operating costs of the Falcon 900 show up as being lower than those of the Falcon 50 (due in part to the fact that the 900 typically carries two more passengers). Thus, the costs of owning and operating a business jet have not been increasing. Prices, viewed in terms of operating costs per seat mile, have in fact been falling, thanks to the artful use of better wings, better engines, better avionics — in general, to improvements that run throughout the whole airplane.

The trend toward lower operating cost <u>and</u> improved performance is the more remarkable when attention is paid to some of the detail. In the case of the BAe 1000, for example, the fuselage was about 3 feet longer than that of the 125-800. If British Aerospace (or operators) had elected to use this space for two more passengers, costs per seat mile would, of course, have decreased far more than they did. Instead, while about 27 inches were added to the length of the cabin, more spacious seating, better galleys, and a better commode were put into the standard design. Fuel capacity, with corresponding weight, was increased to get more range. Thus, a number of the design changes in fact worked against decreases in operating cost per seat mile — and yet these costs did fall. Similar tradeoffs between cost reductions and qualitative performance improvements are involved in the design changes of the other manufacturers, as well. The regression equation on which the data in Table 7-4 are based suggests that operating costs per seat mile have decreased by about 2% per year since 1961 while at the same time, comfort, range and other flight characteristics have improved.

The observed price increases reflect other factors, too. The technological environment may indeed have been more niggardly if, as some feel, a technology plateau has been reached. Without more significant changes in technology, the upfront (and largely sunk) development costs of getting better

Table 7-4 Comparisons of Estimated Total Operating Costs per Seat Mile for Selected Business Jets		
Aircraft	Year Introduced	Estimated Total Operating Costs Per Seat Mile (1980 dollars)
HS-125-3A	1964	$0.50
BAe 1000	1991	$0.21
Citation	1971	$0.30
CitationJet	1992	$0.22
Citation II	1977	$0.23
Citation V	1991	$0.18
Falcon 20	1965	$0.34
Falcon 200	1983	$0.23
Gulfstream II	1967	$0.49
Gulfstream IV	1984	$0.35
Falcon 50	1980	$0.26
Falcon 900	1988	$0.23

Source: Regression equation in Appendix A

performance from the planes were escalating even as anticipated sales volumes were falling. Unit costs were seen to be going up, and this was a condition common to all of the manufacturers. Each perceived — correctly, we think — that the short-term cross-elasticity of demand between its new models and the new models of other manufacturers was low. Morever, the similarity in their cost and demand structures was such that major shifts in relative prices were unlikely. Such changes in price relatives as might occur would reflect differences in development costs associated with differences in the extent of the change from the older to the newer models. That is, the price increases would be greatest where the greatest changes (and highest development costs) were involved. When the improvements are pronounced, however, customers are the more willing to pay the higher prices. The cost increases and the perceived demand conditions led each of the manufacturers to increase prices more or less in proportion to the increases in unit production costs, with hopes that the better airplanes and lower operating costs would make their models sell.

There is another aspect of the cost and revenue structure that made price increases for the new models attractive to the sellers. A decision at one point in time to commit to a new model is made with the recognition that it will be some time in the future before positive returns can possibly be realized. Increases in prices, if they can be made without sacrificing volume appreciably, reduce the time needed to break even. Consider the following example. Assume that a manufacturer anticipates on January 1, 1987, that the development costs for a new model will total $400 million, with $100 million of that in the current year, $150 million in 1988, and $150 million in 1989. In the illustration, assume that deliveries of the new plane will begin on January 1, 1990, with each unit entailing production costs of $8 million. If each plane were sold at $14 million, if 25 could be sold per year, and if the manufacturer reckoned a 10% cost of capital, the break-even point would be realized upon the sale of the 94th plane in September 1993, nearly seven years in the future.[11] As we have seen, a lot can happen in so long a time.

If the same calculations are done assuming a price of $16 million rather than $14 million, the break-even point moves to the delivery of the 67th plane in August 1992, 13 months earlier. An increase in price from $14 to

$16 million, however, could result in sales losses. Even if short-term cross-elasticities between the plane under consideration and substitutes are very low, some losses would be expected in a period as long as that involved here — if the prices of the substitutes did not also increase. If our hypothetical manufacturer recognizes that others in the industry are also developing new planes and that they too envision longer payback periods, some confidence can be placed on an expectation that all of the firms will be pressured to increase prices. Parallel price movements are not likely to result, because different aircraft entail differing R&D costs with differing improvements in performance. Whether our manufacturer eventually realizes profits, of course, depends on whether the development projects, whatever their costs, result in an airplane with such novel performance attributes and operating efficiencies that a sizable niche of buyers is insensitive to the higher price. And therein lies the great risk. It may not work out that way.

Does this mean that the price increases of the 1980s and early 1990s did not contribute to the reduced level of sales? We think not. The typical business customer was far more budget-constrained in 1990 than in 1981. The luxury of a new business jet was less easy to explain to stockholders who were increasingly critical of executive salaries and perquisites. Fleets were sometimes slashed radically in corporate re-structurings, too.[12] These factors, including the criticisms of stockholders and others, may be essentially income effects — effects due to poor business conditions.

Substitution effects were at work, however. One possible substitute for companies already possessing airplanes was to use their present fleets longer. In addition, retrofitted older models, with much the same appearance and performance as the new ones, were available at much lower prices. In fact, sales of used aircraft were flourishing while sales of the new ones fell.[13] In 1986, there were 762 sales of used business jets in the United States. That number reached 892, 928, 587, 700, and 681 in 1987, 1988, 1989, 1990, and 1991, respectively. Thus, we think that the higher prices did have some effect on the sales of new planes.

Government Policies

There have been serious contentions that the policies of the United States have not been favorable to domestic producers of business jets and other types of aircraft. In addition to matters such as tax policy, environmental (including noise) regulations, the system of public education, various regulations covering the workplace and product liability law, it is argued that the U.S lacks an industrial policy favoring the development of new aircraft and, more particularly, that the U.S. government does not subsidize and otherwise support the industry to the same extent that other countries do.[15]

Evidence from the market for business jets does not lead inexorably to the conclusion that the United States is a particularly hostile environment in which to manufacture and sell airplanes. On the one hand, the data in Table 7-2, show that the share of the foreign producers was higher in the 1980s than it had been in the 1960s and 1970s. Foreign manufacturers accounted for slightly more than 22% of the value of deliveries in the U.S. in the years 1968-1976. This share rose to 29.1% in 1977-1979, 41.4% in 1980-1982, 43.5% in 1983-1985, and 47.0% in 1986-1988. It then declined to 40.6% in 1989-1991. On the other hand, the two most successful manufacturers, Gulfstream and Cessna, are U.S.-based companies. Mitsubishi, the Japanese entrant, failed in its attempt to get into the market. Beech was not deterred from taking over from Mitsubishi because of its U.S. home. Under Raytheon's ownership, more of the content of the BAe planes is likely to be built in the United States. Swearingen, a U.S. firm, is currently the strongest potential entrant. The Canadian government certainly rescued Canadair from bankruptcy, but the U.S. government rescued Lockheed. Military work in their respective countries helped Dassault and Hawker-Siddeley enter the market and helped IAI as it took over the Jet Commander line. The same type of work helped North American, Lockheed, Grumman and Cessna to enter. Lear received little direct government support and its weaknesses after the early 1980s can hardly be attributed to the government. Patterns are far from clear.

There have been numerous instances in which foreign governments supported the development and production of particular business jets. We noted in Chapter Three that the Italian government was involved in several of the programs undertaken in that country. None of them was successful. The

French government supported the MS-760 and the Aerospace Corvette SN601. Neither was successful. The German government at least indirectly supported the HFB 320, another plane that failed to gain market acceptance. The Saab 105 entry was supported by the Swedish air force; the Hispano Aviacion HA-230, by the Spanish air force. One would be hard pressed to argue that government involvement in a specific development program provides assurance that a successful airplane will emerge. If anything — considering especially the records of Lear, Cessna and Gulfstream — the weight of the evidence is to the contrary.

At a more general level, the role of government is even more difficult to discern. Over the years, U.S. government-financed R&D and procurement has contributed heavily to the development of business jets and other aircraft — not always to the exclusion of providing benefits to foreign manufacturers as well. The NASA supercritical wing is really an isolated, albeit important, example. An OECD (Organization for Economic Development and Cooperation) study shows that the U.S. government paid directly for 76.2% of the R&D undertaken by U.S. aerospace firms.[16] The governments of Germany, France and the United Kingdom each provided about 62% of the aerospace R&D finding. The Japanese government paid for only 9.3% of aerospace R&D.

One way of looking at such data is to look at the reverse side. That is, one could interpret the data to suggest that, in the U.S., private firms had such weak incentives that they accounted for only 23.8% of aerospace R&D funding. In Japan, private firms found adequate incentives to fund up to 90.7% of that investment. Actually, the high percentage in the U.S. reflects the fact that the military and space programs of that country dominate government-funded aerospace R&D. The "aeronautics" part of NASA (the National Aeronautics and Space Administration) has been a declining part of the program.[17] Thus, U.S. manufacturers of business jets are advantaged by the relatively high U.S. government aerospace R&D only to the extent that there are positive spin-offs from the R&D related to business jets. Construction materials, construction techniques, CAD/CAM programs, engines, avionics — name it — more often than not trace directly or indirectly from military and/or aerospace applications.

As federal and military R&D support in the U.S. has shifted from air-craft to space programs and as support of aircraft has shifted from several small programs to one or a few large ones, firms producing aircraft for other purposes have found a less friendly technological environment from which to draw new concepts and techniques.[18] That U.S. firms are disadvantaged rela-tive to foreign companies is still not clear, however. Indeed, even the deter-mination of what constitutes a "foreign" company or a "foreign" airplane is not without problems. Today's manufacturers are multinational firms, with roots in particular nations due largely to history. And their products derive from various countries. The first BAe's 125s had Rolls Royce Viper engines. Then U.S.-made TFE731 engines were used. The 1000s will have Canadian P&W PW305 engines. The interiors and the avionics are from the U.S., as has been the case from the beginning. The Gulfstream III and IV had Rolls Royce engines, while the G-V will use BMW/Rolls Royce engines. Parts of the G-IV are built in several foreign countries. Virtually all commercial and all business jets are currently equipped with avionics equipment built largely in the United States. Again, the patterns are not clear.

Whatever the evidence from business jets, we think it would be a mis-take to trivialize the importance of taxes, educational programs and other poli-cies and laws to the U.S. industries generally and to aviation and the business jet industry more particularly. Go back again to the illustration we used to show the sensitivity of the break-even point to prices. That example can be amended to show the effects of a 50% R&D tax credit. With all of the origi-nal assumptions, including the $14 million price, a 50% tax credit on the $400 million in development costs would bring the payback point back from the 94th airplane in September 1993 to the 44th airplane in September 1991. The credit can be seen as a device for improving the returns on R&D investments, for reducing risks and, by mitigating somewhat the pressures for price in-creases, for increasing total sales. Recent contributions to the theory of in-ternational trade suggest that such a policy — as part of a nationwide indicative program for industrial priorities — might have an especially strong impact on the comparative advantage of U.S. firms in world markets.[19] We re-frain from arguing that the business jet industry has high priorities in such positive programs for U.S. industrial development, but neither would we now argue to the contrary.

What of Tomorrow?

When Pittsburgh Plate Glass was operating *The Glasshopper*, military jets were flying in large numbers, the Comet, while not successful, had been in operation, and Boeing, Douglas and Lockheed were known to be developing or thinking of developing jet airliners. The technical feasibility of a business jet seemed reasonably certain. Jet technologies were well enough developed so that the military and businesses could meaningfully express a "demand" for a business jet. This demand had by then gone far beyond mere expressions of displeasure with certain attributes of *The Glasshopper*. The performance attributes of business jets could be defined with some precision to compare with those of The Glasshopper and other propeller-driven business aircraft. At the same time, aircraft manufacturers could envision how further to hone available technologies to produce what businesses apparently wanted.

Analogous conditions do not now exist with respect to the next radically new business aircraft. The technologies underlying supersonic flight in the Mach 1.5-Mach 2.5 range are reasonably known. Demand for a supersonic business jet (SSBJ) is not now discernible, however. Transcontinental supersonic flight is impractical because of "profligate fuel use, ozone-depleting emissions, and noise pollution."[20] While transoceanic supersonic travel involves fewer environmental hazards, it suffers from the same high costs. In addition, transoceanic travel constitutes so small a part of total business use as to make questionable the payoff from developing an SSBJ.

Considerable research has been done on SSBJs. We mentioned the Gulfstream/Sukhoi joint venture in Chapter Six. Sukhoi is a manufacturer of supersonic fighter aircraft and the initial plans were for Sukhoi to do the physical development work to Gulfstream's specifications. A source for the $1 billion needed for the project has not been found; Chrysler sold its interests in Gulfstream Aerospace in 1990 when Paulson, disturbed that "an anticipated synergism between the companies never materialized," led a successful effort to take the company private. A project such as the SSBJ would hardly have fit Chrysler's idea of diversifying to spread risks even if it had had that amount of money to invest.

Preliminary specifications for the Gulfstream/Sukhoi SSBJ were for a twin-engined, 8-12 passenger plane capable of a Mach 2.0 cruise at 50,000-60,000 ft and a range of 4,600 miles. The plane was also to be certifiable for flight over land at Mach 1.5 at acceptable noise levels. This joint venture was terminated in 1992. The SSBJ, it was determined, was "not commercially viable." Surveys showed little buyer interest and intractable environmental problems remained. Governmental restrictions on technology sharing also contributed to the difficulties.[21]

A number of other SSBJ projects preceded the Gulfstream/Sukhoi research. We noted in Chapter Three that Ted R. Smith proposed a five-to-six place SSBJ in 1964. Smith thought that his plane could be priced in the $750,000-$1,250,000 range. The plane was not built. Four years later, Edward Swearingen suggested an SSBJ.[22] A British Company, Super Dynamics International, announced its 04-1B Robin SSBJ in 1976.[23] The Robin was to use 2 GEJ97-17 engines, each with 11,750 lb st. The plane was to weigh 52,150 pounds, carry eight passengers, cruise at Mach 2.0, have a range of 3,680 miles and be capable of flying over land without creating objectionable noise. It was said that 38 orders were in hand and that 250 would be in use by 1985. The plane was not built.

Gates Learjet explored the possibility of an SSBJ in 1981.[24] The Gates plane was to carry 10 passengers at a Mach 1.8 cruise speed over a range of 4,600 miles. A price of about $15 million was foreseen. Students at Parks College designed an SSBJ in 1984.[25] Their drawing-board model was a 19-passenger craft with a range of 4,600 miles. The students thought that it would take $1 billion to develop the plane and up to $6.6 million per unit to produce it. BAe considered an SSBJ in 1986.[26] None of these planes came close to even prototype production.

Unless more commercial and/or military vehicles in the Mach 1.5-Mach 2.5 performance class lead the way, we believe that the introduction of a successful SSBJ within the next decade is unlikely. That, of course, does not mean that limited development efforts — exploratory research — on

SSBJs will not continue. In fact, an SSBJ could actually reach the market in that time, but there is substantial risk that it — like the MS-760 of forty years ago — will not embrace the combination of technologies necessary to be a market success.

Models of Mach 2.5-Mach 7.0 aircraft now exist. These are far from commercial use, however. The engines needed to power them and the materials necessary to produce them are in the very early stages of development. Some observers believe that Japanese companies, adopting a long-term R&D strategy, may "leapfrog into the hypersonic aerospace plane market," leaving U.S. and European manufacturers behind.[27]

Research on commercial versions of tilt-rotor and other types of V/STOL aircraft is in the very early stages. It is easy to envision wide business use of a vehicle that does not require large airports and that still flies at high, subsonic speeds. Less easy to envision are the technology paths from where we are today to where we need to be to get such a vehicle. It is a long way off under the best of circumstances and, again, some think that the U.S. is lagging.[28]

This brings us full circle. We saw the important role of the government in the development of the first business jets. The same sort of situation exists in 1993. We are not advocating, but we are calling attention to the essential role that government will have to play if substitutes for today's business jets are to be developed in the near future.[29] Both SST and V/STOL technologies are in such formative stages that private investment is unattractive even if today's Schumpeterian entrepreneurs would like to go ahead. The financial requirements are massive. Incentives are lacking. Technological risks are extreme. Appropriating for private gains the benefits from such huge R&D projects — even if successful — is likely to be all but impossible. We suspect that today's equivalents of *The Glasshopper* will be with us for many years. If there exist major new technologies that provide opportunities to displace the business jet as *The Glasshopper* was displaced, they are not apparent today in the same sense that they were in 1957.

Notes

1. See note 5, Chapter One.

2. F. M. Scherer, "Schumpeter and Plausible Capitalism," *Journal of Economic Literature*, September 1992, p. 1416, provides a review of the evidence relating to the influences of market structure on technology and innovation. The paper barely mentions studies of the influences of technology and innovation on market structure.

3. For detail on the Herfindahl Index, see A. O. Hirschman, "The Paternity of an Index," *American Economic Review*, September 1964, p. 761; M. A. Adelman, "Comment on the 'H' Concentration Measure as a Numbers Equivalent," *Review of Economics and Statistics*, February 1969, p. 99; W. A. Kelly, "A Generalized Interpretation of the Herfindahl Index," *Southern Economic Journal*, July 1981, p. 50.

4. See note 23, Chapter Three.

5. A. Phillips, *Technology and Market Structure*, Lexington, MA.: Lexington Books, 1971.

6. R. R. Nelson and S. G. Winter, "Forces Generating and Limiting Concentration Under Schumpeterian Competition," *Bell Journal of Economics*, Spring 1978, p. 524.

7. U.S. Department of Justice and Federal Trade Commission, *1992 Horizontal Merger Guidelines*, Washington, D.C., 1992. For antitrust purposes, the market might well include certain commercial aircraft as substitutes for "heavy iron" business jets, turboprop aircraft as substitutes for some low-end business jets, and used business jets as substitutes for new ones.

8. D. Hughes, "Bombardier Optimistic Despite Slow RJ Sales," *AWST*, September 28, 1992, p. 42.

9. A. Lewis, "The Lagging Market for Business Jets," *B&CA*, September 1985, p. 153; D. M. North, "First Quarter General Aviation Sales Hit 40-Year Low," *AWST*, April 29, 1985, p. 229; "Business Aircraft Deliveries Still at Record Low," *AWST*, July 29, 1985, p. 61; "Product Liability is Key Problem for General Aviation Companies," *AWST*, May 13, 1985, p. 71; P. Proctor, "U.S. General Aviation Slump Deepens," *AWST*, January 19, 1987, p. 26; E. H. Phillips, "Economic Concerns Threaten Growth of Corporate Aviation," *AWST*, October 1, 1990, p. 40; "Stormy Future in Business Flying," *AWST*, September 21, 1992, p. 40; "Aerospace," Chapter 37, *U.S. Industrial Outlook, 1987*, U.S. Department of Commerce, 1987; *The Competitive Status of the U.S. Civil Aviation Manufacturing Industry*, National Academy of Engineering, Washington, D.C.: National Academy Press, 1985.

10. Lewis, *op. cit.*

11. The break-even point is defined here as the point in the delivery schedule where the present value (as of January 1, 1987) of the streams of future revenues and costs becomes non-negative. The present value was calculated assuming that one-twelfth of the year's total is delivered at the end of each month, with the discount factor expressed as e^{rt}. It is assumed too that full payment is received on delivery and that there are no customer deposits prior to delivery.

12. E. H. Phillips, "Stormy Future in Business Flying," *AWST*, September 21, 1992, p. 40; B. Bryan and J. Helyar, *Barbarians at the Gate: The Fall of RJR Nabisco*, New York: Harper and Row, 1990, especially p. 277.

13. *AWST*, September 29, 1986, p. 93.

14. E. H. Phillips, "British Aerospace to Sell Majority Share in Business Jets, Reorganize U.S. Unit," *AWST*, April 20, 1992, p. 66.

15. See M. Porter, *The Competitive Advantage of Nations*, New York: The Free Press, 1990; G. Dosi, K. Pavitt, and L. Soete, *The Economics of Technical Change and International Trade*, New York: Harvester-Wheatsheaf, 1990; *Technology and Global Industry: Companies and Nations in the World Economy*, Washington: National Academy of Engineering,1987; Gellman Research Associates, *Analysis of Foreign Government Support for Aeronautical Research and Technology Expenditures*, May 1984; *Government Financial Support for Civil Aircraft Research, Technology and Development in Four European Countries*, October 1978; R. S. Gardiner and S. J. Berman, "U.S. Aerospace Industry Dominance Under Siege," *AWST*, October 19, 1992; *FI*, October 26, 1985, p. 13; *Aeronautical Technologies for the Twenty-First Century*, National Research Council, Washington, 1992; A. Phillips, "Changing Patterns in the Costs and Benefits of Technological Change in Commercial Aviation," *Review of Social Economy*, March, 1971, p. 9; U. S. Department of Defense, National Aeronautics and Space Administration and Department of Transportation, *Research and Development Contributions to Aviation Progress (RADCAP)*, Washington, D.C., 1972; D. C. Mowery and N. Rosenberg, "The Commercial Aircraft Industry," in R. R. Nelson, (ed.), *Government and Technical Progress: A Cross-Industry Analysis*, New York: The Pergamon Press, 1982; R. R. Nelson and S. G. Winter, "Appropriating the Returns from Industrial Research and Development," *Brookings Papers on Economics Activity*, 1987, p. 783.

16. R. Ford, *et al, Industrial Subsidies in OECD Economics*, O.E.C.D. Working Paper No. 74, Paris: 1990.

17. See *Aeronautical Technologies for the Twenty-First Century, loc. cit.*; *FI*, April 7-13, 1993, p. 12; A. L. Velocci, "Study Urges More Proactive Government Role in Aerospace," *AWST*, April 19, 1993, p. 49.

18. See, for example, *Economic Analysis of Aeronautical Research and Development*, Gellman Research Associates, Inc. (for Office of Science and Technology

Policy, Executive Office of the President), August 30, 1982; *U.S. Civil Aircraft Industry*, U.S. Department of Commerce, Washington, D.C., March 1984; B. Bluestone, P. Jordan, M. Sullivan, *Aircraft Industry Dynamics: An Analysis of Competition, Capital, and Labor*, Boston, MA.: Auburn House Publishing Company, 1981; *The U.S. Private, Business and Light Transport Aircraft Industry: Its Development, World Market and Foreign Competition*, Washington: Aerospace Industries Association of America, October 1984.

19. See P. R. Krugman, *Rethinking International Trade*, Cambridge, MA.: MIT Press, 1990; P.R. Krugman (ed.), *Strategic Trade Policy and the New International Economics*, Cambridge, MA: MIT Press, 1986; R. C. Baldwin and P. R. Krugman, "Industrial Policy and International Competition in Wide-Bodied Aircraft," in R. C. Baldwin (ed.), *Trade Policy and Empirical Analysis*, Chicago: University of Chicago Press, 1987; D. C. Webb, "Integrated Research Key to Global Competitiveness," *AWST*, April 19, 1993, p. 41.

20. I. Amato, "NASA Urged to Pump Up Its First 'A,'" *Science*, October 16, 1992, p. 394.

21. *B&CA,* May 1989, p. 104; May 1990, p. 117; May 1991, p. 114; *B&CA*, August 1992, p. 17.

22. *AWST*, March 18, 1968, p. 308.

23. *FI*, May 6, 1976, p. 1488.

24. *B&CA*, September 1981, p. 77.

25. *AWST*, October 1, 1984, p. 133; September 23, 1985, p. 67.

26. *AWST*, October 13, 1986, p. 121.

27. R. S. Gardiner and S. J. Berman, *op. cit.*

28. E. H. Phillips, "Vulcan Ends Initial Wind Tunnel Tests on VTOL, Fan-in-Wing Starfire Model," *AWST*, November 13, 1989, p. 64; D. A. Brown, "U.S. Lags in Development of Power-Lift Aircraft," *AWST*, December 24, 1990, p. 46; K. Daly, "US Navy Seeks V-22 Alternatives," *FI*, November 11-17, 1992, p. 20; J. D. Morracco, "ASTOVL Flight Demonstration Pushed Beyond End of Decade," *AWST*, October 26, 1992, p. 21; *AWST*, October 26, 1992, p. 15; P. Sparaco, "Eurofar Team Advances 'Prop-Rotor' Transport," *AWST*, April 19, 1993, p. 36.

29. See H. Mark, "Aerospace," in A. G. Keatley (ed.), *Technological Frontiers and Foreign Relations,* Washington, D.C.: National Academy Press, 1985.

Appendix A

Operating Cost Regression

The estimated costs used in Table 7-4 are based on a regression equation. The regression equation was derived by ordinary least squares, based on 16 observations of operating cost per seat mile as calculated by *Business and Commercial Aviation* and converted to 1980 dollars. The *Business and Commercial Aviation* calculations are based on typical but nonetheless assumed cruise speeds, trip lengths, number of passengers, hours of operations, fuel prices, flight crew salaries, insurance rates, hangar rents, maintenance costs and the physical characteristics of the aircraft and engines.

The dependent variable is the log of 1980 cost per seat mile. The independent variables are the log of pounds of gross takeoff weight per passenger (LOGPASS), the log of pounds of gross takeoff weight per square foot of wing area (LOGFOOT), the "technology age" of the aircraft and a dummy variable. Technology age (TECH) is defined as the number of years after 1960 when the aircraft was ready for commercial service. The dummy variable (IRON) distinguishes between "heavy iron" and other aircraft, with 1="heavy iron" (as of the date of introduction), 0=all other.

The parameter estimates and the data are given in Tables A-1 and A-2 below.

Table A-1 Parameter Estimates					
Variable	DF	Coefficient Estimate	Standard Error	T for HO	Probability
INTERCEPT	1	-5.52	1.82	-3.03	0.01
LOGPASS	1	1.27	0.29	4.39	0
LOGFOOT	1	-1.34	0.38	-3.5	0.01
TECH	1	-0.02	0.01	-2.37	0.04
IRON	1	0.1	0.19	0.53	0.61

The resulting parameter estimates are:

R-Square	0.913
Adjusted R-Square	0.881
Durbin-Watson	1.843

Aircraft	Cost per Seat Mile	Pounds per Passenger	Pounds per Square Foot	Technology Age	Heavy Iron
\multicolumn{6}{c}{**Table A-2** Data}

Aircraft	Cost per Seat Mile	Pounds per Passenger	Pounds per Square Foot	Technology Age	Heavy Iron
JetStar 6	$0.566	5,115	75.4	1	1
Sabreliner 40	$0.460	2,960	51.9	1	0
Learjet 23	$0.282	2,083	53.9	4	0
HS 125-1A	$0.503	3,333	56.7	4	0
HFB-320	$0.405	2,771	59.8	4	0
Jet Commander 1121	$0.436	2,400	55.4	5	0
Falcon 20	$0.388	3,224	59.0	5	0
Citation	$0.356	1,725	39.8	11	0
Sabre 40A	$0.511	3,173	55.6	11	0
Citation	$0.283	1,725	39.8	11	0
BH 125-600	$0.307	3,125	70.8	13	0
Learjet 35	$0.187	2,125	67.1	14	0
Citation III	$0.108	1,683	64.7	22	0
Falcon 900	$0.256	3,792	86.3	26	1
Challenger 601-3A	$0.179	3,089	96.1	27	1
Learjet 31	$0.115	1,969	59.5	27	0

Appendix B

Characteristics of Business Jet Aircraft Available in the United States, 1958-1993

Appendix B lists selected characteristics of the new aircraft that were available for sale in the United States for 1958 through 1993. The data are those publicly announced with respect to the aircraft as of the date they were first offered on the U.S. market. Data on cruise speeds, range and takeoff field requirements often vary considerably from those actually found in practice and from those listed at other times for the same aircraft. Aircraft weights are less variant, but these, too, tend to change with use and re-certification.

The listings are grouped by manufacturer, with the successive manufacturers appearing in the chronological order in which they offered business jet aircraft in the United States. The several models of each of the manufacturers are listed chronologically within that manufacturers set of airplanes. In cases in which the identity of the manufacturers changes through time, the groupings are identified by the name of the company first responsible for a particular series of aircraft. For example, the Gulfstream II, III, and IV are in one set, with the manufacturer first identified as Grumman. The manufacturer's name switches from Grumman to Gulfstream American and then to Gulfstream Aerospace in the Gulfstream Listings.

Appendix B
Characteristics of Business Jet Aircraft Available in the United States, 1958-1993

Manufacturer	Morane-Saulnier	Lockheed	Lockheed	Lockheed
Model	MS-760 Paris	JetStar 6	JetStar 8	Jetstar II
Year Available	1958 (U.S.)	1961	1967	1976
Number of Passengers	3	8-10	8-10	8-10
Wingspan (ft)	33.3	54.4	54.4	54.4
Length (ft)	32.9	60.4	60.4	60.4
Wing Area (sq. ft)	194	543	543	542.5
Gross Takeoff Weight (lbs)	7,725	40,921	42,500	44,000
Wing Loading (lb/sq. ft)	39.8	75.4	78.3	81.1
Engines:				
Manufacturer	Turbomeca Marbore	Pratt & Whitney	Pratt & Whitney	Garrett
Model	II	JT12A-6	JT12A-8	TFE731-3
Power (thrust lbs)	880	3,000	3,300	3,700
Number	2	4	4	4
Power Loading (lbs/thrust lb)	4.26	3.41	3.22	2.97
Maximum Cruise (mph)	415	567	565	567
Normal Cruise (mph)	370	500	500	500
Range (st. mi.)	700	2,000	2,370	3,095
Takeoff Length (ft)	4,135	6,200	6,000	6,200
Initial Equipped Price (current dollars)	$210,000	$1,500,000	$1,650,000	$4,395,000

Appendix B (continued)

Characteristics of Business Jet Aircraft Available in the United States, 1958-1993

	North American	North American	North American Rockwell	North American Rockwell
Manufacturer	North American	North American	North American Rockwell	North American Rockwell
Model	Sabreliner 40	Sabreliner 60	Sabre 40A	Sabre 75
Year Available	1963 (1960 military)	1967	1971	1971
Number of Passengers	6	8	8	9
Wingspan (ft)	44.4	44.4	44.43	44.43
Length (ft)	44.0	46.9	43.75	47.17
Wing Area (sq. ft)	342.1	342.1	342.1	342.1
Gross Takeoff Weight (lbs)	17,760	20,000	19,035	21,000
Wing Loading (lb/sq. ft)	51.9	58.5	55.6	61.4
Engines:				
Manufacturer	Pratt & Whitney	Pratt & Whitney	Pratt & Whitney	Pratt & Whitney
Model	JT12A-6	JT12A-8	JT12A-8	JT12A-8
Power (thrust lbs)	3,000	3,300	3,300	3,300
Number	2	2	2	2
Power Loading (lbs/thrust lb)	2.96	3.03	2.88	3.18
Maximum Cruise (mph)	560	560	538	528
Normal Cruise (mph)	495	528	528	522
Range (st. mi.)	1,770	1,700	1,780	1,800
Takeoff Length (ft)	3,500	4,900	3,300	4,150
Initial Equipped Price (current dollars)	$990,000	$1,300,000	$995,000	$1,600,000

Appendix B (continued)
Characteristics of Business Jet Aircraft Available in the United States, 1958-1993

	Rockwell International	Rockwell International	Hawker-Siddeley	Hawker-Siddeley
Manufacturer				
Model	Sabre 75A	Sabre 65	HS 125	HS 125-1A
Year Available	1974	1979	1964	1965
Number of Passengers	10	10	6-8	8
Wingspan (ft)	44.5	50.5	47.0	47.0
Length (ft)	47.2	46.1	47.4	47.4
Wing Area (sq. ft)	342.1	380	353	353
Gross Takeoff Weight (lbs)	23,000	24,000	20,000	20,000
Wing Loading (lb/sq. ft)	67.2	63.2	56.7	56.7
Engines:				
Manufacturer	General Electric	Garrett	Bristol Siddeley	Bristol Siddeley
Model	CF700-2D	TFE731-3R	Viper 520	BS Viper 521
Power (thrust lbs)	3,500	3,700	≈3,050	3,115
Number	2	2	2	2
Power Loading (lbs/thrust lb)	3.29	3.24	3.28	3.21
Maximum Cruise (mph)	528	552	491	491
Normal Cruise (mph)	495	508	415	415
Range (st. mi.)	1,896	3,222	1,412 @460 mph 1,760 @415 mph	1,412 @460 mph 1,720 @415 mph
Takeoff Length (ft)	4,850	5,895	3,400	3,350
Initial Equipped Price (current dollars)	$1,950,000	$4,575,000	$750,000	$775,000

Appendix B (continued)
Characteristics of Business Jet Aircraft Available in the United States, 1958-1993

	Hawker-Siddeley HS 125-3A	Hawker-Siddeley HS 125-3AR (BH 125-400)	Hawker-Siddeley BH 125-600	Hawker-Siddeley HS 125-700
Manufacturer				
Model				
Year Available	1966	1968	1973	1977
Number of Passengers	8	8	8-12	8-12
Wingspan (ft)	47	47	47	47
Length (ft)	47.4	47.4	50.6	50.7
Wing Area (sq. ft)	353	353	353	353
Gross Takeoff Weight (lbs)	21,000	22,700	25,000	25,000
Wing Loading (lb/sq. ft)	59.5	64.3	70.8	70.8
Engines:				
Manufacturer	Bristol Siddeley	Rolls Royce Bristol	Rolls Royce	Garrett
Model	Viper 522	Viper 522	MK.601	TFE731-3-1H
Power (thrust lbs)	3,360	3,360	3,750	3,700
Number	2	2	2	2
Power Loading (lbs/thrust lb)	3.13	3.38	3.33	3.38
Maximum Cruise (mph)	535	535	508	508
Normal Cruise (mph)	477*	495*	490*	495*
Range (st. mi.)	1,590	1,800*	1,840	2,700
Takeoff Length (ft)	3,450	5,000	5,350	6,200
Initial Equipped Price (current dollars)	$780,000	$820,000	$1,687,000	$3,800,000

* Listed; in practice, less than this

Appendix B (continued)
Characteristics of Business Jet Aircraft Available in the United States, 1958-1993

	British Aerospace	British Aerospace	Lear Jet Corporation	Gates Learjet
Manufacturer	British Aerospace	British Aerospace	Lear Jet Corporation	Gates Learjet
Model	BAe 125-800	BAe 1000	23	24
Year Available	1984	1991	1964	1967
Number of Passengers	8	8	6	6
Wingspan (ft)	51.4	51.4	35.6	35.9
Length (ft)	51.2	53.9	43.3	43.3
Wing Area (sq. ft)	374	374	231.8	231.8
Gross Takeoff Weight (lbs)	27,520	31,000	12,500	13,000
Wing Loading (lb/sq. ft)	73.6	82.9	53.9	56.1
Engines:				
Manufacturer	Garrett	Pratt & Whitney	General Electric	General Electric
Model	TFE731-5R	PW305	CJ610-1	CJ610-4
Power (thrust lbs)	4,300	5,225	2,850	2,850
Number	2	2	2	2
Power Loading (lbs/thrust lb)	3.2	2.97	2.19	2.28
Maximum Cruise (mph)	525	525	535	526
Normal Cruise (mph)	450	450	485	485
Range (st. mi.)	2,610	2,822	1,686	1,600
Takeoff Length (ft)	5,300	5,590	4,300	4,800
Initial Equipped Price (current dollars)	$6,650,000	$12,500,000	$573,500	$649,000

Appendix B

241

Appendix B (continued)
Characteristics of Business Jet Aircraft Available in the United States, 1958-1993

	Gates Learjet	Gates Learjet	Gates Learjet	Gates Learjet
Manufacturer	Gates Learjet	Gates Learjet	Gates Learjet	Gates Learjet
Model	25	Learjet 35/36	Learjet 35A/36A	Learjet 28/29
Year Available	1968	1974	1976	1979
Number of Passengers	8	8-6	8-6	8-6
Wingspan (ft)	35.6	38.1	39.5	43.7
Length (ft)	47.6	48.7	48.7	47.5
Wing Area (sq. ft)	231.8	253.3	253.3	264.5
Gross Takeoff Weight (lbs)	15,000	17000/18,000	17,000/18,000	15,000
Wing Loading (lb/sq. ft)	64.7	67.1/71.1	67.1/71.1	56.7
Engines:				
Manufacturer	General Electric	Garrett	Garrett	General Electic
Model	CJ610-6	TFE731-2	TFE731-2	CJ610-8A
Power (thrust lbs)	2,950	3,500	3,500	2,950
Number	2	2	2	2
Power Loading (lbs/thrust lb)	2.54	2.43/2.57	2.43/2.57	2.54
Maximum Cruise (mph)	526	560	560	540
Normal Cruise (mph)	485	500	500	500
Range (st. mi.)	1,510	3,027/3,621	3,027/3,410	1,575/1,817
Takeoff Length (ft)	5,500	5,500	4,300/4,960	2,993
Initial Equipped Price (current dollars)	$795,000	$1,395,000 / $1,445,000	$1,650,000 / $1,697,000	$1,770,000 / $1,820,000

Appendix B (continued)
Characteristics of Business Jet Aircraft Available in the United States, 1958-1993

	Gates Learjet	Learjet	Learjet	Learjet
Manufacturer	Gates Learjet	Learjet	Learjet	Learjet
Model	Learjet 55/56	Learjet 31	Learjet 31A/31A-ER	Learjet 60
Year Available	1981	1988	1991	1993
Number of Passengers	10-8	4-8	4-8	8-10
Wingspan (ft)	43.8	43.8	43.8	43.8
Length (ft)	55.1	48.7	48.7	58.7
Wing Area (sq. ft)	264.5	264.5	264.5	264.5
Gross Takeoff Weight (lbs)	19,500/20,500	15,750	16,500	23,100
Wing Loading (lb/sq. ft)	73.7/77.5	59.5	62.4	87.3
Engines:				
Manufacturer	Garrett	Garrett	Garrett	Pratt & Whitney
Model	TFE731-3A	TFE731-2	TFE731-2	PW305A
Power (thrust lbs)	3,700	3,500	3,500	4,600
Number	2	2	2	2
Power Loading (lbs/thrust lb)	2.50/2.77	2.25	2.36	2.51
Maximum Cruise (mph)	540	535	533	535
Normal Cruise (mph)	500	500	500	500
Range (st. mi.)	2,767/3,327	1,875	1,797/2,079	3,154
Takeoff Length (ft)	4,715/5,235	2,906	2,930/3,280	5,360
Initial Equipped Price (current dollars)	$3,275,000/$3,360,000	$3,704,000	$4,700,000	$8,866,000

Appendix B (continued)
Characteristics of Business Jet Aircraft Available in the United States, 1958-1993

	Learjet	Avions Marcel Dassault	Avions Marcel Dassault	Avions Marcel Dassault
Manufacturer	Learjet	Avions Marcel Dassault	Avions Marcel Dassault	Avions Marcel Dassault
Model	Learjet 45	Falcon 20	Falcon 20 C/D/E/F	Falcon 10
Year Available	in development, 1993	1965	1967	1973
Number of Passengers		8-10	8-10	4-7
Wingspan (ft)		50.5	53.5	42.9
Length (ft)		56.2	56.2	45.5
Wing Area (sq. ft)		437	441	260
Gross Takeoff Weight (lbs)	19,500	25,794	26,675	18,300
Wing Loading (lb/sq. ft)		59	60.5	70.4
Engines:				
Manufacturer	Garrett	General Electric	General Electric	Garrett
Model	TFE731-20	CF700-2C	CF700-2D	TFE731-2
Power (thrust lbs)	3,500	4,125	4,250	3,230
Number	2	2	2	2
Power Loading (lbs/thrust lb)		3.13	3.14	2.83
Maximum Cruise (mph)		565	560	583
Normal Cruise (mph)		490	516	528
Range (st. mi.)		1,891	1,900	2,200
Takeoff Length (ft)		5,700	5,700	4,550
Initial Equipped Price (current dollars)		$1,094,000	$1,500,000	$1,425,000

Appendix B (continued)

Characteristics of Business Jet Aircraft Available in the United States, 1958-1993

	Dassault-Breguet Falcon 50	Dassault-Breguet Falcon 200	Dassault-Breguet Falcon 100	Dassault-Breguet Falcon 900
Manufacturer				
Model				
Year Available	1979	1983	1983	1987
Number of Passengers	8-14	6-10	5-8	12-19
Wingspan (ft)	61.9	53.5	42.9	63.4
Length (ft)	60.8	56.3	45.5	66.3
Wing Area (sq. ft)	504	441	260	527
Gross Takeoff Weight (lbs)	38,800	30,650	18,740	45,500
Wing Loading (lb/sq. ft)	77	69.5	72.1	86.3
Engines:				
Manufacturer	Garrett	Garrett	Garrett	Garrett
Model	TFE731-3	ATF3-6A	TFE731-2	TF731-5A
Power (thrust lbs)	3,700	5,200	3,230	4,500
Number	3	2	2	3
Power Loading (lbs/thrust lb)	3.50	2.95	2.90	3.37
Maximum Cruise (mph)	565	583	583	528
Normal Cruise (mph)	516	495	528	508
Range (st. mi.)	4,200	3,000	2,210	4,750
Takeoff Length (ft)	4,900	4,600	4,500	5,400
Initial Equipped Price (current dollars)	$6,233,000	$8,850,000	$4,059,000	$17,000,000

Appendix B (continued)
Characteristics of Business Jet Aircraft Available in the United States, 1958-1993

	Dassault Aviation	Dassault Aviation	Dassault Aviation	Rockwell/ Aero Commander
Model	Falcon 900B	Falcon 2000	Falcon 9000	Jet Commander 1121
Year Available	1992	in development, 1993	in development, 1993	1965
Number of Passengers	10-17	9-19	12-19	7
Wingspan (ft)	63.4	63.4		43.3
Length (ft)	66.3	66.3		50.4
Wing Area (sq. ft)	527	527		303.3
Gross Takeoff Weight (lbs)	45,500	35,000	68,000	16,800
Wing Loading (lb/sq. ft)	86.3	66.4		55.4
Engines:				
Manufacturer	Garrett	Garrett/General Electric	Garrett/General Electric	General Electric
Model	TFE731-5BR	CFE738		CJ610-1
Power (thrust lbs)	4,750	5,725		2,850
Number	3	2	3	2
Power Loading (lbs/thrust lb)	3.19	3.06		2.95
Maximum Cruise (mph)	583	561		535
Normal Cruise (mph)	528	528		400
Range (st. mi.)	5,067	3,840		1,688
Takeoff Length (ft)	4,950	5,520		2,810
Initial Equipped Price (current dollars)	$22,850,000	$15,765,000		$595,000

Appendix B (continued)

Characteristics of Business Jet Aircraft Available in the United States, 1958-1993

	Israeli Aircraft Industries	Israeli Aircraft Industries	Israeli Aircraft Industries	Israeli Aircraft Industries
Manufacturer				
Model	Commodore Jet 1121 B/C	Commodore Jet 1123	1124 Westwind	1125 Westwind 1
Year Available	1969	1971	1976	1979
Number of Passengers	8	8	8-10	8-10
Wingspan (ft)	43.3	43.3	44.8	44.8
Length (ft)	50.4	52.5	52.3	52.3
Wing Area (sq. ft)	303.3	303.3	308.2	308.2
Gross Takeoff Weight (lbs)	18,500	20,500	22,850	23,000
Wing Loading (lb/sq. ft)	61	67.6	74.1	74.6
Engines:				
Manufacturer	General Electric	General Electric	Garrett	Garrett
Model	CJ610-5	CJ610-9	TFE731-3	TFE731-3
Power (thrust lbs)	2,950	3,450	3,700	3,700
Number	2	2	2	2
Power Loading (lbs/thrust lb)	3.14	2.59	3.09	3.11
Maximum Cruise (mph)	535	500	500	516
Normal Cruise (mph)	493*	470	475	488
Range (st. mi.)	1,450	2,120	2,800	3,025
Takeoff Length (ft)	3,600	5,350	4,950	4,950
Initial Equipped Price (current dollars)	$650,000	$995,000	$1,897,500	$2,639,000

*Listed; in practice, less than this.

Appendix B (continued)
Characteristics of Business Jet Aircraft Available in the United States, 1958-1993

	Israeli Aircraft Industries	Israeli Aircraft Industries	Israeli Aircraft Industries	Hamburger Flugzeugbau
Model	Westwind 2	Astra	Astra SP	Hansa HFB 320
Year Available	1980	1985	1990	1967
Number of Passengers	8-10	8-9	8-9	7-11
Wingspan (ft)	44.8	52.7	52.7	47.5
Length (ft)	52.3	55.6	55.6	54.5
Wing Area (sq. ft)	308.2	316.6	316.6	324.4
Gross Takeoff Weight (lbs)	23,650	23,650	23,650	19,400
Wing Loading (lb/sq. ft)	76.7	74.7	74.7	59.8
Engines:				
Manufacturer	Garrett	Garrett	Garrett	General Electric
Model	TFE731-3	TFE731-3B	TFE731-3A	CJ610-1
Power (thrust lbs)	3,700	3,650	3,700	2,850
Number	2	2	2	2
Power Loading (lbs/thrust lb)	3.2	3.24	3.2	3.4
Maximum Cruise (mph)	526	560	560	540
Normal Cruise (mph)	495	526	526	490
Range (st. mi.)	3,300	3,842	3,738	1,660
Takeoff Length (ft)	5,250	5,350	5,250	n.a.
Initial Equipped Price (current dollars)	$3,147,500	$5,995,000	$7,500,000	$940,000

Appendix B (continued)
Characteristics of Business Jet Aircraft Available in the United States, 1958-1993

	Grumman	Grumman-American	Gulfstream Aerospace	Gulfstream Aerospace
Manufacturer				
Model	Gulfstream II	Gulfstream III	Gulfstream IV	G-IVSP
Year Available	1967	1980	1987	1992
Number of Passengers	8-19	14-20	14-20	14-19
Wingspan (ft)	68.9	77.8	77.8	77.8
Length (ft)	79.9	83.1	88.3	88.3
Wing Area (sq. ft)	793	934.6	950.4	950.3
Gross Takeoff Weight (lbs)	58,000	68,200	73,600	74,600
Wing Loading (lb/sq. ft)	73.1	73	77.4	78.5
Engines:				
Manufacturer	Rolls Royce Spey	Rolls Royce Spey	Rolls Royce Tay	Rolls Royce Tay
Model	MK.511-8	MK.511-8	MK.611-8	MK.611-8
Power (thrust lbs)	11,400	11,400	13,850	13,850
Number	2	2	2	2
Power Loading (lbs/thrust lb)	2.54	2.99	2.66	2.69
Maximum Cruise (mph)	550	562	585	552
Normal Cruise (mph)	495	528	528	529
Range (st. mi.)	3,200	4,669	5,250	3,840
Takeoff Length (ft)	4,400	5,850	5,180	5,200
Initial Equipped Price (current dollars)	$2,550,000	$10,000,000	$15,800,000	$27,000,000

Appendix B (continued)
Characteristics of Business Jet Aircraft Available in the United States, 1958-1993

	Gulfstream Aerospace	Piaggio-Douglas	Cessna	Cessna
Manufacturer	Gulfstream Aerospace	Piaggio-Douglas	Cessna	Cessna
Model	Gulfstream V	PC-808	Citation 500	Citation I and I/SP
Year Available	in development, 1993	1967	1971	1977
Number of Passengers	14-19	5-8	6	6-8
Wingspan (ft)		43.3	43.75	47
Length (ft)		42.2	46.5	46.5
Wing Area (sq. ft)		225	260	278.5
Gross Takeoff Weight (lbs)		18,300	10,350	12,000
Wing Loading (lb/sq. ft)		81.3	39.8	43.1
Engines:				
Manufacturer	BWM/Rolls Royce	Bristol Siddeley	Pratt & Whitney	Pratt & Whitney
Model	BR710-44	Viper 526	JT15D-1	JT15D-1A
Power (thrust lbs)	14,750	3,330	2,200	2,200
Number	2	2	2	2
Power Loading (lbs/thrust lb)		2.75	2.35	2.73
Maximum Cruise (mph)		560	400	459
Normal Cruise (mph)		485	400	404
Range (st. mi.)		1,400	1,300	1,525
Takeoff Length (ft)		5,600	3,035	2,930
Initial Equipped Price (current dollars)		$870,000	$695,000	$945,000

Appendix B (continued)

Characteristics of Business Jet Aircraft Available in the United States, 1958-1993

	Cessna Citation II and II/SP	Cessna Citation SII	Cessna Citation III	Cessna Citation V
Manufacturer				
Model				
Year Available	1978	1984	1982	1988
Number of Passengers	7-10	7-9	8-13	7-10
Wingspan (ft)	51.7	52.2	53.5	52.2
Length (ft)	47.2	47.2	55.5	48.9
Wing Area (sq. ft)	315.4	343	312	342.6
Gross Takeoff Weight (lbs)	13,300	14,300	20,200	16,100
Wing Loading (lb/sq. ft)	42.2	41.7	64.7	47
Engines:				
Manufacturer	Pratt & Whitney	Pratt & Whitney	Garrett	Pratt & Whitney
Model	JT15D-4	JT15D-4B	TFE731-3B	JT15D-5A
Power (thrust lbs)	2,500	2,500	3,650	2,900
Number	2	2	2	2
Power Loading (lbs/thrust lb)	2.66	2.86	2.77	2.78
Maximum Cruise (mph)	459	485	550	500
Normal Cruise (mph)	421	463	509	491
Range (st. mi.)	2,080	2,000	2,875	2,208
Takeoff Length (ft)	2,900	3,240	4,350	3,160
Initial Equipped Price (current dollars)	$1,363,000	$2,595,000	$5,196,000	$3,795,000

Appendix B (continued)

Characteristics of Business Jet Aircraft Available in the United States, 1958-1993

	Cessna	Cessna	Cessna	Cessna
Manufacturer	Cessna	Cessna	Cessna	Cessna
Model	Citation VI	Citation VII	CitationJet 525	Citation X
Year Available	1991	1992	1993	in development, 1993
Number of Passengers	7-13	7-13	5	7-15
Wingspan (ft)	53.5	53.5	46.8	
Length (ft)	55.5	55.5	42.6	
Wing Area (sq. ft)	312	312	240.2	
Gross Takeoff Weight (lbs)	22,200	22,200	10,400	31,000
Wing Loading (lb/sq. ft)	71.2	71.2	43.3	
Engines:				
Manufacturer	Garrett	Garrett	Williams/Rolls Royce	Allison
Model	TFE731-3B	TFE731-4R	FJ44	GMA3007C
Power (thrust lbs)	3,650	4,100	1,900	6,000
Number	2	2	2	2
Power Loading (lbs/thrust lb)	3.04	2.71	2.74	
Maximum Cruise (mph)	550	550	437	
Normal Cruise (mph)	544	544	358	
Range (st. mi.)	2,699	2,532	1,725	
Takeoff Length (ft)	5,150	4,950	3,080	
Initial Equipped Price (current dollars)	$7,850,000	$9,403,000	$2,862,000	

Appendix B (continued)
Characteristics of Business Jet Aircraft Available in the United States, 1958-1993

	Aerospatiale	Canadair	Canadair	Canadair
Manufacturer				
Model	SN601 Corvette	Challenger CL-600	Challenger 601	Challenger 601-3A
Year Available	1975	1980	1983	1987
Number of Passengers	6-10	11-19	11-19	9-19
Wingspan (ft)	42.2	61.8	64.4	64.3
Length (ft)	45.4	68.4	68.4	62.4
Wing Area (sq. ft)	237	450	450	450
Gross Takeoff Weight (lbs)	14,660	36,000	43,250	43,250
Wing Loading (lb/sq. ft)	61.9	80	96.1	96.1
Engines:				
Manufacturer	Pratt & Whitney	Lycoming	General Electric	General Electric
Model	JT15D-4	ALF502L	CF34-1A	CF34-3A
Power (thrust lbs)	2,500	7,500	8,650	9,140
Number	2	2	2	2
Power Loading (lbs/thrust lb)	2.93	2.4	2.5	2.37
Maximum Cruise (mph)	510	580	571	571
Normal Cruise (mph)	472	506*	506*	506*
Range (st. mi.)	920	4,505	4,256	3,805
Takeoff Length (ft)	4,560	5,300	5,400	5,400
Initial Equipped Price (current dollars)	$1,450,000	$7,500,000	$11,700,000	$12,950,000

*Listed; in practice, less than this.

Appendix B (continued)
Characteristics of Business Jet Aircraft Available in the United States, 1958-1993

	Canadair	Canadair	Canadair	Mitsubishi
Manufacturer	Canadair	Canadair	Canadair	Mitsubishi
Model	Corporate RJ	Challenger 601-3R	Global Exrpess	Diamond 1
Year Available	1992	in development, 1993	in development, 1993	1981
Number of Passengers	18-30	9-19		7-9
Wingspan (ft)	70.3	64.3		43.4
Length (ft)	88.9	68.4		48.3
Wing Area (sq. ft)	520	450		241
Gross Takeoff Weight (lbs)	57,000	45,100	91,000	14,000
Wing Loading (lb/sq. ft)	98	100.2		58.1
Engines:				
Manufacturer	General Electric	General Electric	BMW/Rolls Royce	Pratt & Whitney
Model	CF34-3A1	CF34-3A1	BR710-4862	JT15D-4
Power (thrust lbs)	8,729	8,729		2,500
Number	2	2	2	2
Power Loading (lbs/thrust lb)	3.3	2.91		2.8
Maximum Cruise (mph)	571	571		514
Normal Cruise (mph)	506	506		474
Range (st. mi.)	2,536	3,827		1,800
Takeoff Length (ft)	6,090	6,050		4,100
Initial Equipped Price (current dollars)	$18,000,000	$18,200,000		$2,250,000

Appendix B (continued)

Characteristics of Business Jet Aircraft Available in the United States, 1958-1993

	Mitsubishi	Mitsubishi	Beech Aircraft	Beech Aircraft	Swearingen
Manufacturer	Mitsubishi	Mitsubishi	Beech Aircraft	Beech Aircraft	Swearingen
Model	Diamond 1A	Diamond 2	Beechjet 400	Beechjet 400A	SJ30
Year Available	1983	1985	1986	1990	in development, 1993
Number of Passengers	7-9	7-9	7-9	7-8	5-6
Wingspan (ft)	43.5	43.5	43.5	43.5	36.3
Length (ft)	48.4	48.4	48.4	48.4	42.6
Wing Area (sq. ft)	241.4	241.4	241.4	241.4	165
Gross Takeoff Weight (lbs)	14,630	15,730	15,780	16,100	10,400
Wing Loading (lb/sq. ft)	60.6	65.2	65.4	66.7	63
Engines:					
Manufacturer	Pratt & Whitney	Pratt & Whitney	Pratt & Whitney	Pratt & Whitney	Williams/Rolls Royce
Model	JT15D-4D	JT15D-5	JT15D-5	JT15D-5	FJ44
Power (thrust lbs)	2,500	2,900	2,900	2,900	1,900
Number	2	2	2	2	2
Power Loading (lbs/thrust lb)	2.93	2.71	2.72	2.78	2.73
Maximum Cruise (mph)	514	525	525	520	512
Normal Cruise (mph)	474	495	495	495	475
Range (st. mi.)	1,738	2,129	2,220	2,230	2,050
Takeoff Length (ft)	3,940	3,670	3,950	3,950	3,300
Initial Equipped Price (current dollars)	$2,690,000	$3,190,000	$3,050,000	$4,200,000	$2,932,000

Appendix C

Glossary[1]

ailerons	hinged surfaces on trailing edges of wings to control roll (bank)
airfoil	shape of cross section of wing; a shape that causes air moving over top surface to have lower pressure (and higher velocity) than that of air moving under the bottom surface. Forward motion of an airfoil results in lift
angle of attack	angle formed by a horizontal line and a line passing through the center (chord) of a wing
avionics	collection of radio, air data and inertial equipment to measure position, speed, attitude, heading, altitude and to use these measurements to control and navigate the aircraft
cantilever wing	wing with no struts or other external bracing
critical Mach number	the velocity of the aircraft, measured in Mach numbers, at which the velocity of the air moving over the top of the wing reaches Mach 1.0, the speed of sound
dihedral	angle formed by horizontal line and line through the mid-wing, from fuselage to wingtip; negative dihedral = anhedral
drag	resistance to flow of air past aircraft; caused in part by friction between air and the surfaces of the moving body (friction drag) and in part by differences in air pressures (pressure drag) over different surfaces of the moving body
empennage	rear section of aircraft, consisting of stabilizer, elevator, vertical fin and rudder
empty weight	weight of aircraft without fuel, passengers or baggage

---

[1] Some of the definitions in the glossary are paraphrased from H.C. "Skip" Smith, *The Illustrated Guide to Aerodynamics,* 2nd ed., Summit, PA: Tab Books, 1992, or from J.D. Anderson, Jr., *Introduction to Flight,* 2nd ed., New York: McGraw-Hill, 1985. Greater detail is available from these sources.

flaps | any of several types of devices to increase chord of wing and/or area of the wing to increase lift at low speeds.

fuselage | the body of an aircraft

green price | factory price of an airplane without exterior finish painting (hence, "green," from the color of the oxidization-preventative coating on the skin) and without interior finishing and the full array of avionics equipment

gross takeoff weight | maximum permissible weight at initiation of takeoff roll

IFR | instrument flight rules

knot | a unit of speed; one nautical mile per hour

landing distance | the distance required to land and stop with specified weights and payloads

lb | pound of avoirdupois weight

lb st | pounds of static thrust; a unit used to measure the power (force) of jet engines; thrust equals pounds per second (mass flow) multiplied by change in velocity of that mass

lift | net upward force; difference between pressure force on top and pressure force on bottom of wing

lift-drag ratio | lift force divided by drag force; a measure of efficiency; one design objective is to maximize the lift-drag ratio at normal cruising speeds

Mach | velocity measured relative to the speed of sound; Mach 1.0 equals the speed of sound at a given altitude; named for Ernst Mach; the speed of sound decreases as altitude increases (temperature decreases). Mach 1.0 equals 761 mph at sea level at 59°F; Mach 1.0 equals 707 mph at 20,000 feet where the temperature is -12°F and 660 mph at 40,000 feet with a temperature of -70°F.

mph | miles per hour

NACA/NASA airfoil	an airfoil design originating from research at the National Advisory Committee for Aeronautics or its successor organization, the National Aeronautics and Space Administration
nautical mile	a unit of linear measurement equal to 6080.6 feet
power loading	gross takeoff weight divided by total pounds of static thrust of engines
shaft horsepower	power delivered to propeller of a propeller-driven airplane; usually used in reference to turboprop aircraft
stall	loss of control of aircraft when, given its angle of attack, airspeed is insufficient to provide adequate lift to maintain flight
stick pusher	a device to avoid stalls. The control column (stick) is automatically pushed forward when the aircraft is approaching stall conditions.
stick shaker	a device to warn the pilot that the aircraft is approaching stall conditions. The control column (stick) is made to shake to signal the pilot of near-stall conditions.
subsonic	speeds less than Mach 1.0
supercritical wing	airfoil that increases speed of aircraft before critical Mach number is reached; increases efficiency at high cruise speeds; invented by NASA scientist Richard Whitcomb
supersonic	speeds in excess of Mach 1.0
swept wing	wing design with leading edge of wing swept back to an angle substantially beyond the perpendicular to the fuselage. Sweep angles of 25° to 35° are common; swept wings effectively increase the critical Mach number and reduce drag relative to lift. Low-speed performance is degraded with wing sweep.
takeoff runway length	runway distance up to a point that, should one engine become inoperative, the pilot should abort plus the distance from that point to the point at which, with one engine inoperative, the aircraft will take off or, if it is greater, the distance required to bring the aircraft to a stop

tip tanks	external fuel tanks mounted on tips of wings
transonic	speeds in the vicinity of Mach 1.0; speeds between Mach 0.80 and Mach 1.20
turbofan	jet engine with a ducted fan mounted ahead of main compressor, with portion of incoming air bypassing the burners; more efficient (and quieter) than a pure turbojet engine
turbojet	jet engine with incoming air compressed and forced into burning (hot) section, where air is mixed with injected fuel and ignited. Expanded exhaust gases drive a turbine which connects by a shaft to the compressor to bring in more air. Acceleration of mass of gases in the engine produces thrust
turboprop	aircraft powered by a turbine engine that turns a propellor shaft
VFR	visual flight rules
VSTOL	aircraft designed for vertical and short take-offs and landings
wing loading	gross takeoff weight divided by the wing area; pounds of lift per pounds of gross weight
wing root	section of wing where wing joins fuselage
winglets	tilted and tapered surfaces at the tips of wings; improve efficiency by reducing drag caused by complex of air currents at wing tips; invented by NASA scientist Richard Whitcomb

INDEX

Falcon 50, 6, 51, 116, 120, 130, 133,
143, 169, 171, 175, 176, 207, 215,
218
Falcon 100, 171
Falcon 200 (20H), 173, 174, 218
Falcon 900, 6, 112, 118-120, 130,
133, 172, 218
Falcon 900B, 120, 175, 178
Falcon 2000, 120, 174, 184, 211
HU-25A, 173
Mediterrane, 27, 50
Mirage fighters, 27, 170, 171
Mystere 20, 27, 39, 50
AVRO C.102, 18

Avro Lycoming, 122, 125-126

– **B** –

Baldwin, R. C., 230

Baldwin, W. L., 8

Baumann Aircraft Corp., 22

Beech Aircraft Corp., 48

Beech Aircraft
Beechjet 400, 182, 184
Beechjet 400A, 183
King Air 100, 78
Model 18, D18S, 13
Model 50 (Twin Bonanza), 14, 21
Model 73 (Jet Mentor), 26
Model 90 (King Air), 175
Starship 400 (T-1A), 183
Super King Air 200 (King Air 200),
80, 90, 155
Bell Aircraft Corp.

Bell Aircraft
Bell XP-59A, 18
F-83, 18
Bendix, 109

Berman, S. J., 229, 230

Bluestone, B., 230

Boeing Aircraft Co., 18

Boeing Aircraft
B-47, 18, 23
B-707, 23, 54, 91,
B-727, 37, 58, 107
B-737, 58,
B-757, 111
B-767, 111

Bombardier, Ltd., 92, 128, 159–160,
170, 184, 206, 211

Bowers, P. M., 32

Branthoover, W. T., 8

Brazilian Air Force, 27

Brigadier 290, 22

British Aerospace Corp., 165, 168, 218
(*see also de Havilland Aircraft Co.*
and *Hawker-Siddeley Aviation, Ltd.*)

British Aerospace Aircraft
BAe 125-800, 50, 65, 165, 168-168,
177
BAe 1000, 168-169, 173, 216

British Aircraft Corp. (BAC 1-11), 82,
168

British Overseas Airways Corp.
(BOAC), 19, 93

Brown, D. A., 67, 69, 70, 71, 135, 136,
185, 188, 189, 230

Brownlow, C., 68

Bryan, B., 229

Economics of Science, Technology and Innovation

KLUWER ACADEMIC PUBLISHERS – DORDRECHT / BOSTON / LONDON